MAY 0 2 2019

DISCARD

100 Greatest Film Scores

100 Greatest Film Scores

Matt Lawson
Laurence E. MacDonald

ROWMAN & LITTLEFIELD
Lanham • Boulder • New York • London

Published by Rowman & Littlefield
An imprint of The Rowman & Littlefield Publishing Group, Inc.
4501 Forbes Boulevard, Suite 200, Lanham, Maryland 20706
www.rowman.com

Unit A, Whitacre Mews, 26-34 Stannary Street, London SE11 4AB

British Library Cataloguing in Publication Information Available

Library of Congress Cataloging-in-Publication Data

Names: Lawson, Matt, 1987– author. | MacDonald, Laurence E. author.
Title: 100 greatest film scores / Matt Lawson, Laurence MacDonald.
Other titles: One hundred greatest film scores
Description: Lanham : Rowman & Littlefield, 2018. | Includes bibliographical references and index.
Identifiers: LCCN 2018001293 (print) | LCCN 2018002292 (ebook) | ISBN 9781538103685 (electronic) | ISBN 9781538103678 (hardback : alk. paper)
Subjects: LCSH: Motion picture music—Bibliography.
Classification: LCC ML128.M7 (ebook) | LCC ML128.M7 A15 2018 (print) | DDC 781.5/42—dc23

LC record available at https://lccn.loc.gov/2018001293

Printed in the United States of America

To my wife, Nichola, my son, Harry, and my
parents and in-laws for their invaluable support, patience, and understanding
during the writing process.
—Matt

To my wife, Carolyn, for being patient, kind, and
understanding throughout the many months of planning, writing,
and editing. She's a SAINT!!
—Larry

Contents

Introduction

Since the invention of the motion picture in the 1890s, music has been an integral part of the film medium. Since the arrival of synchronized sound in the 1920s, musical scores have been written for countless numbers of films. The power that film music has over an audience is unquestionable. It can make us laugh, cry, feel anxious, feel excited, and completely alter the way we view a film. It is almost unthinkable to imagine the shower scene from *Psycho* without hearing Bernard Herrmann's stabbing string sounds, or to see "A long time ago, in a galaxy far, far away . . ." without then following it with the bombastic opening fanfare to *Star Wars*. As Martin Scorsese once said, "Film and music are inseparable. They always were, and always will be."

The purpose of this book is to celebrate music in film by singling out one hundred films with original scores that we, the authors, feel are especially significant. When we accepted this project, we were fully aware that it would be virtually impossible to feature all of the scores that we thought should be recognized for both their musical originality and for the unique contributions that they have made to the films they accompany.

We therefore offer this book as our attempt to acknowledge one hundred exemplary musical works. The selection process we adopted was an ambitious attempt that, together with our editor, Stephen Ryan, resulted in the submission by each of us of lists of films that we felt included outstanding musical scores. We were each given some leeway in the selection process, which in making the final choices involved some compromises by all concerned. These compromises were essential, as both authors, and the editing team, all had differing opinions on what constitutes a memorable or successful film score. For Lawson, born in the late 1980s, the more modern repertory of John Williams, Hans Zimmer, or Michael Giacchino was dominant in the original suggested films, whereas MacDonald suggested some films which were less well known, requiring Lawson to purchase several DVDs for research purposes! Both authors agree that this collaborative process was enlightening and not without its challenges but ultimately provides a rewarding glimpse into what is considered a significant enough score to make our final one hundred. An appendix offers an additional list of one hundred films that did *not* make the book. The caliber of some of those films will highlight just how impossible our task was.

In preparing this book, we were guided by the following dictates: the films should be narrative in nature; that is, they should not be documentaries such as *Winged Migration*; nor should they be nonnarrative in substance like *Koyaanisqatsi*.

We also ruled out musical films such as *The Wizard of Oz*, even though *Oz* features an Academy Award–winning score, because films such as this one include so many musical performances that are visible to the viewer. Our goal has been to feature films in which the music is generally unseen, but still an integral part of each film.

In no way did we intend this book to concentrate on composers who are white males, who are also either American or European. Some suggestions were made concerning the inclusion of scores by such prominent musicians as Quincy Jones, Duke Ellington, and Rachel Portman, but in the final analysis, it was the music, not the composers, that led us to the final list that forms the basis for this book. For this reason, composers such as John Williams are featured on numerous occasions, simply because the music they compose is so memorable and recognizable. Indeed, Williams's scores account for almost 10 percent of the entries in this book. It is partly a reflection of the industry during the Golden Age of Hollywood that this unintentional bias of gender and race occurs, but it is hoped that the twenty-first century will provide more opportunities for women and non-Caucasian composers to write memorable film scores.

The one hundred films we selected have been arranged in alphabetical order. There is no ranking system within the book, and in no way is this book intended to be a countdown to the single greatest film score of all time. We all have our personal favorites among the countless film scores that have been written, but this book does not dwell on the personal choices of its authors.

Each entry features a short synopsis of the film, followed by a detailed article about the music itself, with analyses of the thematic materials and how they are used. Each entry also includes the film's public recognition, including awards it may have won, and anything else that we thought was significant about a particular film. Finally, the entries include recommended recordings in the CD format, and may also include bibliographic information on sources that were consulted.

Since each of us wrote fifty of the articles that appear in this book, we have included our initials after each of the entries that we submitted. Thus, Matt Lawson's articles are identified by ML, and those written by Laurence E. MacDonald are tagged by LEM.

At the back of the book, you will find brief biographies of the fifty composers whose scores are featured in this book.

We sincerely hope you enjoy this excursion into the world of films and their music, spanning eighty-three years from our earliest entry, *City Lights* (1931) to our most recent, *Interstellar* (2014).

A

THE ADVENTURES OF ROBIN HOOD

(1938)

Erich Wolfgang Korngold

The Film

The legendary Robin Hood, the bandit of Sherwood Forest, has been portrayed on film by many prominent stars, including Douglas Fairbanks (in a 1922 silent film), Richard Todd (in a 1952 live-action Disney film), and such diverse actors as Kevin Costner, Cary Elwes, and Russell Crowe. But arguably the best cinematic Robin Hood is Errol Flynn, who gave a delightfully energetic performance in the 1938 film *The Adventures of Robin Hood*.

This beautifully shot Technicolor film, set in England during the late twelfth century, begins with the news that King Richard the Lionheart (Ian Hunter) has been captured and is being held for ransom in Austria. The film concerns the treacherous plot by Prince John (Claude Rains) to usurp his older brother's throne. Robin, who is loyal to King Richard, seeks to thwart the prince's skullduggery by forming his band of Merry Men and seeking refuge at an elaborate compound in Sherwood Forest. Robin becomes the enemy of the prince's ally, Sir Guy of Gisbourne (Basil Rathbone), but King Richard's ward, Maid Marian (Olivia de Havilland), becomes sympathetic toward Robin and his fight for justice.

The Music

Having scored three earlier adventure films that starred Errol Flynn (*Captain Blood*, *Another Dawn*, and *The Prince and the Pauper*), Korngold was an ideal choice as the composer of *Robin Hood*. Despite his own misgivings about scoring such an action-filled movie, Korngold created a lavish orchestral score that fills 70 percent of the film's 102-minute running time.

A helpful clue to the nature of Korngold's music may be found in an interview with cellist Eleanor Slatkin that appeared in a 1995 PBS documentary called *The Hollywood Sound*. According to Slatkin, Korngold's approach to scoring differed from that of fellow Warner Bros. composer Max Steiner: "Max Steiner and Erich Korngold were opposite, because Max treated [film music] as a film totally, and

Basil Rathbone and Errol Flynn engaged in one of cinema's great swordfights. *Warner Bros. / Photofest © Warner Bros.*

Erich treated it like an opera." She also said that in his operas Korngold treated the orchestra and the singers as equals. He did the same with the films he scored, only with actors speaking their lines instead of singing them.

Korngold's score for *Robin Hood*, which highlights almost every scene, employs the leitmotivic method, wherein a musical motif identifies a person, place, or thing. Especially memorable is Robin's theme, which is prominently featured during the opening titles. Against a march-like brass background, violins proclaim a rousing motif of nine tones that starts with a rising octave.

A dramatic six-tone motif that begins with a single tone repeated three times serves as a confrontation theme. This idea is first introduced by brass when Robin gatecrashes a banquet in Nottingham Castle toting the carcass of a deer that one of his men has poached for food.

After Robin rebukes both Prince John and Sir Guy for their inflated taxation policies, he has to fight his way out of the castle, with several repetitions of this motif occurring in Korngold's rousing musical cue.

Two other noteworthy motifs enter as volunteers join the Merry Men. The first to arrive is Little John (Alan Hale), a strapping fellow that Robin encounters at a stream. As the two engage in a rather light-hearted duel with walking sticks, A seven-tone idea is introduced by French horns. Soon thereafter, when Friar Tuck (Eugene Pallette) is invited by Robin to minister to his followers, a jaunty motif for bassoon and other woodwinds is introduced.

Another significant motif is a soaring theme for strings that is associated with Maid Marian, who grows fonder of Robin as the film progresses. Her theme is first heard when she becomes a visitor at Sherwood and sees firsthand the ill effects of Prince John's villainy on the downtrodden villagers who have come to Robin's compound after being brutally evicted from their homes by tax collectors. This theme later sweetens a romantic balcony scene clearly inspired by Shakespeare's *Romeo and Juliet*.

The centerpiece of the film, an archery tournament that is planned as a way of trapping Robin, includes two principal melodic ideas. The first is a trumpet fanfare that announces the beginning of the competition; this is followed by a rousing march-like theme as the contestants take the field. Both ideas return periodically as the tournament progresses.

The most dramatic music in the score occurs during the closing sequence when a fateful duel between Robin and Sir Guy is intermixed with shots of the climactic battle involving the prince's knights and Robin's Merry Men. Korngold's furiously paced music punctuates the action, which includes acrobatic jumps by Robin as he attempts to subdue Sir Guy and rescue the captive Marian. When King Richard regains the throne and decrees that Robin and Marian should wed, Robin's theme is heard a final time in a joyous rendition that clearly announces a happy ending.

Korngold's music has helped this version of the Robin Hood legend to become an enduring example of Hollywood's Golden Age, and his score clearly deserves to be included in this book.

Recognition

Nominated as Best Picture of 1938.

Academy Awards in Art Direction, Editing, and Original Score. Korngold's second Oscar win (he won in 1936 for *Anthony Adverse*).

Recordings

Charles Gerhardt, National Philharmonic Orchestra, *Captain Blood: Classic Film Scores for Errol Flynn*. Includes excerpts from Robin Hood. Fine recording. ****

Charles Gerhardt, National Philharmonic Orchestra, *The Sea Hawk: The Classic Film Scores of Erich Wolfgang Korngold*, RCA, 1991. Part of the Classic Film Scores Series with excerpts from Robin Hood. Fine recording. ****

Varujan Kozian and the Utah Symphony, *Erich Wolfgang Korngold: Music from The Adventures of Robin Hood*, Varése Sarabande, 1987, CD. Topnotch sound. ****

Bibliography

Karlin, Fred. *Listening to Movies: The Film Lover's Guide to Film Music*. New York: Schirmer Books, 1994.

—LEM

ALEXANDER NEVSKY

(1938)
Sergei Prokofiev

The Film

There have been many successful collaborations between film directors and composers. Among the most successful are those of Alfred Hitchcock with Bernard Herrmann and Steven Spielberg with John Williams. Besides these pairings is the one involving Russian filmmaker Sergei Eisenstein, who worked with Sergei Prokofiev on several films, most notably *Alexander Nevsky*.

Eisenstein's film, which is set in the thirteenth century, documents the heroics of Prince Alexander, who earned the nickname Nevsky after leading a Russian army in a decisive battle against the invading Swedish army that took place on the river Neva in 1240. This victory led to Alexander's unification of Russian duchies to defeat an army of German knights on the river Chudskoye in 1242. The film culminates with his victorious entry into Pskov, where he is celebrated as a national hero.

Nikolai Cherkasov as Alexander Nevsky. *Amkino Corporation / Photofest © Amkino Corporation*

The Music

A proper appreciation of Prokofiev's achievement as composer for Eisenstein's film is difficult to achieve, primarily due to the poor quality of the film's original soundtrack recording, which was sanctioned by Stalin without either Eisenstein or Prokofiev's involvement. Fortunately, in 1986, a restored version of the score was authorized by music producer John Goberman with the assistance of orchestrator William D. Brohn. This version was used in place of the original soundtrack when a restored print of the film began to be shown in concert halls with a live orchestral performance of the score. In 1993, the St. Petersburg Philharmonic recorded the score for a VHS release of the restored film. It is this version of the film and the RCA Victor CD of the score that have been examined for the present article.

Instead of the original film's silent credits, the restoration features opening music that was composed for the 1939 *Nevsky* cantata. Thereafter the restored version's music duplicates that of the original film.

The film's opening scene shows a barren Russian landscape following a battle with a Swedish army that has scarred the land with dead bodies and abandoned weapons. Stark unaccompanied tones by woodwinds and strings are heard first, followed by a mournful-sounding theme for oboe with sustained string chords.

In the next scene a Mongol leader and a small attachment of his soldiers pass by a lake where several men are fishing, including Prince Alexander (Nikolai Cherkasov). At this point, an unseen choir begins singing about Alexander's victory over the Swedes at the river Neva. Alexander, now dubbed "Nevsky" for his leadership in that battle, refuses to join the Mongols because he insists that he must remain with his own people. The words of the song reflect his patriotism with such phrases as "We shall not yield the Russian land," which are sung to a noble melody that goes up and down the scale in stepwise motion.

The main part of the film soon begins when hordes of Russian people leave their homes en route to Novgorod to mount a defense against German invaders. As they march toward the city, a rousing choral piece is introduced. This music, which begins with the words "Arise you people of Russia, for the glorious battle," is repeated when Alexander takes command of the army. This music, based on a repeated nine-note motif, has a very upbeat sound that evokes a patriotic feeling about repulsing the German knights, who have already pillaged the city of Pskov.

A third choral piece is set to Latin words beginning with "Peregrinus expectavi"; this short song, which at one point is sounded on an organ, is associated with the German knights who head the invasion.

The centerpiece of the film is the battle fought on Lake Chudskoye in April of 1242. These scenes include a great deal of music, some of which Prokofiev wrote before the scenes were shot; thus Eisenstein edited some of the film to the music.

There are several musical ideas heard during the start of the battle, at around 58:00, that are associated with the German invaders. The first is a repeated three-note pattern played by low brass. The second is an ominous seven-note motif based on two tones played by trumpets that is heard several times. The third is a repeat of the "Peregrinus expectavi."

The most uplifting cue in the battle sequence comes when the Russians gain the upper hand. At around 1:04:40 a new theme is introduced that features a soaring trumpet idea accompanied by rhythmically driven drums as Russian cavalry and foot soldiers dash into battle. Moments later, a second robust theme is introduced by high woodwinds and fast, rhythmically driven drum sounds, as cavalry soldiers charge into battle and force the Germans to retreat.

In the battle's final moments, when the lake ice begins to break, a musical cue mostly for percussion accompanies the watery deaths of scores of German knights.

After the battle there is memorable music, including a mournful piece that features a mezzo-soprano whose singing forms a lament for the dead (note that in the restored version the vocal part is replaced by violins). At the conclusion of the film, Alexander arrives triumphantly in Pskov, with a closing majestic choral rendition of his theme.

Seldom has a more memorable musical score been written for a film, and thankfully the rerecorded soundtrack can at last allow viewers to experience the film as Prokofiev and Eisenstein must have originally wished.

Contributing to the fame of this film is the *Alexander Nevsky* cantata, which Prokofiev created in 1939. This has become a frequently performed concert work and has helped to confirm the view that *Nevsky* is among the greatest of all film scores.

Recognition

Winner of the 1941 Stalin prize for best film.

In 2011 conductor Valery Gergiev called the score "the best ever composed for the cinema."

Recordings

André Previn and the Los Angeles Philharmonic, *Alexander Nevsky*, Telarc, 1987, CD. Top-notch performance and sound. ****

Yuri Temirkanov and the St. Petersburg Philharmonic, *Alexander Nevsky*, RCA, 1993. Rerecording of score CD. Excellent sound. ****

Bibliography

Jaffé, Daniel. *Sergey Prokofiev.* London: Phaeton Press, 1998.

—LEM

AROUND THE WORLD IN 80 DAYS

(1956)
Victor Young

The Film

Of the many films based on Jules Verne's novels, including Walt Disney's 1954 *20,000 Leagues under the Sea*, *From the Earth to the Moon* (1958), *Mysterious Island*

(1961), and two versions of *Journey to the Center of the Earth* (1959 and 2008), Michael Todd's 1956 version of *Around the World in 80 Days* is perhaps the most exceptional.

Todd conceived his film as a widescreen spectacle to be shot in Todd-AO, a process that Todd developed in partnership with the American Optical Company. He then approached author S. J. Perelman to adapt Verne's book, selected Michael Anderson as director, and engaged over forty-two international stars to appear in cameos. Todd also hired thirty-three assistant directors to oversee the multiple-location shooting demanded by the film's screenplay.

In the film, the punctilious Phileas Fogg (David Niven) accepts a wager by fellow members of the all-male Reform Club in London that challenges him to circumnavigate the globe in eighty days or less. Fogg accepts the bet, enlists his trusty valet, Passepartout (Cantinflas), to accompany him, and thus begins a journey that includes many unexpected adventures.

The Music

Victor Young's score, which cleverly reflects the various locales of Fogg's intercontinental journey, includes leitmotifs for the major characters, with most of the melodies borrowed from existing sources. For example, Fogg is represented by the refrain of "Rule, Britannia," while Passepartout's motif is based on "La Cucaracha" (a nod to Cantinflas's Mexican nationality).

Two other motifs are associated with characters that join Fogg's team while en route. The first is a waltz theme associated with Aouda (Shirley MacLaine), an Indian princess that Fogg rescues during a ceremony when she is supposed to join her deceased husband on a funeral pyre. Her theme is first heard in the French sequence when Fogg has to improvise the departure from Paris due to an avalanche that forces the planned train trip over the Alps to become a flight over the Pyrenees en route to Spain. The lilting melody of Young's tune, which is the most prominent theme in the film, creates a feeling of floating in the airborne sequence and later hints at a budding romance between Fogg and the princess.

The motif for Inspector Fix (Robert Newton), who joins the team in order to verify his suspicion that Fogg has robbed the Bank of England, is a purposely clichéd minor-key idea that resembles old-time movie music associated with a villainous character.

Another original theme in Young's score is a rhythmically energetic idea that is heard in the film's opening scene as Passepartout bicycles his way to an employment agency, where he is hired to work for Mr. Fogg, whose eccentricities have driven the last valet to tears. This jaunty tune is recognizable by the ascending seventh that occurs between its first two tones.

Yet another original theme includes sets of cascading string sounds that descend the scale in a succession of semitones. This idea occurs when Fogg and Passepartout travel east from Bombay aboard a train. Another melodious theme, based on a smoothly flowing motif of seven tones, accompanies the group as they travel by train through the American West. This melody has a decidedly out-of-doors flavor that suggests the expansiveness of the terrain.

Cantinflas and David Niven in a hot air balloon, one of their modes of transportation. *United Artists / Photofest © United Artists*

The film includes a multitude of other borrowings, prominent among which is "La Sorella," a dance melody that Young used as a motif for Passepartout's flirtations. Each time Passepartout notices a young lady, the first part of the tune, beginning with a rising set of five tones, is quoted. "La Sorella" is also heard as part of Young's piano music featured in the film's prologue, when Edward R. Murrow introduces footage from Méliès's pioneering 1902 film *Trip to the Moon*.

Another quotation is the French tune "Auprès de ma blonde," which is heard alternately with "La Sorella" as Fogg and his valet arrive at a Paris train station. "The Bear Goes over the Mountain" (perhaps better known as "For He's a Jolly Good Fellow") is heard as source music during a political rally in San Francisco. "Yankee Doodle," "Shoe Fly," "The Girl I Left Behind Me," and "Oh Susanna" also appear in this section of the film, along with part of Rossini's "William Tell Overture," which underscores the scene in which the U.S. Cavalry rides in search of Passepartout, who has been captured by Indians.

Since the beginning of the film follows the prologue without intervening credits, the leading players and all of the cameo actors are named in an animated epilogue designed by graphic artist Saul Bass. Young's music during the epilogue represents a reprise of the film's music, since it reflects the musical motifs associated with the actors in their scenes, which follow the order of their appearance in Fogg's travels. The credits end with a restatement of the waltz theme that accompanies a shot of a pocket watch that is one of Fogg's most valuable possessions. As the music continues the pocket watch opens, its contents fly out, and a heart appears at the center of the watch. This clearly reflects the romantic feelings that Fogg has repressed for much of the film but finally is able to verbally express.

To be evaluated properly, *Around the World* must be seen on a large screen in its original Todd-AO format. On a small computer screen, much of the visual element is lost. However, Victor Young's music remains one of the film's most valuable assets. It is an exceedingly clever combination of the new and the borrowed, with its many musical styles reflective of the various locales where the segments of the film take place. This score deserves to be ranked among the most memorable of all film-music creations.

Recognition

Highly acclaimed by critics.

Four Academy Awards for Best Picture, Adapted Screenplay, Editing, and Original Score.

Victor Young was awarded posthumously, since he died shortly after the film's premiere.

Recordings

Richard Kaufman, the New Zealand Symphony Orchestra, *Shane: A Tribute to Victor Young* (anthology of Victor Young's music), Koch International Classics, 1996. Includes the entire epilogue music. Good sound. ***½

Victor Young, *Around the World in 80 Days*, Decca Records, 1957. Rerecording of the score, reissued on MCA Records CD. Rather dated sound. ***

Bibliography

Cohn, Art, ed. *Michael Todd's Around the World in 80 Days Almanac.* New York: Random House, 1956.

—LEM

AVALON
(1990)
Randy Newman

The Film

Many filmmakers have created motion pictures that are autobiographical in nature. In 1987 both John Boorman and Barry Levinson used their childhood memories as source material; while *Hope and Glory* (1987) depicts Boorman's family struggling to survive in England during World War II, *Avalon* centers on Levinson's family members adjusting to changing times in Baltimore in the 1950s.

Although in Levinson's script the street his family lives on is fictionally named, much else about the film's story is factual. *Avalon* depicts an immigrant family of five brothers who have come to America from Poland during the first part of the twentieth century.

One of the central characters in the film is young Michael Kaye (Elijah Wood), whose father, Jules (Aidan Quinn), changes his surname from Krichinsky to Kaye for business reasons. Michael's grandfather, Sam Krichinsky (Armin Mueller-Stahl) loves to relate to his grandchildren the story of how he arrived in Baltimore on the Fourth of July, 1914.

The Music

Randy Newman's score injects a lyrical atmosphere into *Avalon*. Among the most prominent musical ideas in the film is a minor-key theme in waltz time that is first heard at the start of the film when Sam is telling his grandchildren about his first day in Baltimore. A solo piano is heard in the first segment of the theme that begins with a six-note idea that revolves around a single tone. Soon strings are added as Newman's idea becomes a fleshed-out theme. There is a tinge of melancholy about the music, which is in striking contrast to the amazement that the young Sam displays as he sees fireworks lighting up the sky and children running about with sparklers to celebrate a holiday that is completely foreign to him.

A variation on the first theme is heard as source music toward the end of Sam's recollections, when he describes the first time that he saw Michael's grandmother, Eva (Joan Plowright). Sam remembers playing the violin along with his brothers in a small ensemble that is standing on a balcony overlooking a ballroom where Eva is dancing. The strings play a waltz theme that incorporates the six-note idea from the opening of the film.

Michael Krauss as the young Sam Krichinsky, family patriarch. *Tri-Star Pictures / Photofest* ©
Tri-Star Pictures

A third occurrence of this music is heard in a scene when Michael accompanies his father on his route as a door-to-door salesman. After Jules is stabbed during a robbery, a solo piano starts the theme while Michael and his father ride in an ambulance. As Jules starts to recall his own childhood memories, strings join with the piano in an expressive version of the theme.

A second prominent idea is introduced briefly when Michael's family is packing to move to their new home in the suburbs. As the movers are carrying out furniture there is a sprightly theme for piano with the accompaniment of strings and a soft flute. This theme is heard again as Sam and Jules look around the house they are vacating and Sam recalls Michael taking his first baby steps there. Although the music, which features strings and woodwinds, is kept to a soft level, it adds a feeling of nostalgia about the memories that families accumulate over time.

This theme recurs when a circus troupe comes parading down the street past the home of one of Jules's uncles where a family circle meeting is taking place. First there is lively circus music, but when Michael and his little cousins run outside and are gleefully jumping about, a louder version of the second theme is heard, with a solo trumpet sounding the melody. This music, which also features strings, horns, and woodwinds again adds a nostalgic feeling.

This theme continues in the next scene when Sam takes Michael and some of their cousins to a local park to spend the night during a hot spell. When Sam tells the kids about the small nightclub he used to own, first there is lively source music in the form of a swing piece featuring a solo trumpet, alto sax, piano, and a female singer. When Jules's cousin Izzy (Kevin Pollak), and Jules dance with their brides after having just gotten married by a justice of the peace, Sam recalls this as the best wedding he ever went to. The trumpet again is heard as the second theme returns to add more nostalgia to this happy recollection.

One of the most extended cues in the film features a piano version of the first theme that bookends a five-minute segment of the film. After a feud erupts at one of the family circle meetings, Sam and his side of the family drive off in anger, with the piano sounding the theme. This is the most developed version of the theme, with an add-on section that hasn't been heard before. This theme continues with Sam playing it on a piano at their home. At this point the theme becomes source music, but after a moment strings are added to the theme as underscoring. Music continues as a montage of short scenes begins; a new theme is added as Sam is wallpapering and showing Michael how to do it; then Sam announces that he and Eva are moving into their own place. This theme continues into the departure scene when Sam picks up Michael to say his goodbyes. At this point the solo piano repeats the first theme.

Avalon is about the day-to-day events that define family life, with a score that avoids loud intrusive statements of themes but adds a subtle and lyrical quality to the film. The music is one of Randy Newman's most tuneful works. Although this score lacks the big emphatic moments of his memorable music for *The Natural*, it is still one of his most melodiously haunting film scores and one that should be included on a list of the best film scores of all time.

Recognition

Oscar nominations for Best Screenplay; Best Music, Original Score; Best Cinematography; and Best Costume Design.
Golden Globe nomination for Best Picture.

Recording

Randy Newman, *Avalon: Music from the Motion Picture*, Reprise, 1990, CD. Evocative trumpet solos by Malcolm McNab, with Randy Newman playing piano solos on two tracks. Other piano solos by Michael Lang, with lyrical violin solos played by Stuart Canin. Excellent sound. ****

Bibliography

MacDonald, Laurence E. *The Invisible Art of Film Music*. Second edition. Lanham, MD: Scarecrow Press, 2013.

—LEM

B

BACK TO THE FUTURE

(1985)
Alan Silvestri

The Film

Back to the Future, directed by Robert Zemeckis, is a popular science-fiction adventure comedy film that has gained somewhat of a cult following and inspired two sequels. Starring Michael J. Fox as the teenager Marty McFly and Christopher Lloyd as the loveable mad scientist Doc Brown, the film explores time travel in a unique, quirky fashion. Its success is reinforced by theme park ride adaptations, an animated series, video games, and an upcoming musical.

The plot centers around Fox and Lloyd's characters and their adventures in Hill Valley, California. In 1985, the year in which the film was set and released, the two characters meet for the first time in a shopping mall parking lot. Doc shows Marty a modified car, the DeLorean, which can travel back in time using stolen plutonium from Libyan terrorists. As the Libyans arrive and attack Doc, Marty escapes with the car but unwittingly travels back in time to 1955. In the past, Marty tries to find the younger Doc, but almost inadvertently erases himself from history by preventing his own parents from meeting. Eventually, after several clever plot devices that examine time-travel paradoxes, Marty returns to 1985 while Doc travels to 2015, setting up the first sequel. *Back to the Future* is highly regarded and regularly appears in lists of the top fifty or one hundred greatest films of all time.

The Music

The score to *Back to the Future* was composed by Alan Silvestri, who was thirty-five years old when the film was made. It was the first time in his career that he had been nominated for awards (Saturn and Grammy). He would go on to form a strong collaborative partnership with Robert Zemeckis, composing for every Zemeckis film since *Back to the Future*.

The score is a mixture of grandiose orchestral music and popular songs, most notably two new songs by Huey Lewis and the News. The main orchestral theme is divided into two musical cues. The first is a fanfare and the second a heroic,

14

Christopher Lloyd and Michael J. Fox preparing to travel back in time. *Universal Pictures / Photofest © Universal Pictures*

majestic march-like theme. Both make extensive use of brass, such as trumpets and French horns, and crashing percussion. The strings interject with flourishes and connecting melodic passages. Neither the fanfare nor march is heard in its entirety during the film itself, but the audience instead hears fragments that advance the narrative at crucial moments. It is worth mentioning at this juncture that the film does not open with music. The opening five minutes contain only the sound of ticking clocks, before Marty almost blows himself up by plugging his electric guitar into an extremely large amplifier. The first music we hear in the film is "The Power of Love" by Huey Lewis and the News.

The full theme is heard only during the closing credits, but it is used more frequently in the two sequels. It is a memorable melody and arguably remains one of Silvestri's finest musical achievements. He composed the piece at the piano, experimenting until he had just the melody, and worried about orchestration and harmony afterward. While the entire theme is twenty notes long, oftentimes only the first three notes, a descending fifth followed by an ascending diminished fifth (or tritone), are used, thereby suggesting the theme without playing all of it.

The first music we hear by Silvestri in the film is in the cue "The DeLorean Revealed," but it has also been given the name "The Magic of Time Travel" by film music journalists Jon and Al Kaplan. This twinkling, dissonant cue consists purely of two arpeggiated chords played a half step (or semitone) apart, creating a musical clash but also a sense of wonderment and enchantment. This short, seconds-long musical interjection becomes a signifier (and leitmotif) for the time-travel element of the film.

There are other instrumental cues of importance in the film. Doc Brown has a theme that is playful and comedic in nature. The quick shifts in instrumentation, along with the sometimes otherworldly harmonic accompaniment, ensure that the Doc is portrayed as both slightly zany but also mysterious.

It would be incorrect to dismiss *Back to the Future* as being totally bombastic in nature in terms of its score. There are also much-needed moments of relief, such as in the cue "Marty's Letter," where a soft string ensemble performs a delicate theme, reflecting the softer side of the protagonist's character.

This combination of musical themes, from the fanfares, to the heroic march, to the arpeggiated dissonance depicting time travel exemplifies how Silvestri creates an appropriate accompaniment to an adventurous, romping science-fiction comedy. In contrast to a more "serious" science-fiction film, such as *Blade Runner*, the score allows itself lighter moments in keeping with the nature of the narrative, and this more jovial approach complements the visuals wonderfully, cementing its place as among the finest film scores of all time.

Recognition

Nominated for Saturn Award for Best Music.
Nominated for Grammy Award for Best Score Soundtrack for Visual Media.

Recording

Alan Silvestri, *Back to the Future*, Geffen Records, 1985. This is the an expanded edition of the original motion picture soundtrack. ***

Bibliography

Fhlainn, S. N. (ed.). *The Worlds of "Back to the Future": Critical Essays on the Films.* Jefferson, NC: McFarland, 2010.

—ML

BATMAN

(1989)
Danny Elfman

The Film

This superhero film, directed by Tim Burton and starring Michael Keaton as Batman, was the first in a Warner Bros. series of Batman films that, at the time of writing, has reached ten in number, with an eleventh in the planning stage. Keaton would go on to star in the next film in the series, *Batman Returns*, in 1992.

The film was both critically acclaimed and commercially successful. With a box office return of over $400 million, it was then the fifth-highest-grossing film of all time. It won an Academy Award for Best Art Direction and was nominated for a Golden Globe and six BAFTAs (British Academy Awards.)

The film is set in the fictional Gotham City during its bicentennial year, where the mayor wants to make the city safer. Batman, a vigilante who targets the city's criminals, is investigated by journalist Vicki Vale (Kim Basinger), and Bruce Wayne, Batman's alter ego, begins a relationship with her. Batman continues to fight crime in the city, but soon meets a more deadly foe in the Joker (Jack Nicholson). The Joker lures Vale into a trap, but Batman arrives to rescue her. Later it is revealed that the Joker was the mugger who killed Wayne/Batman's parents years ago. Batman eventually defeats the Joker, and peace is restored, temporarily, to Gotham City.

Batman (Michael Keaton) confronts the Joker (Jack Nicholson). *Warner Bros. / Photofest © Warner Bros.*

The Music

The score to *Batman* was composed by Danny Elfman. The composer was fairly inexperienced at this time, having collaborated for the first time with Tim Burton on *Pee-Wee's Big Adventure* in 1985. Burton had seen Elfman performing in a band and had always considered his music to be very filmic in nature. As is often the case with directors and composers, this collaboration has blossomed into a long-term relationship. Elfman has scored all but three of Burton's feature-length films since. It should also be noted that 1989 was a particularly successful year for Elfman because besides scoring *Batman*, he composed the theme music for a new cartoon series called *The Simpsons*.

Elfman's inspiration for the music originally came from walking around the London-based set of Gotham City at night, with the studio lights switched off. The main theme is at first a slow, rising, dark sequence of brass chords, but then suddenly develops into a heroic fanfare that takes the slow first theme and speeds it up, adding a great feeling of momentum. The theme fits perfectly with Batman's character, a man who moves in the shadows, an uncelebrated, mysterious hero in his vigilante actions in Gotham City. The theme itself is very simple, yet this simplicity lends itself to development throughout the film. Whether it is the melody or a simple harmonic progression that is used as the basis for new variations, the music is easily adapted to fit differing scenes and moods.

The Joker, the main villain in the film, is not scored as heavily as Batman. There is, however, one memorable scene where the Joker is underscored by a jovial waltz. The juxtaposition of images of gunfire and violence set against the sickly sweet waltz creates real impact. The perception of the waltz changes dramatically depending on whether one listens to it with or without the visual. With the visual, the saccharine nature of the music becomes twisted, inappropriate, and altogether terrifying. It almost resembles music one might find in a haunted house or ghost train ride at an amusement park.

Elfman's music is unique in that it is at times heavily percussive and full of momentum, yet through the use of clever orchestration it never becomes overbearing or too saturated with noise. The influence of Elfman's popular music background can be heard, as well as certain jazzy inflections that result in his unique style, one that has stayed with him through his entire film music career.

Elfman's score is not all about swelling orchestral lines and driving percussive motifs, however. There is also a love theme, soft and tender on harps, strings, and woodwinds, offering a welcome respite from the more intense musical moments. It is never without a sense of danger, though, suggesting that this is a romance that will be fraught with anxieties and uncertainties. It demonstrates that Elfman is by no means a one-trick pony in his stylistic output and can offer a full range of moods to suit the relevant scenes.

In the final moments, with explosions and ferocity seen nowhere else in the movie, Elfman responds in kind with a grandiose eruption of sound. It begins to resemble not merely a film score, but a Wagnerian finale to an opera on screen. Composers often are able to stretch their metaphorical legs at the close of a film, and Elfman does so here with real aplomb. It is not overbearing or sensationalist, but rather an orchestral cacophony of sound that creates a real feeling of apocalyptic heroism and magnificence, a fine conclusion, showing the world what was later to come from the composer.

Recognition

BMI (Broadcast Music, Inc.) Film Music Award.
Brit Award for Best Soundtrack.
Grammy for Best Instrumental Composition.

Recordings

Danny Elfman, *Batman: Original Motion Picture Score*, Warner Bros., 1989. The Sinfonia of London conducted by Shirley Walker performs the official soundtrack, which contains twenty-one tracks and runs to just over an hour. Recommended. ****

Prince. *Batman*. Warner Bros., 1989. The score also contained nine songs by Prince and this recording contains these songs but none of Elfman's music. A must for fans of the film or artist. ***

—ML

A BEAUTIFUL MIND

(2001)
James Horner

The Film

Directed by Ron Howard and starring Russell Crowe and Ed Harris, *A Beautiful Mind* is a biographical drama based on Nobel Laureate John Nash. The film opens with Nash (Crowe) arriving at Princeton University, where he meets other graduate students and his roommate. Under extreme pressure to publish, he insists on his own original idea, which develops from the theory that a cooperative approach is likely to be more successful than "every man for himself" in all situations. Nash joins MIT and is later invited to the Pentagon to help crack enemy telecommunications. He becomes obsessive about his work, namely attempting to thwart Soviet plots through analyzing newspapers and magazines.

Nash falls in love with Alicia Larde (Jennifer Connelly) and marries her; however, his paranoia reaches new heights. He attempts to flee from a lecture at Harvard, fearing that he is surrounded by Russian agents. After punching a professor, he is sedated and admitted to a hospital where he is diagnosed with paranoid schizophrenia. After being released, Nash stops taking the medication given to him. Suspecting this is the case, Alicia rushes home to find their baby submerged in the bathtub due to Nash obsessing over newspaper articles once more.

Eventually, Nash returns to Princeton and learns to ignore his hallucinations. By the late 1970s, he is allowed to teach again. In 1994, Nash wins the Nobel Memorial Prize in Economics for his revolutionary work on game theory.

The film was critically successful, being nominated for eight, and awarded four, Academy Awards (Best Adapted Screenplay, Best Picture, Best Director, and Best Supporting Actress for Jennifer Connelly). The film also won two BAFTAs.

The Music

The score to *A Beautiful Mind* was composed by the late James Horner. The composer and director Howard worked together on six films before Horner's

Russell Crowe as brilliant but troubled mathematician John Nash. *Universal Pictures / Photofest © Universal Pictures*

untimely death in a light aircraft accident in 2015. Horner wanted a haunting female voice to feature on his score, and he strove for something "reminiscent of being midway between a girl and woman." He chose to bring fifteen-year-old Welsh singer Charlotte Church on board for the film, and the artist later said the music for the film was among the "most haunting and beautiful I have ever performed." The notion of a kaleidoscope was adopted by Horner to represent the beauty and complexity of mathematics. In the opening theme, titled "A Kaleidoscope of Mathematics" on the recording, a wordless vocal line performed by Church is underscored with constantly evolving harmonies in orchestral ostinatos. The piano later takes over as the dominant accompanying instrument, and this, along with Church's haunting vocals, gives the score a humanized, poignant feel that represents the tragic genius of Nash's character.

In "First Drop-off, First Kiss," the opening theme is recapitulated in the strings. A simple, homophonic string chordal movement is complemented by arpeggios in the harp. It is the epitome of romantic film scoring, and the bittersweet melody on English horn adds to this moment of peace and love.

In a code-cracking scene at the Pentagon, the kaleidoscopic music comes to the fore. Constantly shifting harmonies and textures in the music, without melody, contribute to the feeling of immense genius at work. The music represents the cogs in a machine, whirring in perfect synchronicity in Nash's mind. Neither grandiose nor minimalist, it is an evolving, adapting, dreamlike cue that feels like it is alive. No music could underscore such a complex, powerful mind more effectively, as Nash stares intensely at the numbers, trying to work out the meaning within them. A subtle French horn appears as the answer draws near, hinting at the heroic trope that the instrument has for centuries represented. This short two-minute scene exemplifies the wonders of Horner's score. The music is foregrounded without being overbearing; surely the sign of a great film score is that it is noticeable but not forcibly present.

The whole score, based on the kaleidoscope concept and Church's voice, is an emotional suite of soundtracks to a descent into madness and the ultimate acceptance and redemption at the film's conclusion. The voice of Charlotte Church is a key component in the score's success, as it ultimately bared the soul of Nash to the audience. The use of voice in film scoring to represent the human condition is a common technique, but it is rarely so evocatively successful as in Horner's score to *A Beautiful Mind.*

Recognition

Nominated for Academy Award for Best Original Score.
Nominated for Golden Globe for Best Original Score.

Recording

James Horner, *A Beautiful Mind,* Decca Music Group, 2002. The official soundtrack album, running to seventy-one minutes across sixteen tracks. This includes a song, "All Love Can Be," performed by Charlotte Church. Some of the cues sound a little isolated when separated from the rest of the score, so it is recommended that the recording be listened to as a whole entity. ***

Bibliography

Neary, Lynn. "Analysis: Film Scores for *A Beautiful Mind* and *A.I.: Artificial Intelligence.*" *Highbeam,* March 10, 2002. https://www.highbeam.com/doc/1P1-51458075.html.

Nicholl, Katie. "Charlotte Has an Oscar in Her Beautiful Mind." *Mail on Sunday,* October 21, 2001.

—ML

BECKET

(1964)
Laurence Rosenthal

The Film

French playwright Jean Anouilh's award-winning play was adapted in 1964 into a lavish film with a pair of award-worthy performances. It is a fictionalized version of the relationship of Henry II (Peter O'Toole), the English monarch who reigned in the latter part of the twelfth century, and his chancellor and best friend Thomas Becket (Richard Burton). When Henry made the fateful decision to appoint Becket as the archbishop of Canterbury, his attempt to consolidate his temporal powers with those of the Catholic Church led to a series of struggles that culminated in the murder of Becket in Canterbury Cathedral. The film portrays the camaraderie of the two men in their younger years and the collapse of their friendship when Becket advises that he will serve the church first and Henry second. The latter part of the film focuses on the struggles between the two men and the events that lead up to Becket's death.

King Henry II (Peter O'Toole) and his close friend turned adversary Thomas Becket (Richard Burton). *Paramount Pictures / Photofest © Paramount Pictures*

The Music

The choice of Laurence Rosenthal as composer for *Becket* was an easy one, since he had composed incidental music for the Broadway stage production of the play. In creating the film score, Rosenthal incorporated Gregorian chant melodies from the Middle Ages and blended them skillfully into a score that also includes music with a modern melodic and harmonic context.

The music for the opening credits illustrates how Rosenthal incorporated the score's varied melodic materials into this medieval drama. The film's first sounds are tolling bell tones and a chant melody sung by a male choir. This is soon followed by dramatic brass sounds along with a continuation of the choir's unison singing of the chant tune. A rousing fanfare for trumpets and French horns is then introduced, followed by an emotional melody for strings, harp, and French horns. Then more choral singing returns, but this time in a parallel vocal harmony ending with the singing of the word "alleluia."

This combination of musical styles continues in the opening scene in which King Henry arrives at Canterbury Cathedral to pay his respects to the deceased Becket. As Henry arrives, the music features a string version of a chant melody, plus a collage of sounds, including a tolling bell, a brass fanfare, and overlapping melodic lines that feature trumpets, trombones, and French horns. An unseen choir then intones the start of the "Dies Irae," a Gregorian melody from the ancient Catholic funeral liturgy. This singing is softly accompanied by repeated tremolo string tones and low drum sounds.

Once Henry kneels before Becket's tomb, he remembers their friendship and the circumstances behind their falling out. While Henry talks to the tomb as if Becket could hear him, the music features soft woodwind and harp tones, along with sustained string harmonies and muffled drum sounds.

The film's central story then begins in flashback fashion, with a raucous musical cue that accompanies a comical escapade in which Henry has spent the night frolicking with a country lass, while Becket provides the means for their hasty departure on horseback. Music with a carnival atmosphere begins as they climb out a window. When they ride off together on a single horse, the music features the score's principal theme, an energetic idea for strings based on a repeated five-note motif with full-orchestra accompaniment.

There are a few other themes in the film, including a pompous march that is heard when Henry and Becket ride through a French town that the English army has vanquished. The sounds of brass and drums add a regal quality to this music, which unfortunately is compromised by the din of the cheering crowds. The music continues with military drum sounds when news arrives that the old archbishop of Canterbury has died. At this point Henry conceives the clever idea of making his loyal chancellor the replacement for the dead archbishop. There is no music when Becket tries to convince Henry not to carry out his plan, but when the king receives the keys to the town a chant melody is sung by male voices in parallel harmony. Orchestral harmony is added to the music as a suggestion of both Henry's victory over the town and also his dominance over Becket, who reluctantly agrees to the appointment as the new primate of the English Catholic Church.

At this point in the film Becket's character changes from the fun-loving personal friend of Henry to a serious-minded leader of the Church. The music of the consecration scene reflects this change by including unison singing of several chant melodies, including the Litany of the Saints and "Veni Creator Spiritus." When Becket exits the cathedral a majestic brass theme accompanies his presentation to the crowd.

The score's main theme returns late in the film when Becket and Henry meet in France, where Becket has been living in exile to escape Henry's wrath over Becket's excommunication of one of Henry's knights. As they approach each other on horseback from a distance, the music swells with brass harmonies, and a full orchestra sounds a majestic brief version of the main theme.

By restricting the music in *Becket* to certain select moments the makers of the film have preserved the dialogue of Anouilh's play without much interference. Still, Rosenthal's score enhances the emotional elements in this drama of two men whose devoted friendship has been compromised by their conflicting positions. With his ingenious blending of the medieval and the modern Rosenthal's music is a praiseworthy film-music achievement.

Recognition

Twelve Oscar nominations, including Best Picture and Best Score.
Edward Anhalt won the Oscar for his adapted screenplay.

Recordings

Laurence Rosenthal, *Becket*, Decca Records, 1964. Original soundtrack, available only on vinyl. Good sound. ***½
Laurence Rosenthal, *Laurence Rosenthal: Film Music*, 1994. This two-CD set contains excerpts from *Becket* and other films. It was produced by Windemere Music Publishers for promotional use only. Excellent sound. ****

Bibliography

Becket Souvenir Book. New York: National Publishers, 1964.
Rosenthal, Laurence. Liner notes. *Becket* Original Soundtrack. Decca DL-9117, 1964, LP.

—LEM

BEN-HUR

(1959)
Miklós Rózsa

The Film

Stories associated with the Bible have inspired some of cinema's most expensively produced films, including William Wyler's 1959 widescreen version of *Ben-Hur*, which broke existing records with a budget of $15 million. What most significantly sets this film apart from other costly biblical spectacles is the quality of its script, adapted from Lew Wallace's novel, and Wyler's incisive direction. Charlton Heston is another asset, with his virile characterization of Judah Ben-Hur, a Jewish prince who is enslaved by the Romans following a minor incident that occurs during a military procession in Jerusalem.

The biblical connection in *Ben-Hur* stems from Wallace's idea that Judah's life has links to that of Jesus of Nazareth. Both are about the same age, and their lives converge on two fateful occasions. Wallace's story also involves Judah's relationship with his childhood friend, Messala (Stephen Boyd), whose ambition as a Roman soldier is fueled by his military training in Rome. It is Messala who arrests Judah and has him condemned to slavery. After regaining his freedom, revenge spurs Judah to oppose his former friend in a spectacular chariot race.

Charlton Heston as slave Judah Ben-Hur. *MGM / Photofest © MGM*

The Music

Miklós Rózsa created a lavish orchestral and choral score for *Ben-Hur* that is the longest and most grandiose of his career, with leitmotifs for the major characters in the film and music of pomp and splendor that defines the Roman occupation of Palestine during the first century.

A twelve-minute prologue that precedes *Ben-Hur*'s opening credits is worthy of careful observation since it is filled with Rózsa's music. A pair of motifs is heard as the MGM lion is shown, with the film's title appearing immediately thereafter. In these two motifs Rózsa's music helps establish both the ancient time frame of the story and its Middle-Eastern locale. The first motif has three tones, the middle one of which is a whole step lower than the other two.

Superimposed over these three tones is a mostly descending-pitch six-note idea that uses the old Dorian mode with its lowered pitches on the third and seventh scale steps.

Another element in the music is a tendency for parallelism in the harmonic progression of chordal harmonies and the avoidance of middle tones in those chords.

The prologue music also features two lyrical pieces in depicting the birth of Jesus. The first, "The Star of Bethlehem," includes a sweet melody for violins, while the "Adoration of the Magi" music is a lyrical piece for strings and woodwinds that has the flavor of a children's lullaby, with the harmonic addition of two descending tones that resemble a "mooing" effect, since there are animals in the stable where Jesus's birth takes place.

Then the film's credits begin with a dramatic motif for trumpets and lower brass that leads to the Christ theme, which features the five-note pattern F-E-C-D-B♭. Judah's theme, which comes next, is based on a five-note march-like idea that ends with a rising octave.

Two other themes are introduced during the credits: a flowing love theme for Judah and Esther, plus an emotional idea for strings that defines Judah's family (referred to on the recordings as "A Mother's Love"). An especially noteworthy scene comes after Esther, the daughter of Judah's chief steward, is granted the permission to marry. When she comes to Judah to express her gratitude, first there is a gentle version of the love theme for a low-range flute and harp, and then an emotional version for strings and harp accompanies the moment when he gives her a goodbye kiss.

Beyond the motifs for the various characters, Rózsa's score is filled with music of pageantry played by brass instruments, especially when Arrias (Jack Hawkins), head of the Roman fleet, brings Judah, now his adopted son, triumphantly to Rome to meet the emperor following a sea battle in which Judah saved the admiral's life.

Especially noteworthy in Rózsa's score is the "Parade of the Charioteers," which precedes the climactic chariot race. This music is based on two motifs introduced earlier in the film. The first is a six-note marching idea that signifies the Romans in general and Messala in particular. Then Judah's theme returns in a dramatic statement, with the melody played by strings with a repetitive brass and percussion accompaniment. Significantly, there is no music during the actual race. The grinding of wheels, the thunderous sounds of racing horses, plus the cheering by throngs of spectators provide all the sounds that are needed in this spectacular scene.

An especially glorious musical cue is heard during the storm following Jesus's death on the cross, when his blood trickles down and becomes mixed with rain and then flows into a vast sea. During this scene the music is in the form of a canon (also known as a round) in which the Christ theme is heard as overlapping musical lines, with the strings repeatedly beginning a phrase and the brass sounding the same melodic tones two beats behind the strings. This emotion-filled moment, in which Judah's mother and sister are miraculously cured of leprosy, is followed moments later by a glorious closing choral rendition of the Christ theme.

This is not only Rózsa's musical masterpiece, but in terms of its emotional themes and majestic instrumentation one of the greatest of all film scores.

Recognition

Eleven Oscars, setting a new record, including awards for Best Picture, Actor, Supporting Actor, and Director.

Rózsa earned his third Oscar for this score.

Recordings

Miklós Rózsa, *Ben Hur*, Sony, 1991, two-disc set. Includes contents of two studio recordings released in 1959–1960 in place of the actual soundtrack. Includes a few cues from actual film recording sessions. OK performance and sound. ***

Miklós Rózsa, *Ben Hur: A Tale of the Christ*, Rhino Movie Music, 1996. This is a two-CD remastered recording; it includes a booklet and all of the film's original music tracks. Wonderful performance and sound. ****

Miklós Rózsa, National Philharmonic Orchestra and Chorus, *Ben Hur*, London Records, 1985. Studio recording with Rózsa conducting. Excellent performance and sound. ***½

Bibliography

Bradford, Marilee. Liner notes. *Ben-Hur: A Tale of the Christ*. Rhino Movie Music R2 72197, 1996, CD.

Rózsa, Miklós. *Double Life*. New York: Wynwood Press, 1982, 1989.

—LEM

THE BEST YEARS OF OUR LIVES

(1946)

Hugo Friedhofer

The Film

Some noteworthy films about World War II were made during the war, including *Mrs. Miniver* and *Casablanca*, but perhaps the greatest film about the war came after it ended, when Samuel Goldwyn produced *The Best Years of Our Lives*, the definitive film about the struggles faced by returning veterans in putting their lives back together. Robert E. Sherwood's screenplay (based on a story by MacKinlay Kantor) depicts the experiences of three men who return to Boone City (a fictional city akin to Des Moines, Terre Haute, or any other in America's heartland).

In the film, directed by William Wyler (a veteran himself), these three men represent different aspects of the war and also varying strata of society. Al Stephenson (Fredric March), a middle-aged bank executive with a wife and two teenage children, served as an army sergeant in Europe. Fred Derry (Dana Andrews), a soda jerk born on the wrong side of the tracks who got married only days before shipping out, has come home a decorated captain who served as a bombardier in

From left: Harold Russell, Dana Andrews, and Fredric March as WWII veterans who face ob-stacles returning to civilian life. *RKO Radio Pictures Inc. / Photofest © RKO Radio Pictures Inc.*

the Army Air Corps. Meanwhile, Homer Parrish (Harold Russell), a navy ensign from a typical working-class neighborhood, was badly burned in a Japanese attack on his ship. Homer is engaged to his childhood sweetheart, Wilma (Cathy O'Donnell), but he resists her affections because he doesn't want to be pitied for the hooks he wears for hands.

The Music

After many years as a Warner Bros. orchestrator, Hugo Friedhofer became an independent composer in the 1940s, with *Best Years of Our Lives* earning him lasting recognition.

The score for this film has a decidedly American quality, with an orchestration that avoids the kinds of unusual sounds that added a special ambience to some other 1940s scores such as Miklós Rózsa's Oscar-winning music for *Spellbound*, with its use of the theremin.

The music in the opening credits exemplifies the heroism of those who served during World War II. A horn motif, which begins after a few seconds, clearly suggests the military aspect of the story, with its first three ascending tones mimicking the sounds of a bugle. The rising tones, first heard as G-C-E, recur throughout the film as a reminder of a military call-to-arms. Even though Al, Fred, and Homer are no longer in the service, the music suggests that they are haunted by their experiences in the war.

The music in the credits also includes sets of four tones added onto the three-note horn motif that produce a seven-note theme characterized by rising leaps of an octave. The ascending nature of Friedhofer's melodies is an essential ingredient in the score.

One of the longest cues begins during the homecoming sequence, when the three men are on an overnight flight to Boone City. The cue begins with the soft sounds of strings as Homer sees the dawn breaking. When Al and Fred awaken, the music shifts into an up-tempo version of the score's primary horn motif, with overlapping soundings of the four-tone extension of the motif by string instruments. This is followed by bits of another bugle-like idea for trumpets as they observe Boone City from the air. The music continues as they now observe the city from the back seat of a cab. Various energetic melodic ideas appear as commentary on the changes that have taken place in their hometown, with shots of hot dog stands, used car lots, and various other businesses. When the cab turns onto Homer's street, the music slows down. As they pull up in front of Homer's house, the score includes a sweet violin theme for Wilma, who comes running from her home next door. When Homer raises an arm to wave as the cab pulls away, a minor-key variant of the horn motif suggests Homer's mixed feelings at coming home.

In the following scene, when Al is dropped off in front of his up-scale apartment building, there is no music until he gets into an elevator. At this point, a solo cello plays a sentimental tune that evolves into a poignant string theme as he enters his apartment and his wife, Milly (Myrna Loy), spots him from the end of a long hallway. As they embrace, the strings play an emotional theme that incorporates several repetitions of the rising four-note extension of the horn motif.

Among the other noteworthy themes in the score is a lilting blues idea that is first heard in a scene involving Fred and Al's daughter, Peggy (Teresa Wright). When Al suggests that the drunken Fred spend the night at Al's apartment, as Peggy helps Fred out of his shoes, the sounds of a saxophone suggest a warmth of feeling even before the two are formally introduced.

There is much source music in the film, including music in several scenes that take place at a club owned by Homer's Uncle Butch (Hoagy Carmichael), who is seen mostly at a piano playing tunes while talking with customers.

One especially dramatic cue involves Fred remembering his war experiences as he sits in the cockpit of a soon-to-be dismantled plane. Without a single shot of bombs dropping onto their targets, Friedhofer's strongly accented brass harmonies clearly suggest the war's deadly impact.

This is a lovely score for a truly memorable film. Friedhofer's work, the best of his career, belongs on a list of all-time best scores.

Recognition

The Best Years of Our Lives was the most awarded film of 1946.

Oscar wins for Friedhofer's score as well as Best Picture, Actor (March), Supporting Actor (Russell), Director (Wyler), and Editing.

Recording

Hugo Friedhofer, *Samuel Goldwyn's The Best Years of Our Lives*, Entr'acte Records, 1978, LP. A reconstruction of the score by Tony Bremner performed by the London Philharmonic conducted by Franco Collura. A Preamble CD was released in 1988. Not as dynamic as the original soundtrack but excellently recorded. ***½

Bibliography

Cook, Page. Liner notes. *The Best Years of Our Lives*. Notes reprinted from original vinyl album. Preamble PRCD 1779,1988, CD.

—LEM

THE BIG COUNTRY

(1958)
Jerome Moross

The Film

From the lineage of such classic western films as *Stagecoach* (1939), *High Noon* (1952), and *Shane* (1953), comes William Wyler's *The Big Country* (1958), a widescreen film that centers on a feud between two Texas cattle ranchers during the 1880s.

In Wyler's film, adapted from Donald Hamilton's novel, Gregory Peck plays Jim McKay, a ship's captain from the eastern United States who travels west by stagecoach to wed his fiancée, Pat Terrill (Carroll Baker), at the Ladder Ranch, owned by her father, Major Henry Terrill (Charles Bickford). Jim soon learns about a dispute between Major Terrill and Rufus Hannassey (Burl Ives), patriarch of a neighboring ranch and father to four unruly sons.

Animosity between the two ranchers stems from their mutual desire to own the Big Muddy, a plot of land with a river that that runs between their ranges. The plot's owner, Julie Maragon (Jean Simmons), a local schoolteacher who has allowed the cattle from both ranches to drink from the river, refuses to sell it to either rancher in order to ensure drinking water for both herds. Jim's decision to act as arbiter in the dispute results in dire consequences for both families.

The Music

Wyler apparently wanted Aaron Copland to score the film, but Copland had vowed never to work in Hollywood again after the tampering that had occurred with his score for Wyler's 1949 film *The Heiress*. It has been speculated that Copland recommended his good friend Jerome Moross as composer and Wyler accepted the idea.

Burl Ives, Chuck Connors, Charles Bickford, Alfonso Bedoya, Gregory Peck, and Charlton Heston in the sweeping epic *The Big Country*. *United Artists / Photofest © United Artists*

Since the story is set in the American West, Moross attempted to achieve a sense of grandeur through the repeated use of mostly pentatonic-scale melodic ideas above basic chordal patterns.

Especially vibrant is the opening-credit music, which begins with a repeated pattern of fast-moving violin tones plus a chordal trumpet fanfare. This very energized idea leads directly into a nine-note motif for strings that melodically resembles the beginning of the song "Let Me Call You Sweetheart." This theme is accompanied by syncopated harmonies that change between the second and third beats of each four-count measure and these rhythmic "bumps" add a rugged quality to the imagery of a stagecoach crossing the prairie.

This grandiose theme returns several times. Its second appearance occurs when Jim first looks at a vast landscape from the porch of the Ladder Ranch. Moross's theme aurally reflects the wide-open expanse of the Terrills' cattle range. A lyrical version of the theme is heard in a later scene in which Jim uses a compass as he rides on horseback to get a look at the Big Muddy, which he wants to buy as a wedding present.

Although the score is not leitmotivic in nature, there are themes connected with characters. The Terrills are identified by a six-note idea that uses a pentatonic scale pattern, as in the pitches C-A-C-F-D-C, with long rhythmic pauses on the third tone. The first appearance of this theme occurs when Jim, who has just arrived on the stagecoach, is riding in a buckboard with Pat and headed toward the Terrill ranch. When the Hannassey sons spot them, Pat whips the horses into a full-speed gallop. As the Hannasseys give chase on horseback, the Terrill motif is first sounded by violins and then with trumpets added to the melody. This lively theme, with many syncopated harmonies, continues until the Hannassey boys catch up with them.

The Hannassey motif then begins with an agitated eight-note motif played by trumpets. This raucous music continues while Jim is being teased in rough fashion. Two other melodic ideas are heard in this scene, a fast-paced violin melody that arrives as Jim and Pat start homeward in the buckboard and a second robust idea that enters as Pat initially tries to avoid her neighbors.

One especially noteworthy statement of the Terrill motif occurs when the Major's men ride on horseback through Blanco Canyon to punish the Hannasseys at their ranch as payback for the harsh treatment of Jim and Pat in the earlier scene. This music includes a dramatic statement of the melody with strongly accented syncopated chords and pounding drums in the background.

Among the other pentatonic melodies in the score is a lilting tune for Julie that also represents the Big Muddy itself. Another is a tuneful waltz theme that is heard as source music at the Ladder Ranch during a reception in honor of Jim and Pat's engagement. The waltz is followed by a tuneful polka theme that continues until it is suddenly interrupted by Rufus Hannassey, who makes an unexpected appearance to verbally reprimand the major in response to the destructive raid on the Hannassey ranch.

A syncopated chordal motif is incorporated into the score when Jim enters Blanco Canyon in an attempt to confront Hannassey, who wants to use the kidnapped Julie as a way of luring Terrill's men into an ambush. This motif consists of a basic series of four chords, the first three of which are identical; the fourth chord in the series is a step higher, but upon repetition sounds a step lower. As Terrill and his men enter the canyon, a very rhythmic version of the Terrill motif is heard. The film's final scenes include some of Moross's most dramatic music.

For this almost three-hour film, Moross produced an expansive score that is both tuneful and stylistically captivating. This music surpasses that of other westerns, even *High Noon*, as a classic example of orchestral film scoring. It is truly worthy of being on the top-100 list.

Recognition

Box-office hit and recipient of two Oscar nominations.
Oscar for Best Supporting Actor (Burl Ives).
Oscar nomination for Best Score. Though worthy of the award, Jerome Moross
    lost to Dimitri Tiomkin's music for *The Old Man and the Sea*.

Recordings

Tony Bremner, Philharmonia Orchestra, *The Big Country: Music by Jerome Moross*,
    Silva Screen, 1988. Studio recording of the score on CD. Sound is good, but interpretation not always as vivid as that of original soundtrack. ***
Jerome Moross, *The Big Country*, Screen Classics, 1993. Original soundtrack. Limited edition, with quite good monophonic sound. ***½.

Bibliography

Bremner, Tony. Liner notes. *The Big Country: Music by Jerome Moross*. Silva Screen Records 030, 1988, CD.

—LEM

BLADE RUNNER

(1982)

Vangelis (Evangelos Odysseas Papathanassiou)

The Film

Directed by Ridley Scott and inspiring a 2017 sequel, *Blade Runner* is a science fiction cult classic. Depicting a futuristic (2019), grungy Los Angeles, the aesthetic of the film, caught between science fiction and film noir, resulted in critical acclaim and an enduring appeal to film fans across the globe. It should be noted, however, that success was a slow burner. Initial reactions were mixed, and it only returned $33 million at the box office, a profit of just $5 million. Despite the uncertainty among critics on release, the film was nominated for eight BAFTAs, two Academy Awards, and a Golden Globe. Of these, the film won Best Cinematography, Best

Rick Deckard (Harrison Ford), a blade runner, in 2019 Los Angeles. *Warner Bros. / Photofest* © *Warner Bros.*

Costume Design, and Best Production Design at the BAFTAs. This is understand-
able, as the visual impact of the city skyline of Los Angeles depicted in the future
was (and is) astounding.

Starring Harrison Ford as Rick Deckard in a breakthrough role following his
portrayal of Han Solo in the first two *Star Wars* films in 1977 and 1980, the film
explores the relationship between humans and bioengineered beings known as
replicants. Deckard (Ford) ultimately falls in love with a replicant who thinks she
is human, raising many moral questions about artificial intelligence, which will
surely only become more prevalent as the twenty-first century progresses. Another replicant, Roy (Rutger Hauer), saves Deckard's life when he is hanging off a
tall building. Roy, as he is dying, delivers (and partly improvises) one of the film's
most memorable speeches, one that is widely considered one of cinema history's
finest, about how his memories "will be lost in time, like tears in rain."

The Music

The score to *Blade Runner* was composed by Vangelis. The composer had recently
used synthesizers heavily in his award-winning score to *Chariots of Fire* (1981),
and again he featured them extensively to create dark, moody, atmospheric
soundscapes in the noir landscapes of retro-futuristic Los Angeles.

The opening of the film sets the mood for the remainder. Under a black background with white text introducing the key credits, Vangelis's synthesizer performs an atonal drone, with a higher pitched melodic fragment fading in and out,
but without having a key or destination. This low-level tension continues until
we see "LOS ANGELES, 2019" appear on screen. Then, in a musical moment that
has surely created many goose bumps in audiences, the cityscape enters the full
screen, ablaze with flames from factories and riddled with smog pollution. Vangelis scores this with an arpeggio glissando on synthesized harp, which acts as a
precursor to the first prominent melodic theme. An edgy electronic melody fades
in as the camera pans, tilts, and zooms across the dystopian landscape. The chord
progressions here are undeniably beautiful, a word that one might find inapt
to describe synthesizers. In the hands of Vangelis, though, in a film depicting a
futuristic world, there can be no more appropriate musical accompaniment. The
futuristic, otherworldly sounds are simultaneously harsh and tender, optimistic
and foreboding.

There is a general lack of melodic content in the score in favor of a more ambient soundscape, but there is one noticeable exception with a saxophone solo,
performed by Dick Morrisey, serenading a sumptuous love theme, underscored
with Vangelis's ubiquitous synthesizer. Despite this theme providing some of the
only truly tonal music in the film, it still bears the same mysterious, otherworldly
sound that is heard throughout the rest of Scott's film. Even with this melodic interlude, the atmospheric score was not universally popular. One review claims it
"resides closer to the realm of sound effects and/or new age album atmospherics
rather than anything resembling a truly effective film score." While it is acknowledged that the score does contain new-age elements, it is unfair to say that it does
not resemble an effective film score. Vangelis's silky smooth electronic sounds
glide seamlessly underneath the arresting visuals of a cyberpunk future and

match the genre and aesthetic sublimely. It fully deserves its place as one of the only electronic scores in this book and in our top-100 list.

Recognition

Nominated for a Golden Globe for Best Original Score.
Nominated for a BAFTA for Best Film Music.

Recordings

The score of *Blade Runner* is notorious for having spawned countless bootlegs. The reason for this is that the official soundtrack album was not released until 1994, fully twelve years after the film.

Vangelis. *Blade Runner*, East West Records, 1994, CD, vinyl. The first official release of the soundtrack, and the best sound quality. The bootlegs are to be avoided in favor of this legitimate release. ***
Vangelis. *Blade Runner Trilogy*, 25th Anniversary Box Set, Polydor, 2007, CD. This anniversary edition is spread over three discs. Disc one is the soundtrack, disc two is remastered or reworked versions of the soundtrack, and disc three is works inspired by the film. While some of the new works are not as polished or inspired as the cues on the soundtrack, this is an essential purchase for fans of the film. ****

Bibliography

Filmtracks.com. *Blade Runner* (Vangelis). Accessed December 1, 2017. http:// www.filmtracks.com/titles/blade_runner.html.

—ML

BORN FREE

(1966)
John Barry

The Film

Directed by James Hill, *Born Free* is a 1966 feel-good British film starring Virginia McKenna and Bill Travers about raising an orphaned lion cub. The film received critical acclaim and was one of the highest-grossing films at the British box office that year. Based on Joy Adamson's 1960 book, the film was nominated for two Academy Awards, three Golden Globes, and a Grammy. Unusually, but pertinently for this book, four of the six nominations were for the music. The film was also nominated for Golden Globes in Best Motion Picture Drama and Best Actress.

The plot sees George Adamson (Travers) bring home three orphaned lion cubs after he is forced to kill their mother in self-defense. When the time comes, the two largest are sent to the Rotterdam Zoo, while Elsa remains with Joy (McKenna). After an unfortunate incident with a herd of elephants, Adamson is given three months to either release Elsa into the wild or send her to a zoo. Much time is spent attempting to reintroduce Elsa to the life of a wild lion, and reluctantly, she is eventually returned to the wild. The Adamsons then return to England. A year later, they fly back to Kenya and discover that Elsa hasn't forgotten them.

Elsa the lion is flanked by Joy and George Adamson, played by Virginia McKenna and Bill Travers. *Columbia Pictures / Photofest © Columbia Pictures*

The Music

The score to *Born Free* was composed by John Barry and is perhaps most famous for the title song, which became the signature tune of singer Matt Monro. It is this famous melody that dominates reviews and reception of the score, but while acknowledging the lasting recognition that this theme song enjoys, it would be a disservice to the remainder of Barry's score to ignore the other musical cues found in the film. First, however, we must commence with a discussion of the main theme. The film opens with a majestic French horn proclamation, the instruments soaring to a lofty note before dying away, being replaced with a lilting introduction to the main melody. The strings take the first strain of the melody, which could quite easily be mistaken for a love theme in any other film. The romantic feel of the theme is reinforced when the violins repeat the opening strain an octave higher, ascending into their upper register. A timpani roll introduces the next repeat of the melody, this time played on trumpet with a French horn counter-melody. The horns then take the opening cue through to its quiet, reflective conclusion. The domination of this theme can be heard in the cue "The Hunt," where instead of new thematic material, Barry restates the main theme but in a minor key and lower in the horn's register. The score is rather subdued by Barry's later standards, but it maintains a nobility representative of the vast expanses of the African wilderness and is in line with the tender story of trust and love between human and lion. Indeed, much of the score does consist of further variations of the main theme, with altered tempo, instrumentation, or timbre signifying a mood.

There are occasions where the music moves away from the main theme, such as during the stampede of elephants through the village. The trumpets and lower brass here mimic the sound of the elephants in a clever but not clichéd use of instrumentation.

The score to *Born Free* cannot claim to be as emotive, expansive, immersive, or heroic as some of the others found within this top-100 list, but it more than deserves its place herein, simply because the main title theme, and the variations thereof, are a fine example of the effectiveness of simple, unpretentious film music. The theme is warm, it is gentle, and it is embracing. This matches precisely the narrative of the adopted lion cub. Barry's less prominent themes in the score may at times have been lost beneath the myriad of variations on the main theme, but it is ultimately the main theme that carries the film and gives it its musical identity. With no disrespect meant, it is also arguably an example of a film that becomes more well known for its music than its visual narrative. The awards the film received are affirmation of this viewpoint. Whether over-familiarity breeds contempt is up to the individual, but the score, with Matt Monro, warts and all, cannot be denied a place in the upper echelons of a celebration of film music.

Recognition

Academy Awards for Best Original Score and Best Original Song.
Nominated for Grammy for Best Original Score.
Nominated for Golden Globe for Best Original Song.

Recordings

John Barry. *Born Free*, Proper W/S, 2013. This is a limited-edition rerelease of the original soundtrack, conducted by the composer. Missing some of the cues found on the Varese Sarabande release, with twelve as opposed to seventeen, but still a recommended purchase. ***

Frédéric Talgorn, Royal Scottish National Orchestra, *Born Free*, Varese Sarabande, 2000, 2016. Original motion picture score, running fifty-three minutes, with seventeen musical cues. Unfortunately, the performance lacks some of the vivacity and gentle grandeur of the score. **

—ML

BRAVEHEART

(1995)
James Horner

The Film

Directed by and starring Mel Gibson, *Braveheart* tells the story of William Wallace and the First War of Scottish Independence in the thirteenth century. The film was a critical success and was nominated for ten Academy Awards, winning five of them. These were Best Picture, Best Director, Best Sound Effects Editing, Best Makeup, and Best Cinematography.

A young William Wallace, whose father and brother have been killed fighting the English, returns to his homeland and finds his childhood sweetheart Murron (Catherine McCormack), and the two quickly fall in love. They hear rumors of a revolt against the English, but Wallace is uninterested, wanting only to live in peace. However, when Murron is killed by English soldiers the day after their secret marriage, Wallace single-handedly defeats the whole platoon. The other villagers join him by razing the garrison, and so begins the revolt against the English in what soon turns into an all-out war. Wallace leads his fellow Scots in a series of battles that dent English domination, and he has an illicit affair with the Princess of Wales (Sophie Marceau). He is eventually executed in London, but not before spectacularly shouting "FREEDOM!" in one of the film's most heartbreaking and memorable moments.

William Wallace (Mel Gibson) leads a charge. *20th Century Fox Film Corporation / Photofest © 20th Century Fox Film Corporation*

The Music

In the score to *Braveheart*, composer James Horner unsurprisingly chooses to evoke Scottish ethnicity and culture, but not without controversy. To the untrained ear, it might be bagpipes performing the film's main themes, but it is actually Uilleann pipes. This instrument is considered Irish, so technically, Horner's score could be considered inaccurate. However, the use of the scotch snap, or Lombard rhythm, in many of the themes helps to place the score firmly back across the Irish Sea. The scotch snap is a short-long musical rhythm, where the first, shorter note is accented. It is a common feature in the strathspey, a Scottish dance in 4/4 time.

The main theme to *Braveheart* is simply beautiful. There are few other ways to describe it. It is considered one of Horner's finest works, combining emotional orchestral lines inspired from the great Romantic composers of the late nineteenth century with the aforementioned Scottish and Celtic influences. Add a boys' choir to the mixture and it has the ingredients to be one of the more memorable film scores of the 1990s and one that accompanies some of the most poignant scenes in the film.

The film opens with wide vistas of Scottish mountains and lakes, and this is a common theme throughout the film. Scottish nationalism pervades the narrative, dialogue, and music and extends to the idealistic views of the landscape, even in wet weather. The Romanticization of Scotland and the love stories between Wallace and the two female characters result in a score brimming with amorous, tender, and achingly bittersweet musical themes. There is no clearer example than in the tear-jerking finale to the film, where Wallace is hung, drawn, and quartered. As he lays his head on the block, awaiting the fall of the axe, the orchestra becomes fervent with agonizing passion.

The use of the leitmotif in *Braveheart* is crucial to its success as a score. The theme for Murron is an excellent example of how a musical theme to represent a character can contribute toward an audience's empathy with the film's lead actors. Murron's theme is first heard at Wallace's father's funeral, when she gives Wallace a thorn. The flute is used here as a soft introduction to the character. In later scenes where she courts Wallace, the theme becomes fuller, with harp, woodwinds, and French horn all taking turns in performing the melody. At Murron's funeral, the composer quickly changes the mood from solemn and humanized (oboe) to a forceful furor in brass. This then changes to strings and finally a delicate harp. The fact that Murron's theme continues throughout the film despite her being dead for most of it, suggests that Wallace thinks frequently of her. The music thus becomes her on-screen presence, even when the actress herself is not seen. Appropriately or not, depending on the audience's viewpoint, Murron's theme is later adapted for Wallace's new love interest, the princess. However, it never settles and is not as peaceful as the original, frequently modulating quickly into the film's main theme, or into more militaristic battle music.

This combination of a memorable title theme that evokes the Scottish culture and landscape and the use of leitmotifs that help the audience associate with characters is a classic example of effective film music composition. It is heroic and tragic in equal parts and contains memorable melodies and evocations of sacrifice that live with the audience long after the final credits have rolled. As one of Horner's more accomplished works, it deserves its place among the finest film scores of all time.

Recognition

Nominated for Academy Award for Best Original Score.
Nominated for Golden Globe for Best Original Score.
Nominated for BAFTA for Best Film Music.

Recordings

James Horner, London Symphony Orchestra, *Braveheart*, Decca, 1995. This original soundtrack release is still available. It is seventy-five minutes in length, eighteen cues. Recommended. ****

James Horner, London Symphony Orchestra, *Braveheart*, La-La Land Records, 2015. This two-CD special edition, limited to three thousand copies, covers an astounding forty tracks with a total running time of well over two hours; this is highly recommended if you can find it. ****

Bibliography

Green, Jessica. "Understanding the Score: Film Music Communicating to and Influencing the Audience." *Journal of Aesthetic Education* 44 (4): 81–94.

—ML

BREAKFAST AT TIFFANY'S

(1961)
Henry Mancini

The Film

Breakfast at Tiffany's, loosely based on Truman Capote's short novel, became one of 1961's biggest box-office hits. George Axelrod's witty script, Blake Edwards's perceptive direction, and Henry Mancini's jazz-inflected music all helped in the transfer of the story from novel to film.

The plot of *Tiffany's*, which was updated from Capote's original 1940s setting to the 1960s, concerns a young woman from Texas named Holly Golightly (Audrey Hepburn), who lives in a New York apartment and desires to marry a rich man. Her new upstairs neighbor, Paul Varjak (George Peppard), is an aspiring novelist who becomes infatuated with Holly, even though he is involved with "2E" (Patricia Neal), a wealthy married woman who provides his living expenses. Adding comedy to the film is the wacky landlord, Mr. Yunioshi (Mickey Rooney in Japanese makeup).

Audrey Hepburn singing the Academy Award winning song "Moon River." *Paramount Pictures /* *Photofest © Paramount Pictures*

Paul soon learns that Holly's real name is Lulamae Barnes and that she was married to a widowered veterinarian named Doc Golightly (Buddy Ebsen), who has come from Texas to bring her back home. She reminds Doc that their marriage has been annulled and that she is not Lulamae anymore.

The Music

Any discussion of Henry Mancini's music for *Breakfast at Tiffany's* should start with "Moon River," the song that Mancini created with lyricist Johnny Mercer. The song is heard in a scene where Holly sits on a window ledge strumming a guitar and singing. By studying Hepburn's rendition of "How Long Has This Been Going On" in the 1957 film *Funny Face*, Mancini was able to create a melody that stayed within her limited vocal range. While the song does little to advance the plot, it helps to define the Texas roots of Holly's character and also provides one of the film's most charming moments.

Having already composed "Moon River" for this scene, Mancini worked the song's melody into many of the cues in the underscore. The opening credits include an arrangement of "Moon River" with a solo harmonica on the melody and accompanying strings, guitar tones, and a wordless choir. From the very start of the film, this music provides a significant hint regarding Holly's down-home background.

Mancini inserted the song's melody into several cues. In an early scene, after Holly climbs through the window of Paul's apartment to avoid an obnoxious suitor, the melody of "Moon River" is heard when Holly, curled up with Paul in his bed, has a dream about her brother Fred. The melody is played very slowly, with low woodwinds, strings, and harp adding a moody flavor.

There is much more to the music of *Tiffany's* than the cues based on "Moon River," however. One of the film's most noteworthy musical moments occurs in a scene where a man is seen loitering outside the apartment building. When Paul goes out to investigate and finds this person following him into Central Park, the music starts softly with low piano tones, along with low flute, discordant string tones, and the unique sounds of an organ grinder. The music continues until Paul sits on a park bench and the man, Doc Golightly, sits down beside him. The cue abruptly ends with a stinger chord that features the wavy tones of a vibraphone.

In *Tiffany's*, Mancini punctuated several cues with stinger chords as a way of drawing the viewer's attention to such moments as a character's sudden appearance. Collectively, these chords add a musical effect that is noticeable to the viewer without being too intrusive.

A tuneful theme in an upbeat tempo that appears twice in *Tiffany's* is a swing-flavored melody sung by a choir using the syllables "doo-doo-dah-doo" in a rhythmically energetic style. It is first heard when Holly and Paul attempt to experience things they haven't done before, including a stroll through Tiffany's in search of a purchase that stays within their very limited budget.

The party scene, which includes source music as part of Mancini's original score, features another upbeat piece with alto saxophone, piano, high flute, trumpet, and a rhythmic bongo drum accompaniment. The music gets gradually louder until the police arrive to break up the event.

Mancini's score is a far cry from the typical orchestral film music of its day. For *Tiffany's* Mancini brought the swingy, bluesy sounds of his *Peter Gunn* TV-show scoring to the world of the widescreen motion picture and introduced a younger generation to a kind of music that had seldom before been heard in films. Mancini's music thus provided the spark that ignited a revolution in film music. His work was influential in changing film scoring from the European style, so prominent in scores by Steiner, Korngold, and Rózsa, to a much more distinctively American idiom, with the sounds of a jazz band often replacing those of a symphony orchestra. As such, this score deserves to be recognized as not only one of the most memorable of Mancini's film scores, but one of the best of all time.

Recognition

Five Oscar nominations, including Audrey Hepburn's delightful performance.
Oscar for Best Score.
Oscar for Best Original Song, "Moon River."

Recordings

Henry Mancini, *Breakfast at Tiffany's*, Intrada Records, 1961. This CD is the original soundtrack and includes Hepburn's vocal rendition of "Moon River." Despite being billed as a complete score album, this release does not include track entitled "Mr. Yunioshi." Good sound. ***½

Henry Mancini, *Breakfast at Tiffany's*, RCA, 2010. Digitally updated version of original vinyl album which was studio rerecorded. Musical contents of CD match those on original release, which does not include Hepburn's vocal solo on "Moon River." OK sound. ***½

Bibliography

Mancini, Henry, with Gene Lees. *Did They Mention the Music?* New York: Cooper Square Press, 2001 (reprint of 1989 hardcover edition).

—LEM

THE BRIDE OF FRANKENSTEIN

(1935)

Franz Waxman

The Film

During the 1930s, while other movie studios made films based on the classic novels of such esteemed authors as Charles Dickens and Alexandre Dumas, Universal specialized in adapting horror stories by Bram Stoker and Mary Shelley. When director James Whale's version of Shelley's *Frankenstein* was released in 1931, it became such a hit that Universal soon planned a sequel. The resulting film, *The Bride of Frankenstein*, was based on a subplot in the original story in which Dr. Henry Frankenstein's creature (referred to as "the Monster") desires a mate.

Two actors resumed the roles they played in the 1931 film, including Colin Clive as Dr. Henry Frankenstein and Boris Karloff as the Monster. Ernest Thesiger joined the cast as Henry's crazed colleague, Dr. Pretorius, and Elsa Lanchester played two roles, the Bride of Frankenstein and also Mary Shelley, who in a prologue relates to her husband, Percy, and their friend, Lord Byron, a continuation of her story about the mad doctor and his creation. While Henry, with Pretorius's help, succeeds in creating a bride for the Monster, everything does not go exactly as planned.

The Music

Franz Waxman's music for *Bride of Frankenstein*, which was the first Hollywood assignment for this native of Upper Silesia, represents a major shift in Universal's horror-film series. Instead of music limited primarily to the beginning and ending, as in its predecessor, the sequel features a score that adds atmosphere throughout the film and also includes themes for three of the story's main characters, with the exception of Dr. Frankenstein, for whom there is no specific music.

Elsa Lanchester as the bride and Boris Karloff as Frankenstein's monster. *Universal Pictures / Photofest © Universal Pictures*

The first melodic idea in the score is the Monster motif, a five-note idea in which three short tones of the same pitch lead to a higher long-held tone and then a repeat of the first tone.

The second idea, which is associated with Pretorius, is based on a four-note motif with a rhythmic pattern that reflects the beginning of "La Marseillaise."

The third idea is the Bride theme, which is built on a three-tone idea that greatly resembles the melodic beginning of "Bali Hai" from Richard Rodgers's score of *South Pacific*.

These three motifs are all introduced during the opening credits, with the Monster idea ominously sounded several times, followed by a hint of the Pretorius motif. As the credits conclude, the Bride motif is briefly sounded by strings with accompanying harp glissandos.

During Mary Shelley's narration about what happens in the aftermath of the Monster's supposed death, the first motif returns as a villager named Hans wants to see for himself that the Monster is dead. When Hans falls into an underground tunnel and is killed by the Monster, trumpets sound the motif several times. It returns again when Hans's wife is attacked.

The score's second motif is prominently featured when Pretorious makes a late-night visit to the Frankensteins' residence. Woodwinds and strings combine to sound this sinister idea several times; this motif is accompanied by various music effects, including tremolo strings and a climactic accented chord with added dissonant tones.

A clever variation on the Pretorious motif is heard when the doctor invites Henry to see his laboratory. As the doctor brings out a large wooden case, the motif is repeated twice with tremolo strings adding a mysterious effect. When Pretorious opens the case to show off his miniature human creations that include, among others, a tiny king, a queen, and an archbishop, Waxman's music includes a clever combination of humorous sounds. When Pretorius displays a miniature ballerina, Waxman's music includes a brief reference to Felix Mendelssohn's "Spring Song."

A musically vivid scene begins with the Monster wandering about in the country. Sweet strings, flutes, and harp are heard as he approaches a stream, but when he sees his reflection in the water the Monster motif returns with sinister-sounding trumpets. This motif is then transformed into a dramatic march theme when hostile villagers pursue the Monster and tie him to a wooden log in a ceremony that resembles a crucifixion. As he is dropped into a horse-drawn cart, a downward harp glissando adds a Mickey Mousing effect—a technique where the accompanying music mimics the on-screen action. The following moment includes a victorious version of the march theme as the villagers haul the Monster off to the local jail.

The climax to the film approaches when Henry is forced by Pretorious to create a mate for the Monster. As the two attempt to bring a female corpse back to life, irregular timpani beats suggest that the Bride's newly implanted heart is defective.

The Bride motif is again heard as the female corpse, after a second heart transplant, becomes jolted into life through an electrical current stimulated by lightning. Meanwhile the Monster motif returns as the creature runs amok as he anxiously awaits his mate. Throughout this scene the music features rhythmically steady timpani tones that reflect the Bride's healthy heartbeats.

When Pretorious proclaims "the Bride of Frankenstein," the Bride motif is loudly sounded by trumpets, strings, and chimes in a grandly orchestrated moment.

Not all of the music in the film is original. Borrowed music occurs when the Monster hears a blind hermit playing Schubert's "Ave Maria" on a violin. After the hermit welcomes the Monster into his cottage, the "Ave Maria" melody is featured in the underscore as the hermit offers food to his guest. This music features the vibrato sounds of an organ along with strings.

Waxman's score is groundbreaking in its use of leitmotifs and Mickey Mousing, techniques that were increasingly used by Hollywood composers as the 1930s progressed. This score is a classic example of musical storytelling and richly deserves to be included in this book.

Recognition

Although this film received no Oscar nominations, it is now widely regarded as one of Hollywood's best horror films and one of director James Whale's finest achievements.

Rotten Tomatoes score of 100 percent, based on forty-one reviews.

In 2005, *Time* magazine's film critics, Richard Corliss and Richard Schickel, included *Bride of Frankenstein* on their list of "All-Time 100 Movies."

Recording

Kenneth Alwyn and the Westminster Philharmonic, *Bride of Frankenstein: The Franz Waxman Score*, Silva Screen, 1993, CD. A reconstruction of the score. Excellent sound. ****

Bibliography

Bush, Richard H. Liner notes. *The Bride of Frankenstein: The Franz Waxman Score*. Silva Screen SSD 1028, 1993.

Vermilye, Jerry. *The Films of the Thirties*. New York: Citadel Press, 1993.

—LEM

THE BRIDGE ON THE RIVER KWAI

(1957)
Malcolm Arnold

The Film

Directed by David Lean and starring William Holden, Jack Hawkins, and Alec Guinness, *The Bridge on the River Kwai* is regarded as a classic war film. The film was nominated for eight Academy Awards and won seven, making it the joint fifth-most-successful film in history in terms of awards. The awards won were for Best Picture, Best Director, Best Actor, Best Adapted Screenplay, Best Music, Best Film Editing, and Best Cinematography. The other nomination was for Best Actor in a Supporting Role. It also won three BAFTAs, three Golden Globes, and a Grammy.

Part fact, part fiction, the film is based on actual events when British prisoners of war in World War II were forced to connect Burma and Siam with a rail line. Colonel Nicholson (Guinness) and his fellow officers refused to take part in manual labor, but after being tortured, Nicholson finally agrees to participate. He becomes obsessed with building a bridge over the Kwai, and slowly his view of the bridge shifts from being a testament to British courage to a monument to his inflated ego. On the day of its opening, an Allied Special Forces unit is sent to blow up the bridge. Not wishing to see his efforts destroyed, Nicholson tips off the Japanese commander about the explosives he has found under the bridge. In an epiphany, he realizes that he has been collaborating with the enemy. The film ends with Nicholson collapsing on the detonation plunger, thus redeeming himself by destroying the bridge as the first train passes over.

Alec Guinness (left) and Sessue Hayakawa in front of the bridge on the Kwai River. *Columbia Pictures / Photofest © Columbia Pictures*

The Music

The memorable music to *The Bridge on the River Kwai* is by Malcolm Arnold, who had less than three weeks to compose the score. David Lean was an admirer of Arnold. The composer stated that Lean "adored what I did with the films he made," and that "he never cut a single quaver" of his music. The score is militaristic, daunting, and harsh throughout. The use of marches, fanfares, and aggressive French horn sounds very firmly place it in the context of the Second World War.

While Arnold's music contributed toward an award-winning score, the use of the preexisting "Colonel Bogey March," composed in 1914 by F. J. Ricketts, was undoubtedly one of the enduring memories of the score and film. It was not always certain that this march would make its way into the film, however. The initial screenwriter on the project, Carl Foreman, disagreed wholly with the director's decision to make a full sequence of the troops whistling the march while marching into the camp. Foreman is reported to have said to David Lean: "With all due respect, you are an art house director. You have only made small British films. You have no experience of the international market. They won't stand for all this. You can't take up three minutes with British troops walking into a camp whistling a tune nobody's ever heard of—you can't expect people to sit in their seats. It won't hold." It did hold, of course, and the film and march became famous around the globe. The unusual success of the march as film music was particularly interesting, as it became a musical hit in West Germany. It sold more copies in that country than anywhere else in the world: over one million in five months. This was the first time since the end of the war that a march had been popular in the German nation(s), and it was an interesting turning point in their perspectives on remembering and memorializing the war.

The "Colonel Bogey March" was whistled by members of the Irish Guards for the soundtrack. The director later proclaimed that Arnold had "made the 'Colonel Bogey' twice as good as it was. I love those swaggering marches."

Such was the cultural impact of the march's use in the film that pastiches, parodies, and homages have all appeared in subsequent years, including in the 1980 film *The Breakfast Club*. However, the misappropriation of film music, particularly from war films, sometimes leads to trouble. In 2005, a Nissan advertisement featuring a line of vehicles moving in parade-like fashion used the Colonel Bogey march, but it was forced to change after backlash against using music from a film depicting British POWs in an ad for a Japanese car brand. "You wouldn't consider taking footage from *Bridge on the River Kwai* and using it as an image in the Nissan ad, so you've got to wonder why you would think it would be OK to use the music," claimed one branding consultant.

Recognition

Academy Award for Best Music.
Grammy nomination for Best Dramatic Picture Score.

Recording

Malcolm Arnold, *The Bridge on the River Kwai: An Original Soundtrack Recording*, Legacy/Columbia, 1995. The sound quality does not perhaps match up to modern-day standards, but this is still considered the definitive official soundtrack release and is therefore to be recommended for fans of the film. ***

Note: The "Colonel Bogey March" is featured on numerous other records and compilation albums of film music. The Legacy/Columbia remains the only soundtrack release for the whole film.

Bibliography

Brownlow, Kevin. "The Making of David Lean's Film of *The Bridge on the River Kwai*." Cineaste 22, no. 2 (1996): 10–16.
Phillips, Gene. *Beyond the Epic: The Life and Films of David Lean*. Lexington: University Press of Kentucky, 2006.
Santas, Constantine. *The Epic Films of David Lean*. Lanham, MD: Scarecrow Press, 2012.
Scholz, Anne-Marie. "*The Bridge on the River Kwai* (1957) Revisited: Combat Cinema, American Culture and the German Past." *German History* 26, no. 2 (April 2008): 219–50.
Steinberg, Brian. "Nissan Decides 'River Kwai' Ad Song Is a Bridge Too Far." *Wall Street Journal*, October 18, 2005.

—ML

C

CASABLANCA
(1943)
Max Steiner

The Film

Directed by Michael Curtiz and starring Humphrey Bogart and Ingrid Bergman, *Casablanca* was somewhat of a surprise success, but today it is widely considered one of the finest movies from the early years of the film industry.

Rick Blaine (Bogart) runs a nightclub in Casablanca, Morocco, during the middle period of World War II. The establishment, with its rousing house band and pianist Sam, becomes a popular gathering place not only for German soldiers on tour of duty but also refugees seeking papers that will assist them in their escape to America. An ex-lover of Rick, Ilsa, unexpectedly visits the nightclub, causing emotional conflict for the film's protagonist, culminating in her escape to Lisbon with her new husband, Laszlo. The film was nominated for eight Academy Awards, of which it won three for Best Picture, Best Director, and Best Writing (Screenplay).

The Music

The score to *Casablanca* was composed by Max Steiner. It is a complex score to negotiate, as it relies equally on popular, on-screen songs and Steiner's orchestral underscore. Steiner's underscore develops the songs into his own compositional voice and uses the melodies to create an effective, memorable accompaniment to this wartime, exotic love story. The composer was under demands that differed from his previous films, where he had the freedom to compose in his own style from a blank canvas.

Steiner did have some autonomy to write his own themes, such as the rhythmic representation of Africa in the opening overture. The exoticism of the continent is portrayed by what Martin Marks describes as "pseudo-Arabian" music. This hackneyed theme might be considered the weakest link in a memorable score, being "utterly clichéd and really too savage for a film about such sophisticated characters," according to Marks. It is the adaptations of the songs that instead take center stage.

From left: Paul Henreid, Ingrid Bergman, Claude Rains, and Humphrey Bogart. *Warner Bros. /
Photofest © Warner Bros.*

In *Casablanca*, Steiner had to take music already built into the drama of the film
and use it to manufacture an appropriate musical score. As Scheurer explains, on-
screen (diegetic) popular song in the film was a "force Steiner could not deny."
Songs sung by characters became a dominating factor, and Steiner's score had
no choice but to work with these songs and adapt them into his own writing.
For this reason, continues Scheurer, it might not actually be considered a classic
Steiner score in its own right. But it more than deserves its place in the top 100 for
the way in which the popular music and classical film score intertwine to create
a meaningful whole. Three songs were fundamental to *Casablanca*'s score: "As
Time Goes By," "Deutschland Über Alles" (the German national anthem), and
"The Marseillaise" (the French national anthem). Steiner weaves these themes into
his orchestral underscore, complementing their dominant on-screen appearances
with a subtler underscore presence.

"As Time Goes By," a song that was composed by Herman Hupfeld in 1931, is
first introduced in the film when we see Ilsa's character for the first time in Rick's
club. This then leads into the famous "Play it once, Sam, for old times' sake" line,
where the pianist (Sam) plays the song and then sings it on Ilsa's request. Rick
bursts out of his office to reprimand Sam for playing a song that reminds him
of Ilsa, but stops mid-tirade as he sees Ilsa. Sam has stopped performing, but

Steiner's orchestra takes over. With the melody now firmly in a darker, minor key, the reunion of Rick and Ilsa, underscored by Steiner's take on the music, is a turning point for the musical theme, and from this point on, it belongs firmly in the orchestral underscore as a love theme for the two characters. It is a crucial moment in the score, and as Marks suggests, "Ask an audience to recall the music of *Casablanca*, and chances are that the great majority would point to one, two, or three moments." The first of these moments is this scene in the club, with Sam, Rick, and Ilsa.

The second of these scenes is a memorable moment in the club, when German occupying troops sing "Die Wacht am Rhein" (Watch on the Rhine). The house band is instructed to play the French anthem "La Marseillaise," and the resulting, unintentional duet between the French and the German songs is a rousing, truly wonderful moment in the history of film music. The two songs work with and against each other in a passionate show of patriotism on both sides. This almost transcendental musical moment is cut short when a German officer, underscored by one of Steiner's minor variations on the German national anthem, warns of the consequences of such a show of rebellion. Scheurer credits Steiner with a difficult task that was well executed. He states that "it is to Steiner's credit that, despite having so much of the score dictated by diegetic music ("As Time Goes By" and "The Marseillaise" especially), he was able to craft a score that has his indelible stamp. He took the source music and wove it into the leitmotif structure very effectively, and in the process, he transformed the songs. They seem larger, greater, and better pieces of music than we might think they are." For this reason, working under unconventional conditions and having his hands metaphorically tied by the three existing melodies, this score deserves its place at the top table of film music scores.

Recognition

Academy Award nomination for Best Music.

Recording

Max Steiner, *Casablanca*, Sony, 2010. This is a truly unusual album, as it contains no fewer than ninety-four tracks. Many of these are musical cues, but some include dialogue. It is a unique album and one that is recommended, but some may not enjoy the emphasis on dialogue, as it perhaps feels a little like an audio book of the film at times. ***

Bibliography

Flinn, Caryl. *Strains of Utopia: Gender, Nostalgia, and Hollywood Film Music*. Princeton, NJ: Princeton University Press, 1992.

Marks, Martin. "Music, Drama, Warner Brothers: The Cases of *Casablanca* and *The Maltese Falcon*." *Michigan Quarterly Review* 35, no. 1 (Winter 1996): 112–42.

Prendergast, Roy. *A Neglected Art: A Critical Study of Music in Films*. New York: New York University Press, 1977.

Scheurer, T. E. "The Music of *Casablanca*." *Journal of Popular Film and Television* 32, no. 2 (2004): 90–96.

—ML

CHARIOTS OF FIRE

(1981)

Vangelis (Evangelos Odysseas Papathanassiou)

The Film

Directed by Hugh Hudson, *Chariots of Fire* is a British historical drama film starring Ben Cross and Ian Charleson. The title of the film was inspired by the line, "Bring me my chariot of fire," from the William Blake poem later adapted into the hymn "Jerusalem."

The narrative, told in flashback, focuses on two British sprinters at the 1924 Olympic games. Harold Abrahams (Cross) and Eric Liddell (Charleson) are Jewish and Christian respectively, and the film follows their stories as their paths cross and diverge again. Tragically, the real-life Liddell died in a Japanese prison camp in 1945. Abrahams lived until 1978, when the last remaining member of the 1924 Olympic team read a eulogy at his funeral.

Olympic contenders Harold Abrahams (Ben Cross) and Andrew Lindsey (Nigel Havers). *Warner Bros. / Photofest © Warner Bros.*

The film was hailed by the critics, and this was reflected in the awards it received. It was nominated for seven Academy Awards and won four of these for Best Picture, Best Writing (screenplay), Best Costume Design, and Best Music. It was also nominated for eleven BAFTAs and won three of these for Best Costume Design, Best Film, and Best Supporting Actor. It also won a Golden Globe and a Grammy for Best Foreign Film and Best Pop Instrumental Performance. It is ranked nineteenth in the British Film Institute's top-100 list of British films.

The Music

The score to *Chariots of Fire* was composed by Greek composer Vangelis, who considers the film to be the turning point in his career. The electronic score, making heavy use of synthesizers, was considered unusual for the time. One of the producers of the film, David Puttnam, had admired Vangelis's work for a long time and had ringfenced funds to commission the composer before shooting of the film had even commenced. Vangelis had done work on French television and released an album based on it entitled *Opera sauvage*. He had also released an album of Asian-influenced music entitled *China*. Both influenced the production team's decision to hire him to score *Chariots of Fire*. Vangelis stated in an interview with *Music Maker* magazine that he used the synthesizer for the score because they were in demand at the time, due to the "illusionary effect" the instrument can have. He also stated that the small budget influenced his decision to use only synthesizers and that he only actually began working on the score after the film was finished.

There is no doubting that the main theme to *Chariots of Fire* has embedded itself in many film music charts and lists. Jack Kroll, a *Newsweek* critic, said Vangelis "hit dead center" with the score, stating that there was a universality to the music. The first shot, with the runners on the beach, has a "subliminal suggestiveness." The main theme is deceptively simple. A pulsating, relentless ostinato on one note introduces the cue, followed by a melody so structurally and harmonically simple that it defies a complex analysis. It is as tonal and conventional as one might find in any film score from any period, yet it contains an otherworldly heroism, in no small part due to the instrumentation. In an article for the *Telegraph* in 1982, Andrew Duncan suggested that synthesizers were looked on with suspicion by music aficionados as being "a bit of a fraud" because the music is made by pressing buttons and not, allegedly, by any real craftsmanship. Rick Wakeman, of the rock group Yes, defended Vangelis, claiming that he did not simply use preset modes or functions of the synthesizer, but experimented to create the exact sound he desired. The synthesizer in *Chariots of Fire* is used to build tension, and it pulls the audience into the film as well as any orchestral score would have.

Curiously, Vangelis does not consider the score to *Chariots of Fire* his best. He stated in an interview with *De Telegraaf* newspaper in 1991: "It occurs very rarely that a composer thinks of his most successful work as his best. I am no exception to that rule. I think of my soundtrack for . . . *Mutiny on the Bounty* as endlessly more interesting than *Chariots of Fire*." Regardless of the composer's tastes, it is hard to argue against the memorable, pulsating electronic sounds of *Chariots of Fire* being in any top-100 soundtrack list, so its inclusion here was a straightforward choice.

Recognition

Academy Award for Best Original Score.
Grammy for Best Pop Instrumental Performance (Ernie Watts for dance version of main theme).
Nominated for BAFTA for Film Music.

Recordings

Vangelis, *Chariots of Fire*, UMC, 2006. Running to forty-two minutes over seven tracks, this remastered version of the soundtrack brings Vangelis's music to life and sounds better than previous releases. Well recommended. ****
Vangelis, *Chariots of Fire: The Music of Vangelis*, Castle Music, 1999. This compilation album of Vangelis's music from several of his television works and films is worth purchasing to hear a wider spectrum of his music. ***

Bibliography

Atkinson, Terry. "Scoring with Synthesizers" (Vangelis interview). *American Film*, September 1982.
Dans, Peter E. *Christians in the Movies: A Century of Saints and Sinners*. Lanham, MD: Rowman & Littlefield, 2009.
Duncan, Andrew. "Vangelis." *Telegraph Sunday Magazine*, November 21, 1982.
van Broekhoven, René. "Vangelis, the Sumptuous Synthesizer Saint" (Vangelis interview). *Music Maker*, September 1982.

—ML

CHINATOWN

(1974)
Jerry Goldsmith

The Film

Directed by Roman Polanski and starring Jack Nicholson and Faye Dunaway, *Chinatown* is an American neo-noir mystery film.

Evelyn Mulwray (Dunaway), a concerned wife, appoints JJ "Jake" Gittes (Nicholson), a private detective, to follow her husband whom she suspects of having an affair. Gittes manages to photograph the husband, who works as chief engineer of the LA Department of Power and Water, with a young girl. In a plot twist, it is revealed that an impersonator hired Gittes, not Mrs. Mulwray herself. This thrilling mystery film evolves into a complex whodunnit scenario when Mr. Mulwray is found dead and deals with such challenging topics as incestual rape, murder, and corruption. The film was nominated for eleven Academy Awards and won one of these for Best Writing (screenplay). This makes it the joint fourth-most-nominated

Noah Cross (John Huston) has secrets he must protect from the prying eyes of private detective J. J. Gittes (Jack Nicholson). *Paramount Pictures / Photofest © Paramount Pictures*

film in history. It also won four Golden Globes, for Best Motion Picture, Best Director, Best Actor, and Best Screenplay, as well as three BAFTAs, for Best Picture, Best Actor, and Best Screenplay.

The Music

The score to *Chinatown* was written by Jerry Goldsmith, an established film composer who had already received six nominations for Academy Awards before *Chinatown* became his seventh. Goldsmith stepped in at the last moment to replace Phillip Lambro, whose score was rejected. It is now difficult to imagine *Chinatown* without Goldsmith's score, but Lambro's music was never likely to make the final cut. The director himself said the score turned out to be disappointing and that the music badly impaired the film. Robert Towne, writing about the film, called the original score horrendous, dissonant, weird, and scratchy. Sam O' Steene sums up the original score succinctly and brutally, claiming that everyone in the previews said, "Jesus Christ, that music's terrible!"

Jerry Goldsmith's score was not extensive. For a film over two hours long, only twenty minutes of it were accompanied by music. Goldsmith utilized a small ensemble with a rather unique combination of strings, four pianos, four harps, two percussionists, and a solo trumpet. These smaller ensembles were the norm in film noir of the 1970s, with the addition of new electronic instruments such as the synthesizer adding to the ominous nature of the aesthetic. The main melody, a slightly sleazy love theme, is described by Darby and Du Bois as "tired, perhaps even bored, melancholy." This theme, despite being heard during the opening credits, does not return for quite some time. Instead, fragmented chordal patterns are used to underscore Gittes as he pieces together the mysteries before him. In the cue "The Last of Ida," Ida being the imposter Mrs. Mulwray, Goldsmith calls upon a style of composition similar to that used in his famous *Planet of the Apes* score of 1968. Harsh, dissonant hammerings on the piano are accompanied by violently moving string lines. As the piece progresses, there is a gradual shift toward a more jazzy influence reminiscent of some of Leonard Bernstein's more aggressive compositions.

The score also uses three songs, "Easy Living" by Ralph Rainger and Leo Robin, "I Can't Get Started" by Ira Gershwin and Vernon Duke, and "The Way You Look Tonight" by Jerome Kern and Dorothy Fields. Bunny Berigan and his orchestra perform "I Can't Get Started." The jazz numbers add to the noir feel of the film and place it in its historical and stylistic context.

Perhaps one of the shortest in this book, Goldsmith's score to *Chinatown* is almost a victim of its own success. It is short and in many ways unremarkable, and it simply accompanies a noir film as many noir scores have done before and since. However, it is the remarkable simplicity and sparseness that make the music noteworthy. It fits the film perfectly and is not there when it is not needed. Overuse of music in films is a common curse in the modern era, so it is refreshing to hear a wonderful score that lets the narrative take priority when required. For that reason, the smooth, silky, mysterious jazz of Goldsmith's score to *Chinatown* is fully deserving of its place in the top 100.

Recognition

Nominated for Academy Award for Best Original Score.
Nominated for BAFTA for Best Film Music.
Nominated for Golden Globe for Best Original Score.

Recording

Jerry Goldsmith. *Chinatown*, Intrada, 2016. This recent official soundtrack release is a remastered version of the 1974 album. The first twelve tracks are the original album and not in the correct order. The remaining tracks constitute the score in the correct chronological order for the first time. It includes an informative twenty-four-page booklet with information about the film and music. Well recommended for fans of the film and score. ****

Bibliography

Darby, William, and Jack Du Bois. *American Film Music*. Jefferson, NC: McFarland, 1990.
Goldman, William. *Which Lie Did I Tell? More Adventures in the Screen Trade*. New York: Bloomsbury, 2001.

Ness, R. R. "A Lotta Night Music: The Sound of Film Noir." *Cinema Journal* 47, no. 2 (2008): 52–73.

O'Steene, Sam. *Cut to the Chase: Forty-Five Years of Editing America's Favourite Movies*. Studio City, CA: Michael Wiese Productions, 2002.

Polanski, Roman. *Roman by Polanski*. New York: Ballantine Books, 1985.

—ML

CINEMA PARADISO

(1988)
Ennio Morricone

The Film

Originally entitled *Nuovo Cinema Paradiso*, this is the second and most highly acclaimed film by Italian filmmaker Giuseppe Tornatore, whose original screenplay concerns events in the Sicilian village of Giancaldo following World War II.

Three versions of the film exist. Tornatore's original 155-minute release, first shown in Italy in 1988, met with little success. The theatrical release, which lasts 123 minutes, is the version that won many awards in 1989, including both the Oscar and the Golden Globe as best foreign-language film. Tornatore's *Cinema Paradiso: The New Version*, from 2002, runs 173 minutes.

At the start of the 1988 version, Salvatore Di Vita (Jacques Perrin), a successful filmmaker living in Rome, is informed by his live-in girlfriend that his mother has called from Sicily to inform him of the death of Alfredo (Philippe Noiret), who had been a projectionist at the Cinema Paradiso theater in Giancaldo for many years. Upon hearing of Alfredo's death, Salvatore starts remembering his past and the film goes into flashbacks.

The Music

This commentary on the music refers to the theatrical version of the film.

Ennio Morricone's score for *Cinema Paradiso* is one of his most melodious works. There are three prominent themes, and the orchestration consists principally of strings with the frequent use of two keyboard instruments, the piano and the celesta. The first theme, which is introduced during the film's opening credits, features a lyrical melodic idea based on a ten-note motif that is first sounded by a string quartet with the addition of piano and an alto saxophone. This theme becomes easily recognizable through the use of two musical ingredients; the first is the ascending seventh between the two beginning tones of the motif, and the other is the temporal equality of the first nine of the idea's tones, with a pause on the motif's last note as a means of musical punctuation. Thus this tuneful melody

Projectionist Alfredo (Philippe Noiret) and his young apprentice (Salvatore Cascio). *Miramax Films / Photofest © Miramax Films*

progresses in a smoothly flowing way, with more upward leaps and rhythmic pauses inserted as the theme reaches its conclusion.

The second theme, a tuneful waltz-like idea for celesta, flute, and strings, is associated with the young Toto (played as a young child by Salvatore Cascio). It is first heard when he is an altar boy during a mass being celebrated by Father Adelfio. At first only soft string harmonies are present; after a few moments, the tinkling sounds of the celesta are heard in a melodic idea that moves stepwise within a major-scale pattern with the successive tones arranged into four-note sets. The first two sets include only ascending tones, while the further repetitions include reversals of melodic direction. The flow of the melody is enhanced by the repeated use of a short-short-short-long rhythmic pattern.

Moments later this theme returns as Toto examines pieces of spliced film that he has pocketed without Alfredo noticing his petty thievery. As he fantasizes about what the pieces of film represent, the flute adds a countermotif to the stepwise tones of the celesta melody. The flute idea consists of pairs of tones that alternately ascend and descend in pitch direction.

For much of the film these two themes dominate the scoring. But, when the teenage Toto (now played by Marco Leonardi) starts pursuing Elena (Agnese Nano), a third theme arrives—a romantically tinged melody (identified on the film's soundtrack as the love theme), which was actually conceived by the composer's son, Andrea Morricone. When Elena comes into the projection booth to tell Toto that she loves him, this theme is prominently heard on the alto saxophone with piano chords and strings providing a lyrical accompaniment.

A memorable use of the love theme occurs when Toto reads a letter (with Elena's voice speaking the words) in which she informs him that she will be away for the summer. His sadness is obvious as he mopes around, with lyrical saxophone tones revealing his distress.

The film's most emotional moment comes at the end when the adult Salvatore watches the spliced-together footage of kissing scenes that had been cut out of the films by Father Adelfio, who early in the film is seen ringing a bell during private screenings whenever a loving couple gets too intimate. While Salvatore is watching the censored footage, the clarinet sounds a lyrical rendition of the love theme. When he gets teary-eyed, the music reaches an emotional peak with flute, piano chords, and strings helping to convey the rich romanticism of this lyrical idea, enriched by soaring orchestration.

There is abundant source music from the films shown at the Cinema Paradiso theater. In one instance, Morricone created a sprightly theme in the style of silent movie music for footage from a short Charlie Chaplin film set in a boxing ring, but otherwise the music heard in these scenes is from the actual films themselves.

Few films about the movies have been as emotionally satisfying as Tornatore's film, and few have had such a richly melodious musical accompaniment. This is vintage Morricone, from a time in his career when he was creating fine scores for such other noteworthy films as *The Mission* (1986) and *The Untouchables* (1987).

Recognition

The shorter version of *Cinema Paradiso* released in 1989 won both the Golden Globe and the Oscar for Best Foreign-Language Picture.

Among many glowing reviews Roger Ebert in the *Chicago Sun-Times* wrote, "Anyone who loves movies is likely to love *Cinema Paradiso*."

Recording

Ennio Morricone, *Cinema Paradiso*, DRG, 1990. This disc contains only thirty-eight minutes of music, but includes all the primary themes. Excellent sound. ****

Bibliography

Deutsch, Didier, ed. *VideoHound's Soundtracks: Music from the Movies, Broadway and Television*. Detroit: Visible Ink Press, 1988.

Hickman, Roger. *Reel Music: Exploring 100 Years of Film Music*. New York: W. W. Norton, 2006.

—LEM

CITIZEN KANE
(1941)
Bernard Herrmann

The Film

When *Citizen Kane* premiered in 1941, it received glowing reviews, but the film was a financial flop due to the Hearst newspaper franchise, which sought to thwart Orson Welles's production because the film was believed to be a fictionalized version of William Randolph Hearst's life.

Citizen Kane begins with the death of Kane (Orson Welles) at Xanadu, his palatial home in Florida. This scene is followed by a press screening of a newsreel that covers the facts of Kane's life. After the newsreel ends, a debate ensues about who Kane really was, and a reporter named Jerry Thompson (William Alland) is assigned to learn the meaning of Kane's life, taking as a clue the millionaire's dying word, "Rosebud."

Thompson's task leads him first to the archives of Kane's legal guardian, Walter Thatcher (George Coulouris), from which the viewer learns details of Kane's

Charles Foster Kane (Orson Welles) and Emily Rose Norton Kane (Ruth Warrick) in a scene that captures the disintegration of their marriage. *RKO Radio Pictures Inc. / Photofest © RKO Radio Pictures Inc.*

childhood, but the meaning of "Rosebud" remains a mystery. The story of Kane then unfolds as a series of flashbacks, as Thompson interviews those who knew Kane best: his manager, Mr. Bernstein (Everett Sloane); his college roommate and theater critic, Jed Leland (Joseph Cotten); and Kane's second wife, Susan Alexander (Dorothy Comingore). These flashbacks are constructed in a way that allows the viewer to piece together a chronological sketch of Kane's life.

The Music

Thrust into celebrity by the notorious Halloween radio broadcast of *War of the Worlds* in 1938, Welles signed a contract with RKO that led to the filming of *Citizen Kane*, with Bernard Herrmann, music director of Welles's *Mercury Theatre on the Air* radio series, as its composer. The score's cues resemble musical puzzle pieces that fit perfectly with the visual elements of Welles's unique film. The ominous music that accompanies the opening death scene is based on a five-tone idea that provides the basic leitmotiv for Xanadu and for Kane himself. This lugubrious music features low tones on trombones and bassoons. Herrmann also inserted into this opening scene a second five-note idea that is heard as Kane holds a glass globe with a winter scene inside. This is the Rosebud motif.

Both of these motifs are heard periodically throughout the film and return dramatically in the last scene in which the film has come full circle back to Xanadu. In the final shots, when workers are sorting through some of the deceased Kane's hoarded possessions and throwing some of them into a huge furnace, the film's two primary motifs are combined in a dramatic cue that features a strong blast of orchestral sound.

The operatic music that Herrmann composed for the scene in which Susan Alexander makes her stage debut is a powerful piece of source music. It is heard twice, the first time very briefly during Thompson's interview with Leland. The second iteration, which occurs during Susan's interview, is longer and allows the viewer to hear the conclusion of the work, titled "Salaambo." The vocal part in this operatic scene was planned to be sung by a soprano in an uncomfortably high key, and thus Susan's vocal sound is intentionally compromised (her vocal limitations have already been revealed in Leland's flashback).

A second musical highlight of Leland's interview is the breakfast montage, which occurs during his recollection of Kane's relationship with his first wife, the president's niece, Emily Norton (Ruth Warrick). This montage, which includes a waltz theme that has already been briefly heard during Bernstein's interview, includes six short glimpses of Kane and Emily at various breakfasts during their marriage. Each of these brief shots features the couple seated at the same table, with the musical accompaniment of each vignette incorporating variations on the first three rising tones of the waltz motif. Differing tempos and instrumentation occur during these successive shots.

Since Kane's life covers a period of seven decades, many musical styles are used in the telling of his story. The flashbacks of Kane in the 1890s as a young, newly established newspaper publisher include lively short cues referred to in Herrmann's score as "Galop," "Polka," and "Scherzo." At one point in these cues a syncopated ragtime rhythm is included.

One of the borrowed songs used as source music is "Oh Mr. Kane," by Herman Ruby, which is sung when Kane is being entertained by chorus girls at his newspaper office.

Herrmann's music is a patchwork quilt of different styles, just as the film is a uniquely designed collection of puzzle pieces based on the "Rosebud" mystery. Although there is no big recurring theme such as in *Gone with the Wind*, Herrmann's score, with its unifying use of two primary motifs, is definitely among his most outstanding achievements and deserves to be ranked among the best film scores of all time.

Recognition

Nine Oscar nominations including citations for Best Picture, Actor (Welles), Director (also Welles), and Musical Score, but Academy voters favored *How Green Was My Valley* as best picture.

Oscar for Best Screenplay, credited to both Welles and Herman J. Mankiewicz. Bernard Herrmann wound up winning an Oscar for the music of his second Hollywood film, *The Devil and Daniel Webster.*

Recordings

Tony Bremner, Australian Philharmonic Orchestra, *Citizen Kane*, Preamble, 1991. Studio recording of the complete score. Sound is good, but interpretation is a bit timid. ***½

Charles Gerhardt, National Symphony Orchestra, *Citizen Kane: The Classic Film Scores of Bernard Herrmann*, RCA, 1974. Excerpts from *Citizen Kane*, reissued on CD in 1991. Excellent sound. ****

Joel McNeely, Royal Scottish National Orchestra, *Citizen Kane*, Varese Sarabande, 1999. Studio recording. Good sound, strong interpretation. ****

Note: On all three recordings the singing of the soprano in the "Salaambo" aria is intentionally better than that of the singer in the original film.

Bibliography

Bremner, Tony. Liner notes. *Citizen Kane, Original 1941 Motion Picture Score*. Preamble PRCD 1788,1991, CD.

Kael, Pauline. *The Citizen Kane Book*. New York: Bantam Books, 1974.

—LEM

CITY LIGHTS

(1931)
Charlie Chaplin

The Film

When synchronized sound was introduced in the late 1920s, many film stars adapted to the change from silent acting to the use of spoken dialogue. But one actor who resisted this conversion was Charlie Chaplin, perhaps because his Little Tramp was so famously identified as a silent character. As in his *Modern Times* (1936), Chaplin conceived *City Lights* as a silent film with a synchronized musical score.

In its opening credits *City Lights* is subtitled "A Comedy Romance in Pantomime." Curiously Chaplin's first name is identified as "Charlie" in the cast list, but he is named "Charles Chaplin" as the film's writer, director, and composer.

The film is basically a love story about the tramp and a blind flower girl. When he finds out that she needs money for an operation to help her see again, he attempts to raise the necessary amount. Everything in the film spins off this simple

The Tramp (Charles Chaplin) is beguiled by blind flower girl Virginia Cherrill. *Charles Chaplin / Photofest © Charles Chaplin*

concept, including scenes involving the tramp's relationship with a suicidal millionaire who could help pay for the surgery but who is friendly toward the tramp only when he is drunk.

The Music

Although not a trained musician, Chaplin had experience with music from his early days as a performer in British music halls. Starting with *The Kid* (1921), Chaplin created the musical ideas for all of his later films. Thus he is the composer of *City Lights*, with Arthur Johnston serving as the arranger who wrote down Chaplin's hummed and whistled ideas and utilized them as themes for orchestrated musical cues.

The opening credits include several short bits of music. The movie's title appears with a slow-paced syncopated melody played by woodwinds without any harmonic background. Then the music suddenly shifts to a fast-paced waltz idea for trumpets and strings built on a repeated eight-note pattern. This is followed by a slow and lyrical theme for strings that is heard while the cast list is displayed. Then the film's title is shown for a second time, with the letters spelled out in lights as another syncopated trumpet tune is heard. These ideas will all return later in the film.

In the film's opening scene a trumpet fanfare announces a gala public reception in a city park, where a huge sculpture is about to be unveiled. Furiously fast strings accompany a solo trumpet which mimics the voices of three persons who make speeches to the crowd. First, the mayor "speaks," then a woman whose civic role is not explained; the third "speaker" is the sculptor, who simply says "thank you" three times, again with the trumpet mimicking his voice.

Another trumpet fanfare sounds to announce the actual unveiling. As the little tramp is revealed sleeping in the arms of this giant statue, the music becomes very boisterous, with a fast-paced theme that is interrupted by a band playing the national anthem. The boisterous theme then resumes, while the tramp tries to climb down and leave the scene.

The next scene begins with a lively musical promenade as the tramp walks down a city street. When he stops in front of a shop window to observe a nude statue on display, the music changes to a waltz with several rhythmic pauses as he walks forward and backward, unaware that he is standing in front of a service elevator that keeps going up and down.

When he approaches a street corner and sees the blind flower girl (Virginia Cherrill), the film's most prominent theme begins to sound. It is a habanera-style piece by José Padilla called "La violetera." When she pins a flower onto the tramp's lapel and he discovers that she is blind, the music becomes very emotional, with sweet violin sounds that suggest the tramp's infatuation with the young woman. "La violetera" is heard in various tempos as the film progresses.

When the drunken millionaire first appears, the music includes several moments of Mickey Mousing as the tramp tries to prevent the man from drowning. When the tramp falls in the water, a fast-paced violin theme begins. When the two get out of the water, a slower bassoon theme begins, with "drunken" sliding pitches on trombones adding a comedic effect.

A party scene in a night club features a number of themes, including one of the several recurrences of the promenade melody, plus a raucous tune with trumpets that accompanies a shot of people dancing when the millionaire and his new friend enter the club. This theme returns when the drunken tramp spins a young lady around several times on the dance floor and then spins around a waiter who is carrying a large tray of food.

There is also a party scene at the millionaire's home in which a musical instrument again imitates the human voice. When a man sings to entertain the guests a trombone, with the use of a plunger, makes a funny series of human-like sounds.

The score is not leitmotivic in nature, except for the use of "La violetera." Among the musical ideas that recur in later scenes is the promenade theme, which in the concluding scene has a slow tempo that reflects the tramp's destitute condition after spending several months in jail for allegedly stealing from the millionaire. As the tramp sees the flower girl and realizes her sight has been restored, the strings reprise a lyrical theme from an earlier scene. When she touches his hand and realizes he has been her benefactor, the music adds a heart-rending ambience to the film's final moment.

This is a unique score in many ways. Its simple tunefulness fits the film perfectly, while always expertly highlighting both the humor and the pathos of the story. As such, it deserves to be recognized as one of the cinema's best scores.

Recognition

Selected by the American Film Institute as one of the 100 greatest films of all time.

Recording

Carl Davis, The City Lights Orchestra, *City Lights: A Re-recording of the Original 1931 Score*, Carl Davis Collection, 1989. Reissued on CD by Silva Screen in 2012. Includes fifty-seven minutes of score, with better fidelity than the film's original audio tracks. ****

Bibliography

Robinson, David. Liner notes. *City Lights: A Re-recording of the Original 1931 Score.* Carl Davis Collection CDC015, 1989, CD.

—LEM

CLOSE ENCOUNTERS OF THE THIRD KIND

(1977)
John Williams

The Film

Following the great success of *Jaws* in 1975, Steven Spielberg turned to the sci-fi genre for *Close Encounters of the Third Kind*, which prior to its release was rumored to be an update of such early-1950s alien invasion movies as *The War of the Worlds* and *Invaders from Mars*. But Spielberg's film more closely emulates *The Day the Earth Stood Still*, Robert Wise's 1951 movie about a visitor from another planet who promotes peace and intergalactic cooperation.

Close Encounters begins with the discovery by a team of scientific researchers of World War II–era bombers in a desert area of northern Mexico. The film then shifts to the American Midwest where an air traffic controller in Indianapolis spots UFOs on his radar screen. Soon thereafter, sightings of alien spacecraft near Muncie, Indiana, deeply affect a power company lineman, Roy Neary (Richard Dreyfuss), and an artist and single parent, Jillian Guiler (Melinda Dillon). Roy becomes obsessed with finding out who these aliens are, while Jillian frantically tries to find her young son, Barry (Cary Guffey), who gets abducted by the extraterrestrials. Following their close encounters, these ordinary people become witnesses to a series of extraordinary events.

Barry Guiler (Cary Guffey) welcomes the arrival of aliens. *Columbia Pictures / Photofest © Columbia Pictures*

The Music

John Williams's score differs from the romantically tinged music he created earlier in 1977 for the first *Star Wars* film, which takes place "long, long ago." With its contemporary setting, *Close Encounters* features a score with a modernistic ambiance that initially suggests that the aliens may pose a threat to mankind. In contrast with the dark aspects of the score, Williams was commissioned by Spielberg early in the film's production to create a lyrical idea that would serve as a musical means of communicating with the visitors from space. The result is a series of five tones that are heard as source music in numerous scenes. For example, the same research team seen in the Mexican desert has traveled to India, where villagers are repeatedly chanting the five-note idea. When asked where they heard these tones they point up to the skies. Back in Indiana, little Barry repeatedly plays these same tones on his toy xylophone.

There are several unusual aspects to this score. First of all, instead of an extended musical prelude there is only one bit of music heard during the opening credits. It consists of a single dissonant chord that builds from a barely audible sound in the strings to an increasingly resonant series of long-held tones that culminates in a loud musical "crash" as the screen fades to white.

In the early part of the film there are frequent short cues, some of which combine source music with the score. For instance, in the scene where Barry is abducted, the Johnny Mathis recording of "Chances Are" starts to sound on a phonograph as aliens try to enter Gillian's house. This recording overlays the very dissonant sounds in the underscore that continue until Barry is pulled through an animal flap in the kitchen door.

Several extended musical cues appear in the film's later sequences. One of the most dramatic occurs while Roy is driving with Jillian in a station wagon toward Devil's Tower in northern Wyoming. The music includes brass instruments dramatically sounding a danger motif that consists of two identical sets of four tones, but with the second set a step down from the first (as at the start of Beethoven's Symphony No. 5). When Roy and Jillian leave their vehicle and climb a hill, the danger motif continues until a rising three-note tower motif played by strings gives sound to their sense of awe at seeing the tower in the distance.

In the film's final half hour, there is almost continual music as a planned rendezvous between humans and aliens takes place at the base of Devil's Tower. A synthesized version of the greeting motif is blended with orchestral sounds when the UFOs fly over the tower. As the mother ship lands, the danger and tower motifs are combined into a dramatic musical moment.

A musical highlight of the film occurs when a technician plays the five-note greeting on a computer keyboard. After several repetitions, a duet featuring the computer and the spaceship begins, with the oboe providing the computer's tones, while a tuba represents the voice of the mother ship. This dramatic piece was obviously composed before the scene was shot, since this musical "conversation" could not have been filmed without the music already being in place.

When the aliens choose Roy to board the mother ship, the music consists of the greeting idea plus an ethereal version of "When You Wish upon a Star," with a wordless choir and high violins sounding the melody. When one of the aliens greets a select gathering of scientific personnel, the underscore includes both the greeting idea and a soaring theme based on the tower motif. This soon leads to the shot of the mother ship ascending into the night sky, with the film's final credits superimposed. The film's ending music represents an uplifting musical postlude, with glorious versions of the greeting and tower ideas.

With its ingenious use of short motifs, the score of *Close Encounters* demonstrates a truly high degree of musical creativity and remains one of John Williams's most outstanding achievements.

Recognition

Eight Oscar nominations, including for Spielberg's direction and Williams's score. Vilmos Szigmond won the film's single Oscar for Best Cinematography.
Williams's loss in that year's race was mitigated by his win as composer for *Star Wars*.

Recordings

John Williams, *Close Encounters of the Third Kind*, Arista, 1977. Original soundtrack recording, rereleased on an Arista CD. Contains only forty-one minutes of music. Good sound. ***½

John Williams, *Close Encounters of the Third Kind*, Arista, 1998, CD. Extended version of the score with several tracks of previously unreleased music. Over seventy-seven minutes of running time. Excellent sound. ****

Bibliography

Bouzereau, Laurent. Liner notes. *Close Encounters of the Third Kind, The Collector's Edition Soundtrack*. Arista Records 07822-19004-2, 1998, CD.

Karlin, Fred. *Listening to Movies: The Film Lover's Guide to Film Music*. New York: Schirmer Books, 1994.

—LEM

CONAN THE BARBARIAN

(1982)
Basil Poledouris

The Film

Directed by John Milius, *Conan the Barbarian* is a fantasy adventure film based on written works by Robert E. Howard, starring Arnold Schwarzenegger and James Earl Jones. The film was reasonably successful commercially but performed less well with regard to awards, winning just one major accolade, a Golden Globe for Sandahl Bergman as Best New Star of the Year (female).

Conan (Schwarzenegger) sees his parents murdered by savages led by Thulsa Doom (James Earl Jones), who then take him to the north, where he is overworked and later sold as a slave. His slave master trains him as a warrior to make a profit out of him in fights, but one day Conan gains freedom and uses his new strength to take his revenge on the savages who killed his parents.

The Music

The score to *Conan the Barbarian* is by Greek American composer Basil Poledouris. Poledouris, who died in 2006, was well known for his action and adventure scores

On the verge of stardom: Arnold Schwarzenegger as Conan. *Universal Pictures / Photofest* © *Universal Pictures*

of the 1980s and 1990s and for using traditional orchestral and choral instrumentation in an era when film scores relied heavily on popular music and song. A tribute to his scores in an obituary remarks that his orchestral and choral music are still considered the high point in fantasy film soundtracks. Poledouris's unusual method was to compose the film's music based on the initial storyboards and modify it as the filming commenced. Poledouris conducted and recorded the score over the course of three weeks with a ninety-piece orchestra and a twenty-four-member choir from the Accademia Nazionale di Santa Cecilia and the RAI National Symphony Orchestra in Rome. Director Milius saw Conan as an opera with little or no dialogue, and because of this, Poledouris composed almost two hours of music. Such was the intention of the director to have an epic, classically influenced operatic score, that he sent a copy of the final edit to Poledouris underscored by the music of Richard Wagner, Igor Stravinsky, and Sergei Prokofiev. Poledouris responded to this demand for grandeur by opening the film with twenty-four French horns performing the main theme while ominous drums add a feeling of mystery and intrigue. Listening to the score today, it is clear that Poledouris's music has inspired later fantasy film composers such as Howard Shore in the Tolkien adaptations. It is also clear that the composer looked back for inspiration from the Romantic era, especially to Richard Wagner's complex, sometimes overwhelmingly epic music dramas. Poledouris, in an interview for *Film Score Monthly*, stated that *Conan the Barbarian* was "a real watershed for that kind of film" and that "nobody took fantasy movies that seriously before" *Conan*. The composer highlighted that the seriousness attributed to the lead character by the original author was key to the film's success: "Conan was very much a real guy to [Robert E.] Howard, and a lot like Tolkien, Howard created this world that was . . . just as powerful." Poledouris reflected this world, according to James Caps, by using large choral and orchestral instrumental forces to "stomp his way through the same medieval paths" as composers such as John Barry. Unusually for film music, the score was given room to breathe and to tell the story. It is described by Caps as a "barbaric cantata [that] drives forward with boyish enthusiasm, as if flipping the pages of a comic book."

The score is perhaps best summarized by Michael Goi, a cinematographer, who claims that Poledouris's score "moves from Wagnerian, epic brass, backed by a chorus of bold operatic voices, to gentle themes of profound longing." This myriad of different styles in a fantastical setting ensures that the score to *Conan the Barbarian* acts in an operatic fashion, playing a significant role in taking the narrative forward. The score is powerful, full of energy, and at times brutal, but the lighter moments showcase the composer's adaptability to different scenes and moods. While it may not have been recognized by any awards, it is undoubtedly worthy of a place in the top 100 film scores, simply because it so effectively tells the story as much as the visuals. It is unusual that film music has such a foregrounded, imperative role in a narrative, and for that reason, it is one of the all-time greats.

Recognition

Nomination for the Academy of Science Fiction, Fantasy & Horror Films Award for Best Score.

Recording

Basil Poledouris, *Conan the Barbarian*, Milan, 2017. This reissue of the official soundtrack is, at the time of writing, the only version available. Containing seventeen tracks, it includes scores from *Red Dawn, Farewell to the King,* and *Robocop,* as well as the full *Conan the Barbarian* score. Recommended for fans of Basil Poledouris. ****

Bibliography

Burlingame, J. "Composer Basil Poledouris Dead at 61." *Film Music Society*, November 9, 2006.

Caps, J. "Soundtracks 101." *Film Comment*, 39, no. 6 (2003): 31.

Goi, M. "President's Desk." *American Cinematographer* 93, no. 3 (2012): 10.

Kaplan, J., and A. Kaplan. "Magnificent Movie Music Moments." *Film Score Monthly* 8, no. 3 (2003): 24–31.

MacDonald, Laurence E. "1982—Basil Poledouris: Conan the Barbarian." In *The Invisible Art of Film Music: A Comprehensive History*, 291–94. New York: Ardsley House, 1998.

Morgan, David. *Knowing the Score: Film Composers Talk about the Art, Craft, Blood, Sweat, and Tears of Writing for Cinema.* New York: Harper Entertainment, 2000.

Rhodes, S. M. "A Sprig of Basil." *Film Score Monthly* 9, no. 4 (2004): 26–28.

Thomas, Tony. "More Recently—Basil Poledouris." In *Music for the Movies*, 322–29. Second edition. West Hollywood, CA: Silman-James Press, 1997.

—ML

D

DANCES WITH WOLVES

(1990)

John Barry

The Film

The concept of American Indians as marauding killers was a standard plot device in such John Ford classics as *Stagecoach* (1939) and *The Searchers* (1956), but in his 1964 film *Cheyenne Autumn* Ford adopted a sympathetic attitude toward America's first inhabitants. This revisionist concept is also at the core of Kevin Costner's acclaimed 1990 film *Dances with Wolves*.

After starring in the late-1980s Hollywood hits *The Untouchables*, *Bull Durham*, and *Field of Dreams*, Costner took on the daunting task of producing, directing, and starring in *Dances with Wolves*, which Michael Blake adapted from his own novel. In the film, a Union Army officer named Lieutenant John Dunbar (Costner), after being wounded during a battle with rebel soldiers in Tennessee in early 1863, is rewarded for his bravery by being assigned to Fort Sedgwick, a military post in the Dakota Territory, because he wants to see the frontier before it is gone.

When Dunbar arrives at the fort and finds it deserted, he attempts to befriend members of a Lakota tribe who are encamped nearby. His gradual acceptance as a tribal member causes a crisis of identity that has dire consequences.

The Music

In scoring *Dances with Wolves*, John Barry eschewed the type of western film music popularized by Elmer Bernstein in *The Magnificent Seven* (1960), in which lively, rhythmically syncopated ideas were dominant. The score of *Wolves* is more akin to Barry's earlier Oscar-winning music for *Out of Africa* (1985), with predominantly slow-paced melodic ideas and long-sustained harmonies. The music in Costner's film is distinctive for its tendency to evoke the grandeur of the West, with its rolling prairies and rugged mountain vistas.

The most prominent theme is an idea associated with John Dunbar, first sounded by a solo trumpet during the opening credits. This leisurely paced

Lieutenant Dunbar (Kevin Costner). *Orion Pictures Corporation / Photofest © Orion Pictures Corporation*

melody begins with a five-tone motif that utilizes the pitches of a bugle call. This theme is also prominently featured in a scene where Dunbar, in full military uniform and carrying the US flag, rides his horse Cisco to meet the Lakota at their campsite.

A second prominent theme is first heard while Dunbar is en route to Fort Sedgwick. Beginning with a primarily descending seven-tone idea, this slow-paced theme for strings and horns lyrically evokes the westward journey that Dunbar is now beginning to experience.

A third noteworthy theme is a lyrical idea for solo flute and strings associated with Two Socks, a wolf that hangs around the fort. This theme is based on a six-note tonal pattern that begins with an ascending octave.

Some darker cues are featured in the film, especially the minor-key music that refers to the Lakota Indians when they first observe Dunbar at the deserted fort.

A theme of noble character is heard as Dunbar accompanies the Lakota when they move their campsite to a valley where a herd of buffalo is grazing. This majestic theme features several rising two-note patterns, with French horns and strings alternating in the playing of this idea.

The fastest music in the score occurs during the buffalo hunt in which short melodic motifs are played by horns and trumpets backed by pounding drums. Persistent lively drum sounds also accompany a subsequent scene in which Dunbar, with Two Socks looking on, dances around a campfire outside Fort Sedgwick in celebration of his newfound friendship with the Lakota.

By this point in the film, the music has begun to take on a more Native American sound, just as Dunbar himself is evolving from a properly uniformed US military officer to a member of the Lakota tribe. He has even been dubbed "Dances with Wolves" by the natives who have observed his dancing with Two Socks.

In the film's final section, dramatic drum sounds accompanied by strings and brass are heard as Dunbar, who has been captured by US soldiers, is rescued by the Lakota and then joins them in a bloody struggle against the soldiers who arrested Dunbar on grounds of desertion.

One more theme that should be mentioned is a lyrical idea for flute and strings that is introduced as Dunbar and Stands with a Fist (Mary McDonnell), a white woman who has been raised as a Lakota, find themselves becoming romantically attracted to each other. When he first kisses her, this theme emerges as a musical compliment to their growing physical attraction.

Barry's score captures the romantic aspect of the film not only in the scenes between Dunbar and Stands with a Fist, but also in the feelings that Dunbar expresses in his voiceover narration, taken from entries in his journal, about the American West. In a masterful way, Barry's score describes Dunbar's love affair with the land and its native inhabitants.

Barry's music for *Wolves* became his comeback score after he almost died from complications due to a ruptured esophagus in the late 1980s. And it serves as a beautiful accompaniment for a film that Costner has called "my love letter to the past."

Recognition

Dances with Wolves won seven Oscars, including for Best Picture and Best Director. John Barry won his fifth Academy Award for his score.

Recordings

John Barry, *Dances with Wolves*, Epic Soundtrax CD, 1990. Features most of the music in the film, including all of its prominent themes. Excellent sound. ****
John Barry, Royal Philharmonic Orchestra, *Moviola* and *Moviola* II, Epic Soundtrax, 1985, 1995. Both include excerpts of *Wolves*'s music. The latter contains over twenty minutes of Barry's themes. Good sound. ***½

Bibliography

Costner, Kevin, Michael Black, and Jim Wilson. *Dances with Wolves: The Illustrated Story of the Film*. New York: Newmarket Press, 1990.
Leonard, Geoff, Pete Walker, and Gareth Bramley. *John Barry: The Man with the Midas Touch*. Bristol, UK: Redcliffe Press, 2008.

—LEM

THE DAY THE EARTH STOOD STILL

(1951)
Bernard Herrmann

The Film

Directed by Robert Wise and starring Michael Rennie, Patricia Neal, Billy Gray, Hugh Marlowe, and Sam Jaffe, *The Day the Earth Stood Still* is a science-fiction film based on a 1940 short story by Harry Bates. The film was nominated for two Golden Globes and won one for Best Film Promoting International Understanding. This award, introduced in the immediate aftermath of World War II, was phased out in 1963.The other nomination was for Best Original Score.

A spaceship lands in Washington, D.C. A soldier shoots the solo alien occupant as he leaves the craft. Gort, a large and very powerful robot appears to save him and starts destroying things with only the slightest effort. The injured alien orders Gort to stop, and he is then taken to a hospital. The alien escapes, learns about Earth, and even moves in with a family. When they begin to suspect he is not human, he reveals himself as an alien, along with the fact that Gort is a super-robot

Alien Klaatu (Michael Rennie), left, and Gort (Lock Martin), right, surround human Helen Benson (Patricia Neal). *20th Century Fox Film Corporation / Photofest © 20th Century Fox Film Corporation*

invented to keep peace in the galaxy. The alien warns that his people will destroy the Earth if they are provoked.

The Music

The score to *The Day the Earth Stood Still* was composed by Bernard Herrmann. It is the first score he composed after his move from New York to Hollywood. Herrmann was able to work with fantasy elements for the first time and was delighted with the opportunity to create a soundtrack to the unknown. The unique score he created remains one of the standout scores in the science-fiction genre due to the unusual musical color he used to represent the characters and situations in the film. From his first day on the film, Herrmann declared that he wanted to do something "quite different," and he was successful in this respect.

The first unusual aspect of Herrmann's score was the rejection of the conventional symphonic orchestra, which was the norm for film score recordings at this time. Instead, Herrmann requested a large ensemble of piano, harps, brass, timpani, theremins, electronic violins, electric bass, and electric guitar. He omitted woodwinds. This conscious mixture of acoustic, traditional instruments, and those from the upcoming electronic revolution, resulted in a unique sound world for the film. The ensemble consisted of forty-nine instruments, but no more than twenty-seven were used in any one of the thirty-two individual musical cues on the score.

Herrmann then used these instruments in unusual ways. There would be staggered tritones, glissandi on theremins, and deliberate dissonance to cause discomfort. He would also utilize four tubas at once; unusual in any film score, as they are notoriously powerful, lumbering instruments. Nowhere does Herrmann resort to Romantic, "sweet" music. There is no acoustic string section to provide the classic Hollywood lush string sound, nor woodwinds to provide more delicate colors within the score. Finally, despite a brass section being evident, French horns were not required. Herrmann's goal was, according to the composer, "to characterize a man from another world" and for the music to "reflect an unearthly feeling of outer space without relying on gimmicks." The composer then admitted that his score perhaps inspired the plethora of electronic scores that followed his. Herrmann also employed special recording techniques, considered revolutionary at the time, including layering two separate tracks together to yield a single composite mix.

The score itself revealed Herrmann to be a "musical colorist." The ways in which he constructed harmonies, rhythms, and melodies were simple, and rather than provide the action in the film with grandiose melodies, the composer decided on an accompanying musical color for each scene. Herrmann combines the traditional instruments and the more unusual electronic instruments to portray the humans and alien in turn, with the traditional sounds acting as an invitation to empathize with the characters, whereas the otherworldly timbres and colors warn the audience of impending danger or unusual circumstances in the narrative.

This use of color was a deliberate technique by Herrmann, and he insisted on having full control over his music. He stated: "Color is very important. And this whole rubbish of orchestration is so wrong. I always tell them 'Listen boys, I'll give you a thousand dollars. I'll give you the first page of the *Lohengrin* prelude with all the instruments marked. You write it out. I bet you won't come within 50 percent of Wagner.' To orchestrate is like a thumbprint. People have a style. I don't understand it, having someone orchestrate."

This stubbornness to have control over his compositions cannot be criticized, as he frequently produced works that changed the face of film music composition. *The Day the Earth Stood Still* broke new ground in 1951, and it is still considered one of Herrmann's finest works. For that reason, it is fully deserving of its place in the top 100 film scores.

Recognition

Nominated for Golden Globe for Best Original Score.

Recording

Bernard Herrmann, *The Day The Earth Stood Still* (The Classic Series), Twentieth Century Fox Film Scores, 1993. The original score rereleased on CD. As one reviewer claims: "Thanks to the many eerie, theremin-drenched passages, it's almost impossible to hear that instrument without thinking about guys in space suits. Other great moments: tinkling space pianos, ominous robot monster chords, and weird, plangent orchestrations. One of Herrmann's most visionary and influential scores." For that reason alone, this is a recommended purchase. ****

Bibliography

Fiegel, E. T. "Bernard Herrmann as Musical Colorist: A Musicodramatic Analysis of His Score for *The Day the Earth Stood Still*." *Journal of Film Music* 1, nos. 2–3 (2003): 185–215.

Herrmann, Bernard. Liner notes. *The Fantasy World of Bernard Herrmann*. London Phase 4 SP 44207, 1974, LP.

—ML

DOCTOR ZHIVAGO

(1965)
Maurice Jarre

The Film

Prior to 1965, several classic Russian novels had been adapted for the screen, but until the film version of Boris Pasternak's novel *Doctor Zhivago*, none had achieved such popularity. As a writer, Pasternak attempted to encapsulate the history of Russia during the first half of the twentieth century by creating the fictional character of Yuri Zhivago, who served as an eyewitness to the turbulent events surrounding him.

In the film, Yuri is first seen as a young boy attending his dead mother's burial. He is thereafter raised in Moscow by Alexander Gromeko and his wife, an affluent couple who were good friends of his mother. He also befriends the Gromekos' daughter, Tonya (played as an adult by Geraldine Chaplin). As he grows into manhood, Yuri (now played by Omar Sharif) writes poetry and begins his medical studies. He also becomes an attentive observer of the growing unrest among the working class. When World War I begins, Yuri is married to Tonya and is employed as an army physician; he also meets Lara (Julie Christie), who has become a nurse in hopes of finding her husband, Pasha (Tom Courtenay), a political activist who has disappeared. Their lives are all significantly altered when the Bolshevik Revolution begins.

Lara (Julie Christie) and Yuri Zhivago (Omar Sharif). *MGM / Photofest © MGM*

The Music

Maurice Jarre's score includes the use of an unusually large combination of instruments and voices. In addition to a symphony orchestra of 110 players there is a forty-member choral group, plus an ensemble of twenty-four balalaikas. Additionally Jarre also used such unusual instruments as the Japanese shamisen and koto, plus a novachord, tack piano, and zither, among others.

Balalaikas are prominently used in the opening-credit music, which features two themes, the first of which is a minor-key idea based on an eight-tone motif.

Next comes the first of several renderings of the score's love theme, which has come to be known as "Lara's Theme." This melody, which frequently features the balalaikas plus strings and French horns, begins with an ascending pattern of four tones; the resulting theme is based on multiple variants of this motif, which is easily identifiable by the rising interval between its second and third tones.

Some of the cues in the score are very short and contain only the theme's first four tones. The second appearance of "Lara's Theme" comes after the graveside service for Yuri's mother. As he lies in bed looking at the balalaika that his mother has left him, a solo balalaika is heard in a gentle version of the theme.

The film then concerns the outbreak of World War I and the start of the revolution. As narrated by Yuri's half-brother, Yevgraf (Alec Guinness), this section includes lots of drum-and-cymbal sounds. There isn't much music until deserting Russian soldiers attack military officials who order them back to the front. When Yuri, as a military physician, tends the wounded, he is assisted by Lara, and "Lara's Theme" is briefly heard as a suggestion of their mutual attraction.

The latter part of the film includes a lot of music, but no underscoring is heard during the lengthy railroad journey taken by Yuri, Tonya, and her parents, who have fled Moscow in an effort to reach their country home in the Ural Mountains. Jarre composed three cues for this sequence, but due to the incessant train noises, Lean decided against the use of music. When Yuri and his family reach their destination, a lively minor-key idea is heard as an optimistic reflection on their safe arrival, but nowhere in the film is there a theme representing Yuri's love for Tonya. After becoming separated from his wife, who has fled the country with her family, Yuri finds comfort with Lara. In these scenes, several lushly orchestrated statements of "Lara's Theme" occur as an indication of their mutual love. In the latter part of the film, this theme is clearly the most significant thematic part of Jarre's score.

Borrowed source music occurs early in the film. Just moments before tending Lara's mother, Yuri, sitting beside Tonya at her parents' home, is listening to a pianist who is performing Rachmaninoff's Prelude in G Minor, op. 23, no. 5.

Not included in the film is the song version of "Lara's Theme," called "Somewhere My Love." The Ray Conniff Singers version of this song, recorded after the film's release, topped the record charts through much of 1966 and helped make *Doctor Zhivago* a huge box-office success.

According to Jarre, changes to his score took place during the film's editing process. Many of Jarre's themes were dropped, and consequently, the music in the final version of the film leans more heavily on the use of "Lara's Theme" than had originally been intended. Even so, Jarre's music successfully emphasizes the human drama of the events that took place during and after the Russian Revolution and creates sympathy for the story's central characters. As such, this music deserves a place on the list of the most revered film scores.

Recognition

Despite mixed reviews, received ten Academy Award nominations.
Oscars won for Adapted Screenplay, Color Cinematography, Color Art Direction, Color Costuming, and Musical Score.

Recordings

Maurice Jarre, *Doctor Zhivago*, CBS Special Products, 1990. This is the original soundtrack recording, digitally remastered, Decent sound, but its forty-minute musical content is largely devoted to "Lara's Theme. ***

Maurice Jarre, *Doctor Zhivago*, Deluxe 30th Anniversary Edition, Rhino, 1995. The complete score, containing over an hour of Jarre's music, including outtakes from cues that were dropped from the final version of the film. Of special value for fans of Maurice Jarre's music. ****

Bibliography

Bradford, Marilee. Liner notes. *Doctor Zhivago*. Deluxe 30th Anniversary Edition. Rhino Movie Music R2 71957, 1995, CD.

—LEM

E

EAST OF EDEN

(1955)
Leonard Rosenman

The Film

East of Eden, directed by Elia Kazan, is a filmic adaptation of the 1952 novel of the same name by John Steinbeck. The film starred James Dean in his first major film role. The plot centers around 1917–1918 and is set in central California. It is a complex story of two young brothers, Cal and Aron, striving for the attention of their devoutly religious father. Cal (James Dean) finds out that his mother is still alive, despite what he had been told, and is running a brothel in nearby Monterey. To further complicate matters, Cal also begins to fall in love with his brother's girlfriend, Abra (Julie Harris). Incensed at the preferential treatment his brother is receiving from their father, Cal takes him to see his mother at the brothel. Shocked by this, Aron becomes intoxicated and boards a troop train to enlist for the final moments of World War I. This causes the father to have a stroke. In a final bid to get his father's attention and affection, Cal tries to talk to him, but his father is paralyzed from the stroke. In the end, however, he finally does manage to speak and asks Cal to look after him. Cal and Abra share a kiss, and the film ends on a happy note of acceptance and redemption. The film made the list of the American Film Institute's 400 best American films of all time and was selected for preservation by the National Film Registry.

The Music

The score to *East of Eden* was composed by Leonard Rosenman. Just like James Dean in his star acting role, Rosenman's commission as film composer for *East of Eden* was his first. The composer and director met early in the process to discuss the score, in order to find ways to make the music "inextractable" from the dramatic framework of the film. They agreed that Rosenman should be there for the production of the film and to even write some of the music before the scenes were shot. This resulted in Kazan sometimes shooting scenes to music, as opposed to

Abra (Julie Harris), Aron Trask (Richard Davalos), and Cal Trask (James Dean). *Warner Bros. / Photofest © Warner Bros.*

the far more conventional method of the composer writing music to completed scenes. Rosenman recalls finding himself on the set at Mendocino and Salinas, working on initial musical ideas for the scenes that were about to be shot. While on location, the composer had access to a piano, and he performed his daily musical sketches for the director as they sat and discussed how it fit the scenes shot on that particular day. Because of this collaborative, concurrent method, by the time the film had a rough cut, the music did as well. The only thing left to do was to orchestrate the musical sketches and record the final score.

Rosenman recalls how his concert works were modernist and dissonant and that the director was not especially keen on having a complete score composed in this style. Therefore, the two struck a bargain whereby any music accompanying children characters would be scored in a simple, tonal fashion, whereas adults—more complex characters—would have dissonant music.

Another unusual agreement the two came to was related to the visibility of film music. It is often suggested that good film music is that which is not particularly noticed by an audience. However, Rosenman and Kazan agreed that the score to *East of Eden* should be more intrusive. In other words, the music should be a key component in the plot and not there to simply underscore the narrative. Rosenman stated that "the necessity for music in film is the dramatic necessity for the intrusion of an 'unreal' or illusionary element for the purpose of creating a new and imaginative reality." Thus, in *East of Eden*, the composer wanted the music to illuminate the characters and situations and to "generate the dramatic excitement which the marriage of the arts should bring about." He spoke of the score as being operatic, with the "arias" being spoken as dialogue by the on-screen characters rather than sung on a stage.

Rosenman took the dialogue of the film into account, showing clear consideration of the filmmaking process. He acknowledged that Julie Harris was a soprano, James Dean a tenor, and Raymond Massey (who played Cal and Aron's father) a bass-baritone, and for this reason he designed the instrumentation and the melodic material around the vocal ranges of the main actors and actresses. Rosenman highlighted "holes" that were left in the scoring so that the dialogue could shine through unencumbered. This highly conscious approach to film scoring is undoubtedly why the score is considered one of Rosenman's most successful and why it works with the film in such a cooperative manner.

Recognition

Unusually for a film in this book, Rosenman's score did not receive any major or minor nominations for awards. However, there is no doubt his music helped the film's overall success.

Four Academy Award nominations, winning for Best Actress in a Supporting Role.

Two Golden Globes.

Three nominations for BAFTAs.

Recording

John Adams, London Sinfonietta, *The Film Music of Leonard Rosenman: East of Eden, Rebel without a Cause*, Nonesuch, 1997. This is a compilation of Rosenman's film music. It includes nine tracks from *East of Eden* and a further six from *Rebel without a Cause*. ***

Bibliography

Limbacher, James L. *Film Music: From Violins to Video (Essays & Index of Films)*. Metuchen, NJ: Scarecrow Press, 1974.

—ML

EDWARD SCISSORHANDS
(1990)
Danny Elfman

The Film

In his early films *Beetlejuice* (1988) and *Batman* (1989), director Tim Burton demonstrated a flair for comedy laced with absurd and often darkly dramatic moments. With the help of his longtime musical collaborator, Danny Elfman, this unique blend of stylistic ingredients brought to fruition his next film, *Edward Scissorhands*, in 1990.

This film is a modern Frankenstein story in which an old inventor (Vincent Price) has made a creature who looks human but lacks hands. Edward (Johnny Depp) later recalls that he was prevented from receiving lifelike hands due to the inventor's sudden death.

Edward lives alone in the inventor's old mansion atop a mountain that overlooks a suburban housing development. Peg Boggs (Dianne Wiest), who lives in the suburb with her family, canvasses the neighborhood as an Avon lady, but has little luck selling her products to her neighbors. One day she impulsively drives up to the mansion to find new customers. When Peg meets Edward his appear-

Joyce (Kathy Baker) watches Edward Scissorhands (Johnny Depp) make magic with his hairdressing skills. *20th Century Fox Film Corporation / Photofest © 20th Century Fox Film Corporation*

ance initially frightens her, but she soon sympathizes with his plight of being alone and having an unfortunate skin condition. She invites Edward to her home where she hopes her products will help him. Thus begins Edward's experiences in suburban living.

The Music

The film's score benefits from Danny Elfman's flair for the unusual in terms of orchestration. The first music heard in the film features wordless voices and low strings that accompany the Twentieth Century Fox logo, which is already covered in snow as snowflakes continue falling. Immediately after this image, the film's credits begin with the repeated sounds of a celesta and harp in a waltz-like rhythm. These delicate and tinkling tones provide a harmonic background for the film's first and most prominent theme, a waltz idea first performed by wordless voices and strings. After a few seconds the English horn sounds a melancholy version of this theme, which is based on a seven-note motif of longer and shorter tones in an alternating pattern. The wordless singing by the Paulist Choristers of California adds a uniquely eerie flavor to this music, which injects a fantasy atmosphere that prevails throughout much of the film.

Following the credits, the music continues in the opening scene where an elderly lady (Wynona Rider in old-age makeup) begins to relate the story of Edward to her granddaughter as a bedtime story. During this scene, the music continues with wordless voices and a melody that uses a three-note motif that resembles the last three tones of the opening waltz theme. Unlike the music for the credits the music in this scene is in a major key and provides a more uplifting atmosphere. At the end of this scene, we get the first glimpse of Edward as he looks out of the old mansion at the suburban neighborhood located at the base of the mountain. Elfman's opening cue ends with gentle major-key harmonies after more than five minutes of continuous music.

Another minor-key waltz idea, this time with a lyrical flute melody, is featured as Peg drives up the steep road that leads to the mansion. A menacing flavor by way of loud, low-pitched brass chords is added to the music to suggest the possible danger that lurks inside the house. When Peg enters the garden on the way to the house, wordless voices, harp, and celesta are added to convey the wondrous shapes of the shrubbery. This view of Edward's topiary gives the viewer a preview of his landscaping skills that will be put to later use once he starts living in the suburbs.

The music in the flashback scene, where Edward remembers the old inventor's laboratory in the mansion, has rhythmically driven fast-paced music with the persistent use of repeated tones in an "oom-pah, oom-pah" pattern that emulates moments in Elfman's earlier music for *Pee-Wee's Big Adventure*.

One of the most memorable musical moments in *Scissorhands* occurs when the neighborhood ladies line up with their dogs so that Edward can give the pets a grooming. Before long, one of the women suggests that Edward do a makeover of her hair. Thus the ladies receive the benefit of Edward's ingenious talent. Throughout this scene, Elfman's music is prominent, with two alternate musical ideas used in one continuous cue. The first is a slow-tempo piece in the Spanish style of the habanera that features strongly accented beats, with strings prominently featured in the melody. The other is a very rapid-paced theme with a solo violin playing a boisterous gypsy-style melody. At the end of the scene, when Peg is escorted to the lawn chair for her turn to get a new hair style, the music segues into a second slow rendition by strings of the habanera idea.

A lot of the music of *Scissorhands* is confined to short cues of thirty seconds or less. One of the more noteworthy of these occurs in a morning scene where several residents in the neighborhood leave their homes and drive off in their cars. Fast-paced music begins with "tick-tock" clock sounds played by piano and tonal percussion. Violins provide a short tuneful melodic idea with loud ominous brass chords added in. Wordless voices and bongo drums are also featured.

There are several moments of source music in the film, especially bits of recordings by vocalist Tom Jones. "Delilah," "It's Not Unusual," and "With These Hands" are all associated with scenes involving the sexy neighbor Joyce (Kathy Baker).

Noted film-music commentator Jon Burlingame calls the music for *Scissorhands* an "underappreciated" score. That is putting it mildly. After a career that has lasted more than three decades, this music remains one of Elfman's most imaginatively conceived film scores and one eminently worthy of inclusion on a list of best scores.

Recognition

One Academy Award nomination for Best Makeup.
The film was well received by critics, but unlike the 1989 *Batman*, it was not a huge box-office hit.

Recordings

Danny Elfman, *Edward Scissorhands*, MCA, 1990, CD. Approximately forty-six minutes of score included on this album, along with Tom Jones's recording of "With These Hands." Good sound. ****

Bibliography

Burlingame, Jon. *Sound and Vision: 60 Years of Motion Picture Soundtracks*. New York: Billboard Books, 2000.

—LEM

EMPIRE OF THE SUN

(1987)
John Williams

The Film

In *Empire of the Sun*, Steven Spielberg directed a screen adaptation of J. G. Ballard's novel based on the author's experiences as a boy imprisoned in a Japanese detention camp in China. It was one of two films released in 1987, along with John Boorman's *Hope and Glory*, featuring semi-autobiographical stories about children surviving the perils of World War II.

Empire begins in early December of 1941 with a rehearsal by a boys' choir in a very European-style church. However, the setting is actually an upscale neighborhood of Shanghai, where many English families reside in lavish homes. One of the choirboys is eleven-year-old Jim Graham (Christian Bale), who is chauffeured to and from the church in the family's Packard, driven by one of his parents' Chinese servants.

When Shanghai comes under attack by Japanese bombers, crowds of people flood the streets in an attempt to find shelter. In the ensuing chaos, Jim is separated from his parents and captured by Japanese soldiers. He is loaded onto a truck with other British POWs and winds up in the Soochow Creek Internment Camp. This is a story of survival from a child's point of view.

The Music

For *Empire* John Williams created an emotional accompaniment that reflects Jim's feelings as his world changes so drastically from the contentment of his early childhood to the horrors of the Japanese camp. But instead of an original main-title theme the first music in the film is source music, beginning with a boys' choir in an arrangement of the Welsh song "Suo Gan." Opening shots of the city of Shanghai are followed by quick glimpses of the British sector and the church in which the choir is rehearsing. Jim is first seen as a soloist in the singing of "Suo Gan," with the accompaniment of the choir and organ.

Following the rehearsal scene, when Jim is being chauffeured home, echoes of "Suo Gan" continue but gradually fade as the sounds of his mother playing a Chopin mazurka on the family's piano begin to be heard; the Chopin music continues as Jim rides his bike on the grounds of his family's lavish home.

Williams's original music begins when Jim's mother is sitting by his bed at night. At this point a celesta and high-pitched strings produce ethereal sounds that are followed by a flute introducing Jim's theme, a smoothly flowing melody based on a series of seven tones.

This theme returns in a sequence that connects Jim's arrival at the camp with the second part of the film, which takes place in 1945. The music begins when Jim arrives with a truckload of fellow prisoners at the Soochow camp. When he

A very young Christian Bale. *Warner Bros. / Photofest © Warner Bros.*

climbs a hill and moves among throngs of prisoners, a solo piano sounds Jim's theme with strings in the background. This music continues into the next shot, which shows a Japanese bomber being repaired. As Jim, lured by his fascination with airplanes, sees sparks flying and then puts his hands onto the plane's fuselage, French horns and choral voices, accompanied by strings, are heard in a continuation of Jim's theme. When three Japanese pilots approach him and return his salute, this seven-note idea gradually crescendos into a grandly orchestrated statement.

At this moment, the scene shifts to 1945, with Jim's theme continuing without a break as the thinner and taller Jim, now wearing a bomber jacket instead of his school uniform, watches a toy airplane in flight. After retrieving the plane and sending it over a fence to the Japanese boy who had launched it from the neighboring airstrip, the music suddenly shifts to a new theme for trumpets in a faster tempo that includes a soaring string melody as a high-pitched counterpoint to the trumpet idea. This buoyant music continues as Jim runs about the camp making trades involving food items and articles of clothing. Although this theme seems a bit lighthearted for a scene set in a Japanese internment camp, it signifies the unbridled spirit of Jim, who has learned the art of the deal from an unlikely mentor, an American army deserter named Basie (John Malkovich), who is also a camp detainee. This cue continues until Jim completes his errands and delivers his homework to his tutor, Dr. Rawlins, at a makeshift hospital.

Vocal sounds are a key element in Williams's score. In a scene where allied planes are bombing the nearby airstrip and Jim sees the P-51 Mustangs from the rooftop of a building, wordless women's and boys' voices add an emotional element to Jim's sense of excitement.

Another vocal highlight occurs during the war's final days, when the Japanese have evacuated the camp and Jim wanders about in a way that mirrors his meanderings early in the film. As Jim drags along a parachute filled with food rations that have been dropped from an Allied plane, a choral theme called "Exsultate Justi" is inserted in the underscore; the vocal repetitions of the word "Alleluia" confirm that the war is over.

In the film's final scene, when Jim is reunited with his parents, "Suo Gan" provides a last moment of underscoring that suggests his awakening from a long traumatic nightmare.

Recognition

Although *Empire of the Sun* was not a box-office hit, it had six Academy Award nominations.
Nominated for both Oscar and Golden Globe awards for Original Score.
Williams won a 1987 BAFTA for Music Score.

Recordings

John Williams, *Empire of the Sun*, Warner Bros., 1987. Contains over fifty minutes of music. Good sound. ****

John Williams, *Empire of the Sun* (Expanded edition), La La Land, 2014. Includes over one hundred minutes of music. Limited release of four thousand copies. Excellent sound. ****

Bibliography

MacDonald, Laurence E. *The Invisible Art of Film*. Second edition. Lanham, MD: Scarecrow Press, 2013.

Matessino, Mike. Liner notes. *Empire of the Sun: Original Motion Picture Soundtrack*. La La Land Records LLLCD1300, 2014, CD.

—LEM

E.T. THE EXTRA-TERRESTRIAL

(1982)
John Williams

The Film

E.T. the Extra-Terrestrial is a critically acclaimed science-fiction film and is considered one of the classic Steven Spielberg tearjerkers. The film tells the story of a young boy, Elliot (Henry Thomas), who finds a short-legged alien in his back yard. Trying to find a way home, E.T. is sheltered by Elliot and his siblings, as government officials close in and attempt to take him away to be examined. The famous flying bicycle scene and emotionally charged finale helped to cement the film's place in the history books as an all-time classic. This is backed up by its box-office takings, where it surpassed *Star Wars* (1977) as the highest-grossing film of all time; a record that would not be beaten until the release of another Spielberg film, *Jurassic Park*, in the early 1990s. The film was nominated for nine Academy Awards and won four. Three of these were related to sound and music and another was for visual effects. It missed out on Best Picture to *Gandhi*, directed by Richard Attenborough.

The Music

The score to *E.T.* was composed by John Williams, his sixth collaboration with Steven Spielberg. The main theme can be considered one of Williams's most memorable, with soaring strings, majestic horns, and poignant woodwind interludes using the full capacity of the orchestral palette to create an arresting underscore to a heartbreaking narrative. There are very few film music programs at colleges or universities that do not reference the main theme from *E.T.* at some point in the syllabus. It truly exemplifies Williams's neoclassical or neoromantic style to such a degree of perfection that if film music were allowed one entry in a time capsule, this score would be one of the very top contenders.

Elliott (Henry Thomas) flees with E.T. *Universal Pictures / Photofest © Universal Pictures*

At the start of the film, as E.T. and his fellow aliens survey plant life on earth, the music is soft and slightly mysterious, with slow-moving strings playing glissandi and pitch bends. There is no real melody of note here. E.T. is left behind, and the music turns to sadness temporarily, before the loveable alien takes in his first view of the Los Angeles area from high atop a mountain. The finale to the film, set in a similar location in the woods, sees the spaceship return for E.T., and he says his famous farewell to Elliot. The chase scene that precedes this moment is arguably the finest music ever written for such a scene, with the emotion building in the score until the almost inconceivably heartbreaking moment where E.T. departs. It would be difficult to find another scene in any film where music and image work so intensely together to leave moviegoers without a dry eye. It truly is a moment where Spielberg and Williams combine their talents to create a masterpiece of emotive cinema. Despite all of this poignant grandeur, the more nuanced use of orchestration highlights Williams as a master of his trade. The use of the solo flute to depict E.T. gives the alien character a warmth and likeability that was imperative to the success of the film, and perhaps as effectively as the grandeur of the full orchestra, it offers an emotional connection to the character and his plight.

Williams cleverly self-references his music from *Star Wars* during a Halloween scene. As the children are out trick-or-treating, E.T., wearing a ghost costume, spots a child wearing a Yoda costume heading toward him. Yoda's theme from the *Star Wars* soundtrack is heard momentarily. To all but the trained ear, it might not register, but it is a clever (and admittedly cheeky) use of music by Williams. Indeed, the music preceding the appearance of Yoda, using playful woodwind melodic fragments, sounds very much like it belongs in the musical world of *Star Wars*. This link to another Williams and Spielberg film is reinforced when E.T., seeing Yoda, says excitedly, "Home! Home!" It seems to suggest that the music is not the only link between the two filmic worlds.

There are darker moments in the score. The government agents who attempt to capture E.T. are underscored with sinister organ sounds. It is a rare, but necessary moment of tension in a film that is overwhelmingly full of hope and adventure. Aggressive, jumpy percussion hits add to the scariness of these moments in the film, with the peril in the narrative matched by some of Williams's most agitated accompaniments.

The peril soon gives way to relief, which then gives way to the chase scene and escape. The final ten minutes of the film, as E.T. says his farewells, incorporating the now famous "ouch" dialogue, is without doubt some of the most emotionally involving cinema ever created. It is everything that family-friendly Hollywood can and should be. The visuals are striking, the narrative is heartbreaking, and the music is transcendental.

Recognition

Along with two other Williams scores, *Star Wars* and *Jaws*, *E.T*'s soundtrack won all four major awards (Academy Award, Golden Globe, BAFTA, and Grammy). At the time of writing, only six scores have achieved this, with three of them composed by Williams.

1982 Academy Award for Best Original Score.
1982 Golden Globe for Best Original Score.
1982 BAFTA Award for Best Film Music.
1983 Grammy Award for Best Score Soundtrack.
1983 Grammy Award for Best Instrumental Composition ("Flying Theme").
1983 Grammy Award for Best Instrumental Arrangement ("Flying Theme").
1982 Saturn Award for Best Music.
Voted fourteenth-best American film score of all time by American Film Institute in 2005.

Recordings

John Williams, *E.T. the Extra-Terrestrial*, Universal Island Records, 1992. This official soundtrack release was remastered for the twentieth anniversary of the film's release and is highly recommended. ****
John Williams, *E.T. the Extra-Terrestrial* (35th Anniversary Limited Edition), La-La Land, 2017, two-CD set. Limited to five thousand copies, this edition includes previously unheard cues, as well as the music for the Universal Studios E.T. theme park ride. Well recommended for fans of the film. ****

—ML

F

FARGO
(1996)
Carter Burwell

The Film

Directed by Joel Coen and starring Frances McDormand, *Fargo* is a black-comedy crime film.

In 1987 Minneapolis, Jerry (William H. Macy) comes up with various schemes to clear his financial debt while working at his father-in-law's car dealership. As a last resort, he travels to the small town of Fargo, North Dakota, and organizes the kidnapping of his wife in the hope her wealthy father will pay the requested random figure. The comedic side of the film comes into play as everything that could go wrong inevitably does. The heavily pregnant sheriff, Marge Gunderson (Frances McDormand), does whatever she can to foil the plot as the kidnapping scheme descends into chaos.

The film was nominated for seven Academy Awards, of which it won two for Best Actress in a Leading Role, and Best Writing (screenplay). It was also nominated for four Golden Globes but did not win any, and six BAFTAs, of which it won one for Best Director.

The Music

The musical score to *Fargo* was composed by Carter Burwell, an American who, at the time of writing, has collaborated with the Coen brothers on fifteen occasions.

The score to *Fargo* is fascinating for the complex variety of Burwell's music, but also for its perceived function in a film that highlights the banal in terms of the locations used and set design. The director asked production designer Rick Heinrichs to find the most "soul-deadening, flattened" locations he could. "He'd find some dumpy café, and we'd say, no, it's too good. Less color, less design, less kitsch. . . . We wanted no design. Absolutely nothing."

Frances McDormand in her Academy Award–winning role of Marge Gunderson. *Gramercy Pictures / Photofest © Gramercy Pictures*

The main theme, heard in the cue "Fargo, North Dakota," is based on a Norwegian folk song called "The Lost Sheep." This theme is heard at various points throughout the film. While this book focuses on orchestral scores, the relationship between Burwell's score and popular music in *Fargo* is too important to ignore. Burwell's melodic, flowing score is a blatant contrast to the diegetic Muzak (or "elevator music") that is heard as we follow the story. In an extensive article, Greg Hainge summarizes this relationship by claiming, "Burwell's score aids us less in our attempt to read Fargo than does the Muzak that floods the film's restaurants, hotels, and other public spaces." In other words, Burwell's score is perceived to be less important to the narrative than the popular songs heard throughout the film. Usually, the opposite is true. Incidentally, all the songs heard in the film are featured only as background music, usually on a radio in a restaurant or cafe, and do not appear on the official soundtrack album.

Why then, does the orchestral score appear in this book, if it is allegedly unimportant? The answer to this can be found in the music itself. In a film in which music tells us so much about the characters and locations, the score makes a heavy contribution. According to Phillip Brophy, the score "feels Gaelic, yet . . . moves like a funeral march. Performed with a gypsy waywardness, it climbs in mythical scale." Burwell's use of Norwegian, Gaelic, and gypsy musical styles for a film set in North Dakota is intriguing, yet, lacking the orchestral grandeur often found in other scores, it offers up the impression of banality, which, as Hainge argues, the Muzak also contributes to. The action and dialogue accompanied by background popular music in a run-down, grimy café or lilting Gaelic or gypsy melodies help to establish character and location.

There is a particularly heartwarming and poignant use of the theme in the very last scene of the movie, where Marge and her husband, Norm, lie in bed talking about their relationship and how they are doing "pretty good." The theme appears one last time, but instead of being performed in a folk-like way on strings, it is heard very subtly under the dialogue on a music box. The tinkling, almost unperceivable theme perfectly bookends a film that opens with a full orchestral rendition of the same theme.

Carter Burwell does not receive the same recognition as more "A-list" film composers such as John Williams, Hans Zimmer, Howard Shore, and others, but the score to *Fargo* is a prime example of an effective use of film music that works on many levels. A Norwegian, folksy, gypsy-inspired, Gaelic score perhaps should not work in a film set in a wintery northern US state, but it does. Combined with the use of popular music, it perfectly accompanies the story of Jerry as he blunders his way through this black comedy. The main theme is particularly memorable and heartfelt and is a major contributor to this film making the final cut for this book.

Recognition

The score was not nominated for any major awards.
Awards Circuit Community Award for Best Original Score.
Chicago Film Critics Association Award for Best Original Score.
Nominated for 20/20 Award for Best Score (Drama).
Nominated for Online Film & Television Association Award for Best Score.

Recording

Carter Burwell, *Fargo/Barton Fink: Music of Carter Burwell*, TVT, 1996. This recording combines two of Burwell's Coen collaborations on one disc of twenty-four tracks, running to a total of ninety-eight minutes, roughly half of which is *Fargo*. This is recommended due to the fact you receive two scores for the price of one. It is also the only recording available at the time of writing. ***

Bibliography

Bergan, Ronald. *The Coen Brothers*. London: Phoenix, 2001.
Brophy, Philip. "Muzak for Films and Airports." *Wire: Adventures in Modern Music* 173 (July 1998): 40–41.
Hainge, G. "The Unbearable Blandness of Being: The Everyday and Muzak in 'Barton Fink' and 'Fargo.'" *Post Script—Essays in Film and the Humanities* 27, no. 2 (2008): 38–47.

—ML

FORREST GUMP
(1994)
Alan Silvestri

The Film

Directed by Robert Zemeckis and starring Tom Hanks as the title character, *Forrest Gump* is a comedy-drama based on a 1986 novel of the same name by Winston Groom.

A feather falls from the sky and finds itself at the feet of Forrest Gump, an intellectually challenged man, as he sits at a bus stop in Savannah, Georgia. He begins to tell his life story to a woman seated next to him. Each time the narration returns to the bus stop, a different character is seated next to him.

In school, his ability to run fast gets him into college on a football scholarship. After his college graduation, he enlists in the army and is sent to Vietnam, where he makes fast friends with a man named Bubba, who convinces Forrest to go into the shrimping business with him when the war is over. Bubba is killed in combat, but Forrest is awarded the Congressional Medal of Honor.

Forrest, while in recovery, becomes world famous at table tennis, and he endorses a company that makes ping-pong paddles, earning himself $25,000, which he uses to buy a shrimping boat, fulfilling his promise to Bubba. He eventually earns enough to buy an entire fleet of shrimp boats. After seeing his mother in her last days, he proposes to Jenny, a girl he'd met at school and whose story coincides with Gump's throughout the film. She declines. Forrest goes for a run and keeps running for over three years, becoming famous again.

Back at the bus stop in the present day, Gump reveals he received a letter from Jenny telling him he's a father. They finally marry, but Jenny dies shortly afterward from a virus.

The film ends with father and son waiting for the school bus on little Forrest's first day of school.

The film was an overwhelming success, with thirteen Academy Award nominations, making it the joint second-most-nominated film in history. Of these thirteen, it won six: Best Picture, Best Actor in a Leading Role, Best Director, Best Writer (screenplay), Best Film Editing, and Best Effects (visual effects). It also won three of six Golden Globe nominations and one of eight BAFTA nominations.

The Music

The score to *Forrest Gump* was composed by Alan Silvestri. He composed the film linearly—that is, he approached each scene from the start of the film to the end and decided on the music required, composing as he went along. This is an unusual process for composers, who often write as their inspiration strikes them, regardless of where a scene sits within the film.

Forrest (Tom Hanks) regales fellow commuter (Rebecca Williams). *Paramount Pictures / Photofest © Paramount Pictures*

Silvestri wrote the "Feather Theme," the film's main-title idea, very early in the process, and he completed it in only fifteen minutes. The director had asked for something that captured the essence of the film. Silvestri saw an early mock-up of the film where the feather was actually in the director's hand, but from that, he established the memorable, gentle melody that opens the film and reappears only once at the end. As the feather falls from the sky, a solo piano begins in a high register to play the poignant melody. As it finds its way closer to Forrest, the rest of the orchestra begins to join in, adding an emotive depth to the theme. In an interview with BMI explaining his compositional process, Silvestri stated that he tried to insert the "Feather Theme" into almost every scene in the film where music was required, but it just did not work. For each scene that came up, a new cue or theme had to be written. Only when the feather returned at the end of the film could he reuse what is arguably the most well-known melody from the score.

The music is not always so tender, and Silvestri stretches his orchestra's legs in the cue "Run Forrest Run," where the lead character starts running and decides not to stop. The triumphant, fanfare-like cue utilizes brass and a pulsating string accompaniment. It is grand without being grandiose and still retains the charm and gentle nature of the feather theme, but expanded into a celebratory mood. The music dies down almost immediately, but it is a rare and welcome moment of triumph in a film saturated with poignancy and sadness.

Forrest Gump must have been a challenging film to score, even for as accomplished a composer as Alan Silvestri. It is a difficult subject, and the narrative being so diverse in terms of location and mood means that the music has to be similarly diverse. The evocative "Feather Theme" starting and ending the film is effectively much like a prologue and epilogue to a book that has many varied chapters within.

Recognition

Nominated for Academy Award for Best Original Score.
Nominated for Golden Globe for Best Original Score.
Nominated for a Grammy.

Recordings

Alan Silvestri, *Forrest Gump*, SBME, 2008. This is the orchestral element of the score. The twenty-one tracks last for only thirty-nine minutes, but the quality of the music makes up for the short running time. ***

Alan Silvestri, *Forrest Gump* (Special Collector's Edition), Sony Legacy, 2001. This is the popular music album. It contains two discs with thirty-two songs featured in the film. The very last track of the second disc is an orchestral suite by Silvestri. Recommended along with the orchestral album to complete the collection. ***

Bibliography

"In the Studio with BMI Icon Alan Silvestri." BMI, April 2017. https://www.bmi.com/special/silvestri.

—ML

G

THE GHOST AND MRS. MUIR

(1947)
Bernard Herrmann

The Film

From the many adaptations of Charles Dickens's *A Christmas Carol* to such popular releases as *Beetlejuice* and the *Poltergeist* films, stories about haunting have long fascinated viewers and elicited both fright and laughter. But seldom has the ghost story been a genre for romance. One good example is R. A. Dick's 1945 novel *The Ghost and Mrs. Muir*, which was brought to the screen by director Joseph L. Mankiewicz.

Gull Cottage is a seaside house formerly occupied by Captain Daniel Gregg. Despite being warned of its haunting, a widow named Lucy Muir (Gene Tierney) rents the place and moves in with her young daughter, Anna, and her servant, Martha.

The ghost of Captain Daniel Gregg (Rex Harrison) fails to scare her away. Over time, they become friends, and he helps her financially by becoming the "ghost writer" of a sensational memoir. When Lucy falls in love with Miles Fairley, a writer of children's books, Daniel departs and thus gives her the freedom to choose love among the living. But she soon learns that Miles is already married. Lucy subsequently remains at Gull Cottage as if waiting for Daniel to return.

The Music

Although Bernard Herrmann was never under contract at 20th Century Fox, his long-standing friendship with Fox's music director, Alfred Newman, led to many scoring assignments for that studio. *The Ghost and Mrs. Muir* represents the fourth of those films.

One of Herrmann's many creative gifts as a composer was his uncanny ability to utilize unusual combinations of orchestral sounds. In *Mrs. Muir* Herrmann's ingenious use of woodwinds, from the lowest contrabass clarinet to the high piccolos, helps to convey the mysterious sea that plays a significant role in the film.

Lucy Muir (Gene Tierney) and the deceased Captain Gregg (Rex Harrison). *20th Century Fox Film Corporation / Photofest © 20th Century Fox Film Corporation*

This mysterious aura is evident in the opening credits, where pairs of woodwinds sound the first of three distinct ideas that serve as important thematic motifs. These fast-moving rising tones are followed by a slower-paced four-tone string idea that begins with an ascending leap. Herrmann's combining of these motifs suggests the continual ebb and flow of the incoming waves. There is also a motif for strings and harp with four melodic tones that smoothly descend in pitch. This third idea is used as the basis for Lucy's theme, which arrives immediately following the credits. The lilting music represents both Lucy's loving nature and an inner strength that allows her to confront ghosts.

Among the most prominent of the score's other ideas is a jaunty flute tune played in the style of a sea chantey that represents the ghostly presence of Daniel. It is prominently heard in a scene where Lucy is typing Daniel's reminiscences and she objects to Daniel's salty vocabulary.

Another melodic idea that makes a couple of appearances is the theme for Mr. Coombe, the realtor who tries unsuccessfully to keep Lucy from renting Gulf Cottage. The bassoon is featured in this theme, which begins with a simple ascending pattern of five tones. There is also a lilting idea for solo violin and strings that represents Martha, Lucy's devoted maid.

A romantic theme for strings and woodwinds is associated with Miles Fairley, the deceitful writer who temporarily wins Lucy's heart. The six-note motif heard in this music provides the basis for some of the score's most romantic moments.

There are several short cues in the score that serve as connective tissue between scenes. One example is a short cue for solo oboe heard as Lucy arrives in the seaside town of Whitecliff, where she has decided to live. This idea returns later in the film when Lucy is aboard a train returning from London, where she has gone to get Daniel's memoir published.

There is a prevailing sense of melancholy about much of the score, which helps to convey both Lucy's loneliness and the mysterious aura of the haunted cottage. There is also a powerful presence of sea motifs in two late scenes of waves crashing over rocks, serving to indicate the passing years in which Lucy moves gradually from her youth into old age.

Two scenes deserve special mention. One occurs when Daniel tells the sleeping Lucy that she has only dreamed about him and that she must find happiness among the living. As he speaks, the music features soft strings and woodwinds in motifs from earlier in the film. Brass instruments add a boldly dramatic sound when Daniel wishes they could have seen the world together.

The other standout scene comes when the elderly Lucy sits in a chair holding a glass of milk. When the glass tips over, it is evident that she has died. Daniel then reappears, and for the only time in the film, he touches her, taking her hands and she rises from the chair as a young woman. Lucy's theme then returns in a beautifully romantic arrangement for strings and harp as Lucy and Daniel leave Gull Cottage and walk into eternity. A triumphant return of the descending four-note motif from the opening scene accompanies the film's wondrous ending.

Herrmann's score is remarkable from beginning to end, with a subtlety of style that perfectly captures both the fantasy and romantic elements of the film's story. It is one of the composer's most unique and memorable creations and richly deserves a place of distinction in this book.

Recognition

Oscar nomination for the beautiful black-and-white photography by Charles Lang.

Number eighty-nine on the American Film Institute's list of 100 years of film scores.

Recording

Elmer Bernstein, *The Ghost and Mrs. Muir*, Elmer Bernstein's Film Music Collection, 1975. Reissued on a Varése Sarabande CD in 1985. Excellent sound. ****

Bibliography

Geist, Kenneth L. *Pictures Will Talk: The Life and Films of Joseph L. Mankiewicz*. New York: Da Capo Press, 1978.

Steiner, Fred. Liner notes. *The Ghost and Mrs. Muir: Original Motion Picture Score*. Varése Sarabande VCD 47254, 1985, CD.

—LEM

GIANT

(1956)
Dimitri Tiomkin

The Film

Many of Edna Ferber's novels about life in particular regions of America became successful films. While *Cimarron* was set in Oklahoma, *So Big* took place in the fertile farmland of Illinois, and *Show Boat* was largely set along the Mississippi River, her 1952 novel *Giant* took readers to the sprawling plains of central Texas, a region that director George Stevens vividly depicted through many weeks of location shooting for his 1956 film adaptation.

In *Giant*'s opening scenes, Bick Benedict (Rock Hudson), owner of a huge Texas cattle ranch named Reata, travels to Maryland to buy a horse. He returns with both the horse and its rider, Leslie (Elizabeth Taylor), daughter of the horse's previous owner.

From the moment Leslie arrives in Texas, she turns the lives of Bick and his sister, who lives with him in a large Victorian mansion, upside down. The film depicts several clashes, most of which concern Leslie's negative response to her

Bick (Rock Hudson) and Leslie Benedict (Elizabeth Taylor) are "welcomed" by Luz Benedict (Mercedes McCambridge). *Warner Bros. / Photofest © Warner Bros.*

husband's condescending treatment of their Mexican servants. Leslie also rejects the idea that Texas women do not discuss politics.

By the end of *Giant*, not only has one of the Benedict children married a Mexican woman, but Bick has come to the defense of a Mexican family that is refused service at a local restaurant.

The Music

As with everything else in George Stevens's lengthy film, Dimitri Tiomkin's score is large in scale, with a full orchestra employed in many of the cues. Three themes predominate, the first of which is heard during the opening credits. This theme, which begins slowly with a melodic ascent that mirrors the start of "The Star-Spangled Banner," serves as a call to attention for the family saga that is about to begin. The tempo then increases, with the added sounds of brass instruments supplemented by the wordless singing of a choir. The high soprano notes add a thrilling sound to this music, which represents the film's main melodic idea.

Although the score does not include leitmotifs, the main title theme serves as a musical reflection on the sprawling Texas landscape. Nowhere is this more apparent than in the scene where Bick returns to Texas with his bride. After arriving by train to the area where the Benedict cattle are shipped, Bick drives Leslie the last fifty miles to his home. As the car is seen from a distance with trails of dust that crisscross the screen in cleverly edited panoramic shots, the *Giant* theme returns in a dramatic brassy orchestration enhanced by the pounding of drums.

The score's second theme is a romantic idea for strings that serves as the film's love theme for Bick and Leslie. It is introduced in the early scenes when Bick is immediately smitten by the sight of Leslie. Small portions of the theme occur as Leslie becomes infatuated with Bick and spends hours reading about Texas. When Bick is supposed to catch a train to take his newly purchased horse back to Texas, the strings produce a version of the love theme that soars as Bick and Leslie look ardently at each other. The music fills in the blanks for this scene, in which words of love are never spoken.

The third principal theme is associated with the ranch hand Jett Rink (James Dean), who is first seen from a distance as Bick arrives at Reata with his bride. A harmonica provides the melody for this theme, which begins with a number of short melodic phrases. Its most prominent appearance occurs in a wordless scene that follows the accidental death of Bick's sister, who wills to Jett a small parcel of land on Reata. As Jett walks off the margins of his parcel and then climbs a water tower to have a better look at his inherited property, the theme builds steadily in volume as Jett contemplates the possibility of drilling for oil. The strumming of a banjo often adds a folksy flavor to this theme.

There is much source music in the film, including "The Eyes of Texas Are upon You," which is heard at a banquet held in celebration of a new hotel that Jett has built using his newfound wealth as an oil prospector. "The Yellow Rose of Texas" is prominently featured toward the end of the film as Bick defends his family's honor at Sarge's Diner when the restaurant owner challenges him to a fistfight. When they plow into a jukebox, the song starts to play. It is worth noting that when *Giant* was being filmed in 1955, the Mitch Miller rendition of "Yellow Rose of Texas" was the *Billboard* chart's number-one song. Curiously, the Mitch Miller recording was not used in the film. Instead, a facsimile of the Mitch Miller recording by Warner Bros. music head Ray Heindorf was utilized for this scene.

The brassy orchestrations of Tiomkin were a mainstay in many of his film scores in the 1950s and 1960s, but nowhere are these brassy sounds more relevant to the story than in *Giant*. Tiomkin produced music that gives the film a larger-than-life quality. As such, this music is not only memorable, but it represents one of the high points of his career.

Recognition

Giant became one of 1956's top box-office hits and was awarded ten Oscar nominations, including a citation for best picture. Despite best-actor nods for Rock Hudson and James Dean, plus a scoring nomination for Tiomkin, *Giant*'s only Oscar win was for George Stevens's direction.

Over the years *Giant* has achieved distinction through the cultish lionization of Dean, who died before the film's release. It is also recognized as a breakthrough film in the feminist movement and a noteworthy example of socially conscious cinema regarding Mexican immigrants.

Recording

Dimitri Tiomkin, *Giant*, Capitol, 1955. Reissued on CD in 1989 and mp3 in 2013. Contains forty-two minutes of music. Good monaural sound. ***½

Bibliography

Palmer, Christopher. *Dimitri Tiomkin: A Portrait*. London: T. E. Books, 1984.
Moss, Marilyn Ann. *Giant: George Stevens, a Life on Film*. Madison: University of Wisconsin Press, 2004.

—LEM

GLADIATOR

(2000)
Hans Zimmer

The Film

Directed by Ridley Scott and starring Russell Crowe in his breakthrough role, *Gladiator* was a resounding critical success. The film garnered five Academy Awards and was nominated for seven more, making it the joint third-most-nominated film in history with twelve. Commercially, the worldwide returns of $457 million place it outside the top-grossing films of all time, but it was still a success in movie theaters around the globe.

Set in AD 180, the film focuses on General Maximus Decimus Meridius (Crowe) and his journey through tragedy and betrayal. After leading the Roman army to victory against Germanic tribes, the reigning emperor tells him that he is to be his successor, as Commodus, the emperor's son, is deemed unfit by his father. In a fit of rage, Commodus murders his father and declares himself emperor. After Maximus refuses to pledge his loyalty to Commodus, he escapes captivity, but on his return home finds his family murdered. Maximus is captured by slave traders and sold to a gladiator trainer. After building up his skills as a gladiator in local fights, he enters the Colosseum in a masked helmet and surprisingly wins the gladiatorial combat. Commodus, in attendance, is pleased by this and offers congratulations but is shocked to see Maximus when the helmet is removed. The narrative eventually leads to Commodus and Maximus facing each other in a duel, which ultimately kills them both. Commodus is left dying on the floor, while Maximus, already dead, is carried in a respectful procession to his final resting place.

The film was responsible for an upsurge in interest in the Roman period, and aside from the occasional anachronism or fictional character, it is regarded as a faithful adaptation of life in the historical period it depicts.

Maximus (Russell Crowe) and Juba (Djimon Hounsou) in the Colosseum. *DreamWorks SKG / Photofest © DreamWorks SKG*

The Music

The score to *Gladiator* was composed by Hans Zimmer and features the contralto Lisa Gerrard. The score has several prominent themes, including "Barbarian Horde," "The Might of Rome," and "Now We Are Free."

"Barbarian Horde" underscores the reenactment of a battle in the Colosseum, the one that Maximus surprisingly "wins," in opposition to historical accuracy. The music is a tempestuous, relentless stomp through time signatures of 3/4 and 2/4, giving the feeling of an uneven, off-kilter beat. The melody, such as it is, is occasionally accompanied by a rhythmic ostinato in the strings and brass on the same note, a rhythm mimicked by the snare drum. It is an uncomfortable, oppressive musical cue, which represents effectively the chaos in the gladiatorial arena.

"The Might of Rome" cue underscores the scene where the new (self-appointed) emperor, Commodus, returns to the city. The influence of Richard Wagner's epic Ring cycle is evident here, with the visual imagery also linked heavily to those found in propaganda films of the Third Reich. The composer himself admitted that the nod to Wagner was deliberate, claiming, "Yes, the Wagner was a very conscious choice. The scary thing for me was when after I saw the entry into Rome it seemed so apposite. I managed to assume the style of Wagner so easily that I was able to write that piece in an hour." However, the composer has been known to become frustrated by the comparisons to Wagner, complaining "Yeah, I get a lot of shit about this Wagner thing, and so what if it does? I wanted to be Little Richard Wagner. I wrote that theme in about ten minutes. I'm not saying it is any good, but it was a lot of fun." It is undoubtedly good, and it is a striking audiovisual moment in the film, which, yes, is Wagnerian in style. But it fits the majestic style of the remainder of Scott's film, so it does not in any way feel out of place.

"Now We Are Free" is perhaps the most famous of the *Gladiator* musical cues and is also the gentlest. The most prominent instance of this cue in the film is after Maximus's death. His transition into the afterlife is shown as he runs toward his wife and son, murdered earlier in the film, but seen here greeting him home. Lisa Gerrard vocalizes the melody with wordless singing during this scene. The musical cue continues to build up the levels of poignancy during this emotional climax to the film and transitions into the final credits, where we hear Gerrard performing the song version of the theme.

The score to *Gladiator* is widely regarded as one of Zimmer's finest. The scope of it, ranging from Wagnerian influences to barbaric-sounding battle music and to the emotive, tragic undertones of "Now We Are Free" result in an effective score in a well-respected historical epic.

Recognition

2000 Golden Globe for Best Original Score.
Nominated for Academy Award for Best Original Score.
Nominated for BAFTA Award for Best Score.

Recordings

Hans Zimmer, *Gladiator*, Decca, 2000 (rereleased 2003). The official soundtrack and the first choice for any listeners interested in the score. ****
Hans Zimmer, *Gladiator: More Music from the Motion Picture*, Decca, 2003. An additional release of previously unpublished music from the film. Recommended for hardcore fans only, as this is a compilation of unfinished cues, clips of dia-

logue played over musical cues, and music deemed not required in the final film. **

Bibliography

Lace, Ian. "Hans Zimmer and the Gladiator: An Interview with the Film Music Composer." *Film Music on the Web*, May 2000. http://www.musicweb-interna tional.com/film/Zimmer.html.
Synchrotones. "Interview with Hans Zimmer." *Synchrotones' Soundtrack Reviews*, May 1, 2013. https://synchrotones.wordpress.com/2013/05/01/interview -with-hans-zimmer/.

—ML

THE GODFATHER AND *THE GODFATHER PART II*
(1972, 1974)
Nino Rota and Carmine Coppola

The Films

Directed by Francis Ford Coppola and starring Marlon Brando and Al Pacino, *The Godfather* is an American crime drama that spanned the years 1945–1955. *The Godfather Part II* was released two years later and stars Al Pacino and Robert De Niro. In The *Godfather*, set in the years 1945–1955, the infamous Five Families erupt into open warfare while Michael Corleone (Al Pacino) ascends from relative obscurity to mafia boss. The film is a bloody representation of life in the mafia, with a series of murders and betrayals forming a backdrop to the stories of several individuals whose fates are decided by the feuding families.

Part II is both prequel and sequel to the original film, spanning 1901–1958. It ties up loose ends from Michael Corleone's narrative but also acts as an origin story for some key characters from the first film. Both films set the scene for *Part III*, which covers the period of the late 1970s and 1980s.

The Godfather was nominated for eleven Academy Awards, of which it won three for Best Picture, Best Actor in a Leading Role, and Best Adapted Screenplay. It also won five of seven Golden Globe nominations. Finally, it won one of five BAFTAs. *The Godfather Part II* was again nominated for eleven Academy Awards, of which it won six for Best Picture, Best Director, Best Actor in a Supporting Role, Best Adapted Screenplay, Best Art Direction, and Best Music. It received six Golden Globe nominations and won one of five BAFTA nominations. No other film series has ever won two Academy Awards for Best Picture.

The Music

The music for both films was composed principally by Nino Rota, best known for his scores of Fellini's films. The main themes from the first film have become

The Corleone clan: Sonny (James Caan, left), Don Vito (Marlon Brando), Michael (Al Pacino), and Fredo (John Cazale). *Paramount Pictures / Photofest © Paramount Pictures*

two of film music's most recognizable melodies. The first theme is described by Kristopher Spencer as "nostalgic, tragic" music. The theme opens on a solo trumpet. It is simple, unassuming, but unmistakably, to audiences today, the start of a venture into the shady underworld of the mafia. This trumpet melody is joined by dissonant piano chords and string interjections. The sweet, lilting trumpet is suddenly far more sinister. The solo violin takes over the melody after the harsh piano and strings have seemingly silenced the trumpet. Now, the theme is sad and mournful, before transitioning seamlessly into the waltz, with quirky, almost playful, off-beat accompaniments very clearly letting us know we are in 3/4 time. The clarinet takes on the melody accompanied by French horn, as the music continues to evolve, representing differing emotions and moods.

The second theme, arguably even more famous than the first, is the "Love Theme." This is an evocative, longing melody that oozes with Italian romance. It is haunting and heartbreaking, signifying a tragic romance more than a perfect Hollywood love story. One musical reason for this is that it is in a minor key, whereas many famous, traditional love themes will be in the happier major. Ironically, but certainly intentionally, the love theme is not used for either of the weddings found within the film.

The second film recapitulates the two main themes from the first film, but adds three memorable cues. The most successful of these is often referred to as the "Immigrant Theme," representing musically a young Vito Corleone." It adapts the love theme from the first film and morphs into a symphonic signifier of hope. It is likely that this theme, which was used to open the second film, as well as the reuse of the two successful themes from the first film, contributed to Rota and his associate Carmine Coppola both winning the Academy Award at their second attempt.

The films are not unusual in relying on the same musical themes, but it is unusual that the themes rarely do anything drastically different each time they are heard, yet they do not lose any impact. They are used sometimes subtly, sometimes explicitly, but they are always, generally, the same musically. The interweaving of the key themes throughout the *Godfather* series works in a Wagnerian manner and can be compared to his use of leitmotifs throughout the Ring cycle. The music unites the films in the series as one narrative through the repetition of key themes, becoming as memorable to the audience as the characters and locations.

Recognition

The Godfather:

Golden Globe for Best Original Score.
BAFTA for Film Music.
Nominated for Academy Award for Best Original Score.

The Godfather Part II:

Academy Award for Best Original Score
Nominated for Golden Globe for Best Original Score
Nominated for BAFTA for Film Music

Recordings

Nino Rota, Carmine Coppola, *The Godfather*, Geffen Records, 1991/2010. This twelve-track CD, lasting a little over half an hour, is recommended if you only require the first score. ***

Nino Rota, Carmine Coppola, *The Godfather Part II*, Geffen Records, 1974/2020. This thirty-eight-minute album contains fourteen musical cues from the second film. ****

Nino Rota, Carmine Coppola, *The Godfather Trilogy: New Recordings from the Classic Scores*, Silva Screen Records, 2005. This is a selection of seventeen cues from the three films. ***

Bibliography

Hewitt, Ivan. "Nino Rota: A Musical Offer Coppola Couldn't Refuse." *Telegraph*, November 17, 2011.

—ML

GONE WITH THE WIND

(1939)
Max Steiner

The Film

Immediately upon its arrival in bookstores, Margaret Mitchell's Civil War novel *Gone with the Wind* became a huge best seller and won the 1936 Pulitzer Prize. Producer David O. Selznick bought the film rights and spent three years creating a film version of Mitchell's massive 1,037-page book. Despite a host of production difficulties, Selznick's film premiered in Atlanta on December 15, 1939, and became one of the most acclaimed motion pictures of all time.

The film, which covers a ten-year period from the start of the Civil War to the Reconstruction era, revolves around Scarlett O'Hara (Vivien Leigh), the willful eldest daughter of a prominent Southern family that lives on Tara, a cotton plantation near Atlanta. The plot centers on Scarlett's relationships with several men, including Ashley Wilkes (Leslie Howard), the son of a nearby plantation owner, and Captain Rhett Butler (Clark Gable), a dashing visitor from Charleston, South

Rhett Butler (Clark Gable) and Scarlett O'Hara (Vivien Leigh). *MGM / Photofest © MGM*

Carolina. Although Rhett believes the South cannot win the war, he thinks he can win Scarlett, despite her infatuation with Ashley. The film also depicts her love/hate relationship with Ashley's wife, Melanie Hamilton (Olivia de Havilland).

The Music

Selznick felt that Max Steiner was the only composer who could give *Gone with the Wind* the musical score it deserved. Since Steiner was then under contract at Warner Bros., Selznick's film had to be scored while Steiner was working on other films. Problems emerged when Selznick moved up the release date so that the film would be eligible for the 1939 Oscars. As a result, Steiner sought help from Adolph Deutsch and Hugo Friedhofer in writing a few of the cues. Two cues were lifted from preexisting scores, including Steiner's 1938 score for *The Adventures of Tom Sawyer* and a short piece by Franz Waxman from the 1936 film *His Brother's Wife*.

The lavishly orchestrated score, which accompanies almost three hours of the film's 222-minute running time, utilizes the Wagnerian leitmotiv method that Steiner and Erich Wolfgang Korngold often utilized for Warner Bros. films. Steiner composed themes for the prominent characters as well as motifs for several of the supporting roles. Rhett's theme is a stately march-like tune, while Melanie is represented by a serene three-note motif, and Ashley is musically represented by a lyrical melody based on a descending-tone idea.

The only major character without an original theme is Scarlett, who is musically identified by a lively melody that begins with a motif of seven tones based on Stephen Foster's "Katie Belle," which Steiner may have used because Katie is Scarlett's first name.

Mammy (Hattie McDaniel) is identified by a piece with a jaunty ragtime flavor, while Scarlett's father, Gerald O'Hara (Thomas Mitchell), is accompanied by an Irish jig-flavored melody based on a seven-note motif in a "long-short-long-short" rhythmic pattern. The Tarleton twins, who flirt with Scarlett in the opening scene, are represented by a frolicsome idea that includes an ascending major-scale tonal pattern.

There are also love themes, a descending five-tone idea associated with Scarlett's flirtation with Ashley, and a soaring five-note motif that identifies the relationship of Ashley and Melanie.

Beyond all of these melodic ideas, the most famous theme in the score is "Tara," which represents the O'Hara plantation. The theme's basic four-note motif, with an ascending octave between the first two tones, heroically proclaims the importance of the land.

Over a dozen borrowed melodies, many of which reflect the Civil War era, are in the score, including "Bonnie Blue Flag," "When Johnny Comes Marching Home," "Cavaliers of Dixie," "Tramp, Tramp, Tramp," and especially "Dixie," which is heard several times. Other borrowings include Stephen Foster's "Louisiana Belle," "Ring de Banjo," "Beautiful Dreamer," "Camptown Races," and "My Old Kentucky Home."

A good example of Steiner's mixing of the new and the borrowed comes as the film begins. After bells intone the start of Alfred Newman's motif for the Selznick company logo, a brief quotation of Mammy's theme is heard, followed by a majestic rendition of "Tara." The title music also includes a brief bit of Rhett's theme, followed by a repeat of "Tara" and then a slow-paced wordless vocal rendition of "Dixie."

Of the many key scenes in which "Tara" is featured, two stand out. In the first, Scarlett sulks over Ashley's decision to marry Melanie and then is told by her father that land is all that matters. At this moment, "Tara" begins to crescendo and their silhouetted figures become dwarfed by a huge tree with the facade of their home in the distance.

When Scarlett, hungry and exhausted from trying to run the plantation following the war, pulls a radish from the garden and tries to eat it, "Tara" begins to soar as Scarlett, invoking God as her witness, vows that she will never be hungry again.

Steiner's score also includes lilting dance tunes and moments of highly dramatic music, especially in the wartime scene when Atlanta's munitions depot is being detonated.

A noteworthy use of borrowed music occurs in an emotional wartime scene when Scarlett is in Atlanta with Melanie, who is about to give birth. As Scarlett hurriedly walks to a makeshift hospital located at a train station to find Doctor Meade, a panoramic shot reveals a massive number of wounded soldiers lying in the train yard. This scene features a minor-key rendition of "Dixie," a slow trumpet version of "Taps," and a string arrangement of "Maryland, My Maryland" and "Old Folks at Home."

This score, with its now-famous "Tara" theme and all its other noteworthy motifs, is one of Steiner's best and deserves to be listed among the best film scores of all time.

Recognition

Ten Oscars, including awards for Best Film, Best Actress, Best Supporting Actress (McDaniel), Best Director, and Best Adapted Screenplay.

Steiner was nominated for Best Original Score (the Oscar went to Herbert Stothart for his musical contribution to *The Wizard of Oz*).

Recordings

Charles Gerhardt, National Philharmonic Orchestra, *Gone with the Wind*, RCA, 1973, 1990. Rerecording with Charles Gerhardt conducting the National Philharmonic, released again by Sony in 2010. Includes forty-three minutes of music. ***½.

Max Steiner, *Gone with the Wind: Original Motion Picture Soundtrack*, Rhino, 1996. Digitally remastered two-disc soundtrack. Includes over two hours of music. ****

Bibliography

Behlmer, Rudy. Liner notes. *Gone with the Wind,* in RCA Classic Film Scores Series. RCA 0452-2-RG, 1990, CD.

———. Liner Notes. *Gone with the Wind: Original Motion Picture Soundtrack*. Rhino Movie Music R2 77269, 1996, CD.

Brooks, Herb, and Terryl C. Boodman. *Gone With the Wind: The Definitive Illustrated History of the Book, the Movie, and the Legend*. New York: Simon & Schuster, 1989.

—LEM

THE GREAT ESCAPE

(1963)
Elmer Bernstein

The Film

Directed by John Sturges and starring Steve McQueen, James Garner, and Richard Attenborough, *The Great Escape* is based on one of the all-time great prisoner-of-war escape stories. It focuses on an Allied escape attempt from a German POW camp during World War II. The first half of the lengthy film deals with the digging of three secret tunnels, "Tom," "Dick," and "Harry." After over seventy prisoners escape, the latter half of the film shows the Gestapo tracking them down as they try to make their way to either neutral countries or England. The film was nominated for an Academy Award for Best Editing, and a Golden Globe for Best Picture.

The Music

The music to *The Great Escape* was composed by Elmer Bernstein. The score is quite extensive, in a film that runs to nearly three hours in length. However, it is the main theme, in the form of a march, that has placed the film firmly in the soundtrack canon and propelled it into the top 100 soundtracks of all time.

Jeff Bond, in the notes for a soundtrack release, states: "Bernstein's march from the film, a quirky tune taken up by flutes and woodwinds over a low rhythm of tuba and basses, is one of the most instantly recognizable in a long tradition of military marches from war films, and in fact has outlived many of its contemporaries." The score is dominated by the march, with variations and fragments of the famous theme appearing and reappearing at different moments in the film. The instrumentation, tempo, and pitch of the melody is altered to represent excitement, nervousness, and other moods endured by the characters in their brave quest for freedom. The march has a mischievous, playful undertone that well represents the love-hate relationship between the prisoners and the guards. There is a feeling of mutual respect between the Germans and the prisoners—that is, until the escape attempts begin. At this point, the music takes a darker turn, and scenes that include the mass execution of rounded-up prisoners move well away from the jovial nature of the march. There are darker and more tender moments in the score, reinforcing the fact that despite the main theme's astonishing popularity, Bernstein produced a score of great variety and emotional depth. The cue "The

Captain Virgil Hilts (Steve McQueen) attempting to cross into Switzerland. *United Artists / Photofest © United Artists*

Scrounger/Blythe" is a musical representation of the bonding between prisoners that offers a reprieve from the "overt testosterone and masculinity" of Bernstein's score. The gentle woodwinds in this scene show empathy with Blythe, who is visually impaired. He has a comfortable life in the camp, so escaping for him is full of peril. This almost cozy, gentle, homely musical interlude between the militaristic themes found elsewhere in the film seems out of place initially, but actually humanizes the prisoners and offers an alternative to escape, namely sitting the war out in peace and not risking their lives attempting to flee.

The Nazis have their own theme, which is scored for strings. Every time they are close to discovering the tunnels, or suspect the prisoners, the mysterious cue rears its head. The latter half of the film and latter third of the score combine to create high anxiety as the escape succeeds and the prisoners find themselves well and truly behind enemy lines. The infamous moment where a German says, "Good luck" in English to an escaped prisoner about to board a train, who absent-mindedly replies "Thank you!" is scored by tense, unsettling music. So while the score may be accused of being a one-trick pony by some, it truly is a varied score to a long film, although one that even in its darker moments always returns, eventually, to the march that has become a staple of the film music world—and of British television at Christmas. The score pervades popular culture too.

Such is the catchy nature of the melody and the patriotic nature of the film in which it is found that it has become a regular feature of England soccer matches, with England fans singing the main theme as part of their repertoire of chants. Later films such as *Chicken Run* (2000) also pay homage to the film and music.

Bernstein's score, while not winning any awards, is highly effective at keeping the film's narrative moving forward. Certain films that push three hours might be accused of slowing to a walking pace, but the use of the march as a leitmotif for the ongoing saga helps the audience to bond with the characters and their plight. The payoff is in the final chase scene and escape over the barbed wire at the end, when the theme returns with all its might and militaristic pomp to celebrate the end of a war film classic. Whether you hear it in the film or in a stadium, there is no "escaping" this "great" film score, in all its jaunty, ironically Germanic glory.

Recognition

Nomination for International Film Music Critics Award (IFMCA) for Best Re-Release of an Existing Score in 2004.

Recording

Elmer Bernstein, *The Great Escape*, MGM Soundtracks, 1998. This is a rerelease of the official soundtrack, spread across sixteen tracks. Recommended. ***

Bibliography

Hall, R. "Elmer's *Magnificent 7*: Essential Elmer Bernstein Scores from the 1960s." *Film Score Monthly* 9, no. 9 (2004): 26–28, 47.

MacDonald, D. "Score: Reviews of CDs: 'The Great Escape.'" *Film Score Monthly* 9, no. 9 (2004): 33.

—ML

THE GREEN MILE

(1999)
Thomas Newman

The Film

Directed by Frank Darabont and starring Tom Hanks and Michael Clarke Duncan, *The Green Mile* is often considered one of the greatest tearjerkers of recent times. Based on a Stephen King novel, the film begins with an elderly man, Paul (Tom Hanks), weeping while watching the 1935 film *Top Hat* in his care home. The film reminds him of something that happened while working as a prison officer in the 1930s. The film flashes back to 1935, where the imposing, intellectually challenged but gentle John Coffey (Michael Clarke Duncan) is under supervision from Paul. Sentenced to death for the crimes he allegedly committed, he begins to gain supernatural powers and passes these on to Paul. The two grow to be very fond of one another, and the execution upsets Paul tremendously. Before his death, Coffey reveals he has never seen a film, and so he and Paul sit and watch *Top Hat* together, linking the story to the introduction of the film. The narrative is one of friendship, hope, and redemption against one of cruelty and pain caused by the sadistic officer Percy. This is reflected in Coffey using his supernatural powers for good by resurrecting a mouse in his prison cell and using it for bad by passing on a brain tumour to Percy, which ultimately drives him mad. The end of the film reverts back to the present, where Paul reveals he is well into his 100s, a result of the supernatural powers passed to him by Coffey. *The Green Mile* was nominated for four Academy Awards and one Golden Globe.

The Music

The score to *The Green Mile* was composed by Thomas Newman and was his second collaboration with Frank Darabont after the equally successful *The Shawshank Redemption* (1994).

The main theme to the film is a haunting interplay between woodwinds and piano. A slow, drone-like string accompaniment results in a slow-moving, poignant, yet thoughtful musical introduction to the narrative. It is not a typical Hollywood orchestral main theme. There is no sweeping melody, there are no percussion crashes, and there is no overt emotion. It is withdrawn, subdued, yet extremely contemplative. It is music made for thinking, not for being overwhelmed by.

The most emotionally intense the score becomes is during Coffey's slow march to the electric chair and his execution. For a brief thirty-second spell, the

Death row guard Paul Edgecomb (Tom Hanks) and inmate John Coffey (Michael Clarke Duncan). *Warner Bros. / Photofest © Warner Bros.*

strings do swell, and the orchestra does rise in volume, but this soon withdraws into a smooth, relaxed string accompaniment, with the piano performing the solo arpeggiated melodic line. It is to Newman's credit that he decided against melodramatic excess. The nature of the film, and of Coffey being perceived as a physically imposing gentle giant, seems to call for a more introverted musical score.

There are also darker cues, such as "The Bad Death of Eduard Delacroix." Here, an electrocution sequence lasts for over four minutes, and Newman, perhaps for one of the only times in the whole score, turns to aggression and percussive, dark orchestral scoring. It is a rare moment where Newman threatens to lose control of the tenderness and restraint of the score, but it is a justified exception. Compared to Coffey's death, this disturbing execution would not have been served by a subtler musical accompaniment.

There are moments that represent the Deep South in the interwar period. Banjos and guitars occasionally make an appearance to give some chronological and geographical context, but these moments do not outshine the sensitive orchestral scoring that accompanies the most heartrending moments of the film. The placement of popular songs in the soundtrack does nothing to boost Newman's score, but they are appropriate to the time the film was set. The song "Cheek to Cheek," performed by Fred Astaire in *Top Hat*, plays a large part in the film. It is the only film Coffey has ever seen. After he tells Paul he has never seen a movie, the guards let him watch it, and Coffey becomes very emotional. This links back to Paul's reaction in 1999, as it bring back intense memories of Coffey.

Comparisons are often made to *The Shawshank Redemption*, a film that appears elsewhere in this book, but those comparisons are perhaps unfair. *The Shawshank Redemption* may be a more memorable score, but *The Green Mile* matches it for effectiveness and emotional impact. The two films, while both being set in prison, are very different in nature, and Newman's music reflects this. It is for the sensitivity and thoughtfulness of *The Green Mile* that Newman earns his second entry in this top-100 list. He resisted the temptation to exploit often-used Hollywood orchestral excessiveness in favor of an almost hypnotically ambient score. And to continue this style of composition through one of the most upsetting deaths in cinema history was a brave decision that ultimately paid off.

Recognition

Academy of Science Fiction, Fantasy & Horror Films Award for Best Original Score.
BMI Film & TV Award for Best Film Music.

Recording

Thomas Newman, *The Green Mile*, Warner Bros., 1999/2010. This thirty-seven-track soundtrack consists of all of Newman's orchestral cues, as well as the popular songs featured in the film. As the only official soundtrack release, it is well recommended. It is also conducted by the composer. ***

—ML

H

HENRY V

(1944)
William Walton

The Film

Since the 1930s many Shakespearean plays have been adapted into films, and several of these contain outstanding musical scores that are worthy of consideration in this book. One score is particularly worthy of inclusion—William Walton's atmospheric and often majestic score for Laurence Olivier's screen version of *Henry V*, the first of three film collaborations between director/star Olivier and composer Walton.

Olivier's film begins with a reenactment of a typical stage performance of the play at the Globe Theatre in London in 1600. As with the play, the film includes an opening narration by Chorus (Leslie Banks), who explains that the play is set in England during the early fifteenth century, in the early stages of the Hundred Years War against France. King Henry (Olivier) sails across the English Channel with an army of thirty thousand, places himself in the front lines of battle against the French soldiers, and after two months of fighting rallies the remnants of his army to face the French at a field called Agincourt. During his words of encouragement to his soldiers before the fateful battle he makes them aware that they are greatly outnumbered.

The Music

The cleverly conceived beginning of the film includes an energetic-sounding flute solo that accompanies a shot of a piece of paper being blown about by the wind over London. As this paper comes closer to the camera the printed title of the film is revealed, with a rousing orchestral fanfare.

As the camera then slowly pans the landscape of London, the music includes a dramatic slow-paced idea for strings and wordless choir based on a pattern of low-pitched tones that form a basso ostinato on which several musical variants

Princess Katherine (Renee Asherson) and King Henry V of England (Laurence Olivier). *United Artists / Photofest © United Artists*

are then superimposed. This music establishes the Elizabethan era of this theatrical pageant and captures the viewer's emotions right away, preparing the audience for the play that is about to begin.

As the Globe Theatre comes into view, the music gradually diminishes in volume and ends completely as actors and members of the audience take their places so that the play can begin.

Olivier's adaptation of Shakespeare's play preserves much of the original text, with Chorus providing introductions to various scenes along with Walton's music, which includes both trumpet fanfares and short interludes played by the Globe's band.

There is not much underscoring in the first hour of the film, but one early scene stands out. As Sir John Falstaff lies on his deathbed in a room above the Boar's Head Inn, the strings begin a mournful piece in the form of a passacaglia, with a continuously repeated melodic idea in a minor key that begins in the low strings, gradually ascends in pitch, and then is sounded by violins. Moments later, after Falstaff's death is learned, the music features a very melancholy string theme based on a sweetly soothing six-note motif.

After Henry and his army cross the English Channel to fight the enemy on French soil there is an extended scene without music that takes place before dawn on the day of battle. Then, rousing music begins as Henry's knights get suited up in armor. The strings strongly sound a motif based on the tones of a major triad accompanied by accented brass chords. This music clearly anticipates the drama of the upcoming and crucial battle of Agincourt.

After Henry's speech to his troops, Walton's music creates an emotion-charged atmosphere as the French cavalry soldiers advance on the vastly outnumbered English soldiers. As the horses gain speed, a fanfare-like melody begins with the repeated use of a rising fifth. Together with fast-sounding string tones and persistent drumming, this music adds excitement to the clash that is about to begin.

There is extensive music during the battle that culminates with a duel on horseback between King Henry and the Constable of France. After Henry slays his opponent, Walton's music includes a slow-paced reference to the rousing theme heard in the film's opening aerial shot. After the French surrender, an a cappella choral piece based on the words "Non nobis, Domine" is heard as soldiers march away from the field.

Music of a much lighter tone occurs in the latter scenes when a peace treaty is signed and Henry begins to court Katherine, the French king's daughter. A sweet theme for strings and harp accompanies the courting scenes, and joyous music for strings and wordless choir enhances the scene of Henry and Katherine's wedding.

This film, with a fine cast of character actors recruited from Olivier's Old Vic theater company, which had performed the play on stage, is in every aspect a worthy translation of Shakespeare into film, with a vibrant and melodious score by William Walton.

Walton, who teamed with Olivier again for the Oscar-winning film *Hamlet* (1948) and also for the vivid Technicolor production of *Richard III* (1956), created a multifaceted score for *Henry V* that remains one of his most justly celebrated compositions.

For a different interpretation of the post-battle scene, seek out Kenneth Branagh's 1989 film of *Henry V*, with composer Patrick Doyle's extended musical piece based on the "Non nobis" text. Whereas the Walton music lasts only a few seconds, the Doyle version extends over five minutes and allows the music to more fully express the emotional aspects of both the English victory and the tragic loss of life resulting from the battle.

Recognition

Four Oscar nominations, including Best Picture and Best Original Score.
Honorary Oscar awarded to Olivier for his achievement in producing, directing, and starring in *Henry V*.

Recordings

Patrick Doyle, *Henry V*, EMI, 1989, CD. Original soundtrack, performed by Simon Rattle and the City of Birmingham Symphony. Excellent sound. ****
Sir Neville Marriner, Orchestra and Chorus of the Academy of St. Martin in the Fields, Christopher Plummer, narrator, *William Walton's Film Music, Vol. 3: Henry V*, Chandos, 1992. Hour-long recording on CD. Excellent sound. ****

Bibliography

Thomas, Tony. *The Great Adventure Films.* Secaucus NJ: Citadel Press, 1976.

—LEM

HIGH NOON

(1952)
Dimitri Tiomkin

The Film

Gary Cooper, with his iconic strong and soft-spoken screen persona, starred in several westerns, the best of which is undoubtedly *High Noon*.

Writer Carl Foreman based his screenplay on the short story "The Tin Star," which had appeared in *Collier's* magazine. In Foreman's script, which is set on a Sunday in the small Texas town of Hadleyville during the 1880s, Will Kane (Gary Cooper), the local marshal, is about to get married at 10:30 a.m. and quit his job. But a few minutes after his wedding to Amy Fowler (Grace Kelly), Will learns that an old adversary, Frank Miller (Ian MacDonald), is out of prison and aboard the noon train.

Three of Miller's old gang members have arrived at the train station, and there is little doubt that they will help carry out the death threat that Miller had made against the marshal on the day of his sentencing. Although Will is advised to immediately get out of town with his new wife, he feels compelled to stay and form a posse because he has never run from danger in the past.

High Noon, which runs eighty-five-minutes, is set basically in real time, with shots of clocks appearing in almost every scene to inform Will Kane that his time is running out.

The Music

Tiomkin's music is prominently based on a song, with lyrics by Ned Washington that help tell the film's plot. This song provides the first sounds in the film, with soft muffled drumbeats and strummed guitar chords, followed by the voice of Tex Ritter with an accordion doubling his voice. Parts of this song are heard periodically throughout the film, with Tiomkin's orchestral score being melodically based on the song's two separate melodic motifs (which can be identified as *a* and *b*).

The *a* motif, which is first sung to the words "Do not forsake me, oh my darling, on this our wedding day," is based on a smoothly flowing nine-note idea. The song's middle section, which is based on the *b* motif and sung to the words beginning with "Oh, to be torn 'twixt love and duty," has a different melodic and rhythmic design. This idea is based on a single tone that is repeated seven times in a lively rhythmic patter. The *b* motif also includes one higher tone and then a

Marshal Will Kane (Gary Cooper) and his young bride Amy (Grace Kelly). *United Artists / Photofest © United Artists*

return to the first pitch. In creating this section Tiomkin used the *b* motif six times. The song then concludes with a repeat of the *a* idea.

Following the opening credits, as the Miller gang rides through town toward the train station, the song's *b* motif is heard as the first melodic idea to appear in Tiomkin's underscore.

Although both motifs often appear in abbreviated form, an extended orchestral statement of *a* is heard following the wedding as Will and Amy attempt to leave Hadleyville. The music ends when he stops the carriage and explains that he must go back and face the Miller gang.

Some cues feature a muted use of Ritter's voice in bits of the song that seem to remind Will of the grim task he is facing. Other cues in Tiomkin's music suggest the ominous approach of noon through the persistent use of clock-like "ding-ding" tones on harp and pizzicato strings. Several shots of clocks are musically accompanied by these sounds

Tiomkins's score also features a rhythmic melodic idea that has a Spanish flavor. It is associated with Helen Ramirez (Katy Jurado), the saloon owner and Kane's former mistress, who appears in some scenes with Harvey (Lloyd Bridges), Will's deputy and her new boyfriend.

A clever use of source music occurs in a saloon scene when the song's *a* motif becomes part of the unseen piano player's repertoire (this is clearly an anachronistic use of the tune, since it wouldn't have existed in the 1880s). Following this bit of Tiomkin's theme there is a unique moment when the piano player returns to a jaunty rendition of "Buffalo Gals" that has been heard earlier. This cue begins as source music, but when Harvey looks out the window at Will, who is walking by in the street, the tune begins serving as underscoring since it is unlikely that Will can hear the piano played that loudly from such a distance.

One of the score's most bombastic cues comes as noon arrives. Here the *b* motif is heard in a dramatic cue with brass and pounding drums accompanying an angular shot of a grandfather clock with its pendulum swinging ominously toward the viewer. The music builds in intensity until it suddenly stops when the train whistle sounds.

After the climactic gun battle, in which both song motifs are dramatically combined, the voice of Tex Ritter returns in the last portion of the song that brings *High Noon* to an ending that is as quiet as the film's opening. The muffled drumbeats heard as the film starts provide a bookend device when they serve as the fade-out sounds of the film's ending.

Tiomkin's music was not only a catalyst in the film's critical and box-office success, but it remains to this day a compelling example of dramatic storytelling. The music of *High Noon* had a huge impact on later films, and it remains a classic example of film scoring in westerns.

Recognition

Four Oscars, including one for Gary Cooper for Best Actor and one for Elmo Williams and Harry Gerstad for Editing.
Tiomkin won the awards for Best Song and Best Original Score.

Recordings

Laurie Johnson, London Studio Symphony Orchestra, *The Western Film World of Dmitri Tiomkin*, Unicorn/Kanchana, 1993, CD. Includes thirteen minutes of Tiomkin's score. Very good sound. ****
Sir David Willcocks, Royal College of Music Orchestra, *The Film Music of Dimitri Tiomkin*, Unicorn/Kanchana, 1993, CD. Includes music from *High Noon* in work entitled "A President's Country." Decent sound. ***½

Bibliography

Palmer, Christopher. *Dimitri Tiomkin: A Portrait.* London: T. E. Books, 1984.
Spoto, Donald. *Stanley Kramer: Film Maker.* G. P. Putnam, 1977.

—LEM

HOW THE WEST WAS WON
(1962)
Alfred Newman

The Film

Directed by John Ford, Henry Hathaway, and George Marshall, this epic film, the last of the Metro-Goldwyn-Mayer era, costarred Carroll Baker, Lee J. Cobb, Henry Fonda, Carolyn Jones, Karl Malden, Gregory Peck, George Peppard, Robert Preston, Debbie Reynolds, James Stewart, Eli Wallach, John Wayne, and Richard Widmark.

Unusually, this film is split across five time periods. These are entitled "The Rivers (1839)," "The Plains (1851)," "The Civil War (1861–65)," "The Railroad (1868)," and "The Outlaws (1889)." A final, short epilogue shows the (then) present of the 1960s, with aerial photography above Los Angeles showing how America developed into a modern, bustling world power. The film is a story of America and about America. The narrator opens with the patriotic declaration that "this land has a name today and is marked on maps."

Primarily following the Prescott family, the film spans a wide geographical area from the Erie Canal to the west of the country. The epic narrative is one of survival, love, and hope, with encounters with river pirates and fur trappers interspersing more poignant and tender scenes of love, marriage, and death. The film is unusual not only for the five time periods but also the sheer number of characters introduced. There are almost thirty significant characters across each of the "chapters," as well as a narrator who ties the narratives together. While appearing ostensibly complex, the common thread of following one family's fortunes across several decades resulted in a film epic in scope but with a peculiarly homely feel. The film was nominated for eight Academy Awards, winning three for Best Original Screenplay, Best Film Sound, and Best Editing. In 1997, it was selected for preservation in the National Film Registry of the Library of Congress.

The Music

The score to *How the West Was Won* was composed by Alfred Newman and takes twenty-fifth position on the American Film Institute's top twenty-five film scores of all time list. Newman won nine Academy Awards for music during his career, but was only nominated for Original Score for *How the West Was Won*. The score is said to bear many musical influences from Elmer Bernstein, including wide

Zeb Rawlings (George Peppard) leads the expansion west. *MGM / Photofest © MGM*

intervals and an intense energy, but Newman deserves the credit for producing a memorable musical accompaniment to a film truly epic in scale at almost three hours in duration.

The score blends original music by Newman with preexisting songs. The opening overture parades these themes in the guise of a choral medley. One of these adapted songs, "Promised Land," opens the overture in a rousing, adventurous manner, introduced by a brief brass fanfare and sung by hundreds of voices. This song returns later in the film as a recurring motif. The four-minute overture then segues into the main theme proper, which is performed as a heroic, gun-slinging, pioneering French horn romp. It is inspiring and makes the heart pound with excitement. It transports the audience back to the early 1800s with its sound so typical of the western film genre, one that has been mimicked in countless films and theme parks. In some ways, it is a shame that Newman uses this theme so sparingly, but he composed many other cues in this saturated score. Gregory Peck's character is accompanied by the upper woodwind section, along with bells and a celesta; Zeb is portrayed by strings and French horns, which speaks to his ambitions in life; and the river pirates have sinister music in the lower woodwinds to represent their dastardly deeds. There is also a memorable musical cue for the Indians' attack on the wagon train, with deep contrabass sounds offering a sense of dread and danger to the otherwise generally uplifting score.

A chorus is used at other moments in the score, and not just in the grandiose overture. As Zeb joins the army, a male choir sings "When Johnny Comes Marching Home." This is an excellent example of music acting in an incongruous manner. Zeb is excited, and practically skips down the road, but the music is a dirge and lets the audience understand the true peril in which he places himself. The visuals and the music counteract each other.

Perhaps the most famous song to find a place in the film is "Greensleeves," supposedly composed by Henry VIII. Performed by Debbie Reynolds, this is one of three songs she sings playing Lilith.

Newman's score is reminiscent of Aaron Copland's American style of composition, with the folk songs providing the other half of the musical accompaniment to the film. While these two almost separate scores do not always flow completely smoothly, the combined effect in this epic western generally works well. The fact that the film is split into different eras gives it the feel of an opera, with the music acting as arias would to contextualize the time period and location, as well as the plight of the main characters. The word *epic* is arguably overused today, but the length and scope of the film and score can be described as nothing else.

Recognition

Nominated for the Academy Award for Best Music Score.

Recording

Alfred Newman, *How The West Was Won*, Rhino, 1997. This two-disc, fifty-eight-track remastering of the original 1963 recording is certainly comprehensive in its coverage of Newman's score. The entire score is here in a presentation that has drawn almost universal critical acclaim from reviewers. It is recommended without hesitation. ****

Bibliography

Meyer, D. C. "Music Cue Archetypes in the Film Scores of Elmer Bernstein." *Journal of Film Music* 5, nos. 1–2 (2012): 153–63.

—ML

I

The Film

Directed by Christopher Nolan and starring Matthew McConaughey and Anne Hathaway, *Interstellar* took science-fiction films to a new dimension, both in filmic and narrational terms.

It is a difficult task indeed to summarize the plot of *Interstellar* in the space available in this chapter, as Christopher Nolan takes us on a complex, time-travelling, logic-defying trip through our universe and beyond. In the American Midwest, Cooper (McConaughey) is an ex-science engineer and pilot who lives with his daughter, Murph (Mackenzie Foy as the ten-year-old character). Sandstorms ravage crops around the world, and food begins to run out on a global scale. Cooper, by chance but also for his skill as a pilot, is asked to go with other scientists on a NASA mission into a wormhole to find a new home while Earth slowly dies. Cooper must decide to either stay behind on Earth or risk never seeing his children again. The choice is family or the saving of the human race by finding a habitable planet elsewhere in the universe.

The film was nominated for five Academy Awards, winning one for Best Visual Effects. It also won one of four BAFTA nominations and was nominated for a Golden Globe.

The Music

In an extraordinary interaction between director and composer, Christopher Nolan said to Hans Zimmer, "I am going to give you an envelope with a letter in it. One page. It's going to tell you the fable at the center of the story. You work for one day, then play me what you have written."

The eventual result is arguably one of the finest scores of Zimmer's film music portfolio. The two decided that they wanted a unique sound for *Interstellar*. The composer stated that his usual compositional style would have to be left behind, or at the very least adapted: "The textures, the music, and the sounds, and the

Cooper (Matthew McConaughey) leads a group of astronauts on a mission to save mankind. *Paramount Pictures / Photofest © Paramount Pictures*

thing we sort of created has sort of seeped into other people's movies a bit, so it's time to reinvent. The endless string (ostinatos) need to go by the wayside, the big drums are probably in the bin." After Zimmer had been sent away by Nolan with the envelope and letter, they reconvened. Zimmer recalls the meeting: "I played him the piece, without actually looking at him. As a composer you are very fragile when you play your music for the first time. So I finished, turned around and said, 'What you do think?' He paused and said, 'Well, I suppose I'd better go and make the movie now.' And I said, 'Great, but what is the movie?'" This exchange confused Zimmer, but not Nolan. The director talked of a "vast canvas" for his film, yet Zimmer had composed an intimate piece for a parent-child story (which, incidentally, was kept in its original form for the final credits). The director told Zimmer not to be concerned, as the music provided the heart of the movie, and Nolan's job was to expand that into the epic, almost three-hour space- and time-travel adventure that it became.

The two decided that the film was about celebrating science, and because of this, Zimmer was inspired to use a quite unusual instrument in his score; unusual in the sense that they are not often utilized in film scores, and when they are, it is for often clichéd gothic horror. The church organ plays a prominent part in the score to *Interstellar*, and this was a conscious choice. Zimmer explains how by the seventeenth century, it was the most complex machine invented, and he describes the gargantuan pipes as appearing like the afterburners on space ships. Zimmer visited London where he decided to use the Temple Church's 1926 organ. Roger Sayer, the director of music at the time, began to play, and Zimmer and Nolan knew that it would work in the film. Added to the organ was an ensemble of thirty-four strings, twenty-four woodwinds, and four pianos, plus a sixty-voice choir, creating a musical sound of huge proportions, although curiously without brass. As well as Zimmer's trademark ostinato and almost hypnotic, minimalist sounds, he also decided to include some more avant-garde moments. He asked the woodwind players to make unusual noises on their instruments. The conductor of the score amusingly said to Zimmer: "You know, they've worked their whole lives never to sound like this." The choral elements of the score were also experimental in nature, with breathing used as an instrument to represent wind on alien worlds. Finally, regarding experimentation, the director chose, unusually, to sometimes have the music and sound effects drown out or distort dialogue. He was adamant that the sounds in space should be realistic, and so the on-screen sound is often given a realistic, background role against off-screen music. It is an interesting and daring move, but one that adds an extra layer to the film. Movie theaters had to place notices up warning audiences that this was intentional to dissuade complaints about sound levels being incorrect.

It is estimated that Zimmer wrote two hours of music, ranging from avant-garde experimentation to minimalism and to Romantic excess. It is a score of colossal scope, but one that Zimmer says is ultimately very personal: "This score is incredibly personal to me. How much more personal can you get when somebody says to you, 'Write about your children's future'?"

Recognition

Nominated for Academy Award for Best Original Score.
Nominated for a Golden Globe for Best Original Score.
Nominated for BAFTA for Best Original Score.
Nominated for Grammy for Best Soundtrack.

Recording

Hans Zimmer, *Interstellar*, WaterTower Music, 2014. This sixteen-track album runs to seventy-one minutes and contains most of the music from the film. Some reviewers complained about cues from the film not being included on this album, but it is still recommended as an introduction to Zimmer's unusual and enthralling score. ***

Bibliography

Burlingame, Jon. "Hans Zimmer's *Interstellar* Adventure: Composer Unveils Secrets of Organ, Choir, Orchestra in Nolan Film." *Film Music Society*, November 6, 2014. Accessed November 26, 2017. http://www.filmmusicsociety.org /news_events/features/2014/110614.html.
Chitwood, Adam. "Hans Zimmer Talks Christopher Nolan's *Interstellar* and the Influence of the Dark Knight Trilogy Score on Blockbuster Filmmaking." *Collider*, October 14, 2013. http://collider.com/interstellar-score-hans-zimmer -dark-knight-trilogy/.
Khatchatourian, Maane. "Christopher Nolan Kept *Interstellar* Plot Secret from Composer Hans Zimmer." *Variety*, April 5, 2014.

—ML

J

JAWS

(1975)
John Williams

The Film

Peter Benchley's best-selling novel *Jaws* thrilled readers with the chilling possibility that a giant shark could be lurking in the relatively cool waters of the North Atlantic. The book and subsequent film directed by Steven Spielberg clearly drew inspiration from such horror films of the 1950s as *The Creature from the Black Lagoon*, in which a dangerous underwater creature poses a threat to anyone who dares to swim in potentially dangerous waters.

Jaws begins on Amity Island, a fictional resort off the New England coast, where the pleasures of summer are disrupted by the violent deaths of a female college student and an adolescent boy. After a thorough investigation, Sheriff Martin Brody (Roy Scheider); Matt Hooper, a marine biologist (Richard Dreyfuss); and Quint (Robert Shaw), an eccentric fisherman, conclude that the killer is an enormous great white shark. Using Quint's boat, the three set out to kill the shark but soon find themselves in mortal danger.

The Music

For many filmgoers the score of *Jaws* is instantly recognizable because of a two-note motif that composer John Williams wasted little time in introducing. During the opening credits, first there are several soft sonar sounds; then string instruments introduce the motif as follows: first a single low E is sounded, then two notes are heard that utilize a rising semitone (E to F). While this shark motif continues, with an occasional addition of a lower-pitched couplet (D to E), a French horn introduces a superimposed second motif of three ascending tones. The horn idea continues as the shark motif increases in volume with the addition of high-pitched strings and shrill high woodwinds. The credit music ends just as the opening scene of an evening beach party begins.

Roy Scheider as Police Chief Brody: "We're going to need a bigger boat." *Universal Pictures /*
Photofest © Universal Pictures

There is much more to Williams's music, but the two-note motif dominates
much of the film's score as a musical reminder that the shark is nearby. This suggestiveness is essential, since there is a minimum of actual shark footage. The
horn motif, which conveys the heroism of the three hunters, also has considerable impact, especially in the scene where Hooper goes underwater to inspect the
wreckage of a local fisherman's boat.

Memorable music occurs in a scene where two fishermen attempt to capture
the shark. When part of the dock they are standing on breaks away and one of
the fishermen falls into the water, the music is very dramatic but gets softer as the
dock floats into the distance. When the dunked fisherman starts swimming frantically back to the shore and the dock begins to turn around, the music becomes
more intense. Williams's music cleverly teases viewers with the varying dynamics
and tempo of the shark motif. As part of the tease there is no actual shark footage,
but the music makes its presence keenly felt.

There are many non-thematic short cues, including one where strings and harp
add an eerie sound when part of the college student's body is discovered in the
sand.

Several times Williams's cues feature techniques from the Baroque era. When
a tourist boat arrives on Amity Island on the Fourth of July, the music features
a bass pattern that is repeatedly sounded with superimposed melodic variations

for trumpet and string tones that are added in the style of a chaconne. A Baroque technique heard several times is the fugue, with overlapping musical lines played by strings that are based on a single melodic idea.

The absence of music in certain scenes is significant. Especially noteworthy is the moment when vacationers on a beach panic at the sight of a fin, which turns out to be an adolescent prank. At this point there is no music, but when a real fin appears, the two-note motif dramatically announces that a shark is on the attack.

As the film progresses the shark starts making sudden appearances without the motif being present. This absence of music makes the shark footage even more frightening because the viewer no longer has the motif as a warning.

In the last part of the film several musical motifs are often featured. The three-note horn idea returns in a dramatic cue for strings, brass, harp, and drums when the three hunters get their first good look at the shark. Also heard is a heroic idea for brass and strings as the three bravely attempt to complete their mission.

Nerve-wracking music occurs when Hooper goes underwater in a metal cage to inject lethal chemicals into the shark. The scene begins with an agitated low-pitched string idea, followed by overlapping lines sounded in fugal style by violins and flutes. Also included is a new ten-note thematic idea sounded by woodwinds. The shark motif is heard repeatedly along with very agitated string sounds as the shark begins to smash the cage.

Music in a lighter vein is heard occasionally; there is sea chantey music in the film, including the borrowed song "Spanish Ladies," which Quint sings more than once. This tune is heard instrumentally in the scene where Quint's boat leaves the harbor.

Williams's score is a classic example of thriller/suspense music. It helped make *Jaws* a huge success. In fact, the film's initial release earned more at the box office than any film prior to 1975. Thus it richly deserves to be acknowledged in this book.

Recognition

Four Oscar nominations, including Best Picture.
Three Oscar wins for Sound, Editing, and Original Score.

Recordings

John Williams, *Jaws*, MCA, 1975. Reissued in 1992 on CD. Only thirty-four minutes of music. Good sound. ***½
John Williams, *Jaws: The Anniversary Collector's Edition*, Decca, 2000. Includes the entire score. Excellent sound. ****

Bibliography

Brosnan, John. *Future Tense: The Cinema of Science Fiction*. New York: St. Martin's Press, 1978.
Hickman, Roger. *Reel Music: Exploring 100 Years of Film Music*. New York: W. W. Norton, 2006.

Spielberg, Steven, John Williams, and Laurent Bouzereau. Liner notes. *Jaws: The Anniversary Collector's Edition*. Decca 289 467 045 2, 2000, CD.

—LEM

JURASSIC PARK
(1993)
John Williams

The Film

Directed by Steven Spielberg and starring Sam Neill, Jeff Goldblum, and Richard Attenborough, *Jurassic Park* brought dinosaurs to the big screen as never before. Based on a novel by Michael Crichton, the film had a budget of $63 million and eclipsed this by taking in over $1 billion at the box office. Adjusted for inflation, it is in the top twenty-five films of all time by box-office returns, both domestically and globally. One of its later sequels, *Jurassic World* (2015), performed even better; it sits in fourth place in both rankings.

Tim (Joseph Mazzello), Ellie (Laura Dern), Grant (Sam Neill), and Lex (Ariana Richards) face a fearsome T-Rex. *Universal Pictures / Photofest © Universal Pictures*

Jurassic Park features John Hammond (Attenborough) as an entrepreneur who has re-created dinosaurs from ancient DNA found in mosquitos. He opens a theme park called Jurassic Park on an island off the coast of Costa Rica. Two paleontologists come to visit the island, Dr. Alan Grant (Neill) and Dr. Ellie Sattler (Laura Dern), and Hammond's grandchildren also arrive for a tour of the park. When a tropical storm blows in, the visitors become stranded, the electric fences in the park are deactivated, and the film becomes a survival story. The survivors leave the island at the end, with Jurassic Park seemingly deemed a failure. The film's sequels explore new scenarios of re-created dinosaur environments.

The Music

Jurassic Park was one of the many collaborations of Stephen Spielberg and John Williams. Williams's score was composed in February 1993 and conducted by Williams a month later. Williams was said to be inspired by dinosaur noises at Skywalker Ranch while composing, and he described it as a "rugged, noisy effort—a massive job of symphonic cartooning," while he tried to "match the rhythmic gyrations of the dinosaurs" with a "funny kind of ballet." Williams tried to achieve a sense of fascination through his music and tried to emulate the feelings of overwhelming happiness and excitement that the general public would feel from seeing real live dinosaurs. Technically speaking, *Jurassic Park* is a horror movie. It features close calls with death and attacks by gigantic, carnivorous dinosaurs, and it is largely set in dark, rainy, horrifying conditions. However, we are not presented with a rehash of *Jaws*, but an astoundingly uplifting score.

The orchestration uses a typically large orchestra and includes parts written for choir. The shakuhachi, a Japanese end-blown flute, is also used to add an exotic nuance to certain cues. The celeste, later used very prominently in the *Harry Potter* scores, was also used by Williams, but synthesized rather than acoustically performed.

The main theme from Jurassic Park is split into two key musical motifs. Perhaps the more prominent of the two coincides with the first big reveal of the dinosaurs. The wonderment on the faces of the two paleontologists is matched by the triumphant, awe-inspiring music that accompanies the scene. This theme is heard at various points during the film, ranging from majestic cues depicting the beauty of the island, to more gentle instances orchestrated for just a few woodwind instruments, French horns, or piano.

The second musical motif underscores the journey to the island by helicopter and is a brass-dominated fanfare. Williams described the theme as "adventurous, high-spirited and brassy, thrilling and upbeat musically." Again, as with the first musical cue, the second motif is used in various points in the film, with the instrumentation and tempo dependent on the mood of the scene. These two motifs provide the majority of the score, but a third, more aggressive, motif was composed to depict the threat of the dinosaurs to the park's visitors. Inspired, perhaps, by some of Williams's previous scores, particularly *Jaws*, it utilizes "wild orchestral and choral things; the idea was to shake the floor and scare everybody." Interestingly, Williams describes his score as operatic (a comparison often made with the *Star Wars* score in mind) and explains that it allowed him to explore the more "swashbuckling" aspects of the orchestral sound world.

Despite the majority of the score being either overtly heroic or exultant, the final rendition of the main theme is more somber and altogether elegant. As the survivors leave the island by helicopter, we see a reverse of their arrival. Instead of arriving in a fit of fanfares and high spirits, a poignant rendition of the theme is heard on solo piano. It is a theme of defeat, an elegy for lost lives and of a missed opportunity. This adaptation of main themes for different instruments is a staple of Williams's compositional process and is repeated in several of his other films to great effect.

Jurassic Park, fairly or not, will perhaps never breach the top five of Williams's film scores, but it is still more than worthy of finding itself in this book. The adventurous spirit and excitement it conjures of real, living dinosaurs enchanted many cinemagoers, and it continues to do so on the small screen.

Recognition

Nominated for a Grammy as Best Instrumental Composition Written for a Motion Picture or for Television.

Despite the score to *Jurassic Park* not winning any awards, it should be noted that it was released in the same year as another Williams and Spielberg collaboration, *Schindler's List*, which appears elsewhere in this book and was more successful in terms of awards. Williams also lost to himself in the Grammy Awards.

Recording

John Williams, *Jurassic Park*, MCA, 1993, rereleased in 2000 on CD. The official soundtrack album, conducted and produced by John Williams. ****

Bibliography

Dyer, Richard. "The Williams Whirlwind." *Boston Globe*, May 9, 1993, B1.
Shay, Don, and Jody Duncan. *The Making of Jurassic Park: An Adventure 65 Million Years in the Making*. New York: Ballantine, 1993.
Thomas, David. "John Williams Interview." *Total Film* 8: 74–79.
"A Whole New Level." (Special feature on *Jurassic Park* Trilogy, Blu-ray edition). Universal Studios, 2015.

—ML

K

KING KONG

(1933)

Max Steiner

The Film

The premise of the original *King Kong*, with a giant ape that runs amok in Manhattan, has been imitated several times, especially in the 1950s when the horror film genre benefited greatly from the on-screen destruction unleashed by gigantic dinosaurs, mammoth lizards, huge ants, and various other super-sized creatures.

The 1933 film, based on an original script by Merian C. Cooper and Edgar Wallace, features a movie producer named Carl Denham (Robert Amstrong), who recruits a cast and crew to sail with him to a remote island to shoot a film. Upon reaching the island, they discover a tribe that worships a giant gorilla named Kong. After much turmoil, the beast is subdued and hauled back to New York, where an attempt to feature him as "King Kong, the Eighth Wonder of the World" in a lavish stage show turns to disaster when Kong escapes.

Kong, who has developed an affection for Ann Darrow (Fay Wray), an out-of-work actress that Denham recruited for his film project, captures her and climbs to the top of the Empire State Building. Kong is attacked by pilots, who shoot at him from their airplanes. After Kong falls to his death, Dunham states, "It was Beauty killed the Beast."

The Music

A primary influence in the scoring of *King Kong* was the intervention of the film's codirector, Merian C. Cooper. At a time when scoring at RKO (and at other studios as well) was limited to mostly short bookend pieces played during the opening and closing credits, Cooper authorized Steiner to write a score for *Kong* that would be heard throughout the film.

Steiner's score, which employed an orchestra of forty-six players, is based on three primary leitmotifs. The first motif, which consists of three chromatically descending tones, identifies Kong, while a very similar descending pattern of

137

Atop the Empire State Building, King Kong is attacked by machine gun-bearing planes. *RKO Radio Pictures Inc. / Photofest © RKO Radio Pictures Inc.*

three tones, in a waltz rhythm, represents Ann. The third idea is a rapid-paced four-note idea that underscores several action scenes in the film.

Following the dramatic opening-credit music, based largely on the Kong motif, there is no scoring until, at about twenty-five minutes into the film, the ship nears Skull Island in the fog. Here Steiner employed repeated soft drum sounds, to which harp tones and sustained strings are added, to create an aura of mystery, with unresolved harmonies that evoke the style of the French Impressionistic composers Debussy and Ravel. Ominous brass chords and high-pitched woodwind tones are gradually added to convey a sense of danger in this scene.

Rhythmically driven vocal tones are introduced as some of the ship's passengers, including Denham, Ann, and first mate Jack Driscoll (Bruce Cabot), prepare to go ashore. When they land on the beach the drumming and vocal sounds get louder; accented string and brass harmonies with shrill woodwind tones are added as part of a tribal dance in which the word "Kong" is chanted repeatedly by natives, many of whom are dressed as gorillas.

When the tribal chief sees the ship's passengers, the music suddenly stops. As the chief approaches the intruders by walking down a set of stone-like steps, repeated brass chords begin, with the addition of descending tuba tones in sync with each of the chief's steps. The descending tones continue until the chief stops, at which point the music also stops. When he moves again the tuba tones resume. This is a classic example of a technique that Steiner pioneered called "Mickey Mousing," in which the music mimics the action onscreen.

In a later scene, Mickey Mousing occurs again when Ann, who has now been abducted by the tribe, is forcibly escorted through a huge doorway in the village's wall to the outside of the compound and forced to walk up a series of steps to a raised platform equipped with restraints. As Ann and several tribesmen climb the steps the music includes ascending chordal patterns that are again synchronized with their upward moves.

With its almost wall-to-wall music, *King Kong* represents a pioneering use of music that foreshadows the elaborately scored films that Steiner and Korngold composed at Warner Bros. in the 1930s and 1940s, a period known as the "Golden Age of Hollywood." In a career that spanned over three decades, Steiner's score remains one of his most memorable achievements.

Recognition

King Kong received no Oscar nominations, but Steiner's score would undoubtedly have been nominated if there had been a music award. The music categories were not introduced until 1934, a year after the film's release.

The film is number forty-three on the American Film Institute's list of the 100 greatest American movies.

Recordings

National Philharmonic conducted by Fred Steiner (no relation to the composer), *King Kong*, Entr'acte, 1976, LP. Rerecording of Steiner's score, released on CD in 1984 on Southern Cross. Male chorus used for the original film's tribal dance music not included in this recording. ***

Max Steiner, *King Kong*, Rhino Movie Music, 1999. The original soundtrack, digitally remastered, it includes over twenty-two minutes of isolated music tracks, plus over fifty minutes of the film's actual soundtrack, with music, voices, and sound effects. A real treasure for film-music collectors. ****

William J. Stromberg, Moscow Symphony, *King Kong: The Complete 1933 Film Score*, Marco Polo, 1996. John Morgan is credited with score restoration. As with the Fred Steiner recording, no voices are heard in the tribal dance music. ***½

Bibliography

Steiner, Fred. Liner notes. *King Kong*. Fifth Continent Music Corp., 1984.
Goldner, Orville, and George E. Turner. *The Making of King Kong*. Cranbury, NJ: A. S. Barnes, 1975.

—LEM

KING OF KINGS
(1961)
Miklós Rózsa

The Film

The popularity of MGM's spectacular *Ben-Hur* in 1959 led to a pair of films about the life of Jesus of Nazareth. Both *King of Kings* (1961) and *The Greatest Story Ever Told* (1965) were met with scorn by some Bible scholars who had problems with the scripts of these films, despite the sincerity of their intentions. Of the two, producer Samuel Bronston's *King of Kings* fared well with both critics and audiences as a vivid attempt by screenwriter Philip Yordan to depict the life of Jesus during a politically turbulent time in Palestine, which was then under Roman rule.

The film shows Jesus (Jeffrey Hunter) as preacher, healer, and leader of a small group of followers, along with scenes of battles between Jewish rebels led by Barabbas (Harry Guardino) and Roman soldiers led by a centurion named Lucius (Ron Randell). Although Lucius is a fictional character, his presence in the film serves as witness to the events in Jesus's life, from his birth in Bethlehem to his execution in Jerusalem.

A reverent depiction of Jesus (Jeffrey Hunter) and Mary (Siobhan McKenna). *MGM / Photofest © MGM*

The Music

Miklós Rózsa seemed a natural choice as the composer of *King of Kings*, since he had scored *Ben-Hur* less than two years earlier. One major difference between the two scores is that *King of Kings* is more Jewish than Roman in its conception. Although there are some brass fanfares for the Roman army in *King of Kings*, the bulk of the music is lighter in its orchestration than its predecessor and generally more subdued in style.

The main-title music begins with a solemn theme that is intoned by strings along with a fifty-voice choir. This theme, which represents Jesus, has a two-part melodic construction. The first segment consists of six tones that remain within a confined pitch range while the second part is a set of seven tones that begins with an upward fifth followed by descending tones. During the main title, the second segment is heard repeatedly with each repetition starting on successively lower pitches. Melodic and rhythmic variants of these two segments appear throughout the film.

One of the most creative uses of the main theme occurs when Jesus begins his ministry by going into the desert, where he is tempted by the Devil three times. Several variants of the Jesus theme appear, including thematic fragments played by an oboe. Wavy high-pitched flute tones add an eerie resonance to the scoring, which also includes a temptation theme, played by a solo violin, that uses the twelve-tone technique. The modernistic harmony used in this scene brings to mind the music that Rózsa had previously conceived for such film noir classics as *The Killers*.

A second theme is a lyrical idea based on an eight-note motif that is associated with Jesus's family. It is introduced by oboe, harp, and sustained string chords when Lucius travels through Nazareth and discovers that Mary and Joseph have a twelve-year-old son that was somehow not registered when he was born in Bethlehem. This melody returns several times, including a later scene in which Mary Magdalene comes to thank Jesus for convincing a crowd not to stone her.

A third theme, associated with John the Baptist (Robert Ryan), is based on an eight-note motif that begins with a single pitch sounded four times. When John is baptizing in the Sea of Galilee this theme is prominently featured, along with a moment of the Jesus theme. When Lucius comes to John's cell after the latter is arrested for insulting Herod and his family, the low strings repeatedly sound this motif's last four tones.

An ingenious combining of all three themes occurs in a touching scene following Jesus's baptism when John comes to Jesus's home to speak with him. The cue begins with the family theme played eloquently by a solo cello with soft string harmonies. A moment of the Jesus theme arrives when the conversation centers on Mary's son, and then low strings feature the eight-tone motif of John's theme.

One of the film's dramatic highlights occurs when Jesus preaches to a large crowd from a high hill (this is known as the "Sermon on the Mount"). During this scene there is initially little underscoring, but at the words "Ask and ye shall receive, seek and ye shall find" the Jesus theme begins softly and gradually increases in volume when sounded by French horns, strings, and wordless voices in an emotionally moving statement. Toward the end of this scene a soaring new theme is introduced (which is also featured in the film's closing Resurrection sequence). It accompanies the words of "Our Father," which Jesus teaches in response to a question about how to pray. The new theme gets more intense when the chorus joins the instrumentation.

There are other musical motifs in the score that appear only once. One is a lilting lullaby for oboe and strings that occurs when the three wise men come to honor the newborn child. Another theme is heard in the exotic dance that Herod's stepdaughter Salome performs for him with the guarantee that she can have anything in return. For the Middle-Eastern-flavored dance music the English horn and bassoon play the melody, accompanied by other woodwinds and drums.

While this score is less grandiose than the majestic music of *Ben-Hur*, it is tastefully composed and repeatedly illustrates Rózsa's masterful handling of thematic ingredients. As such, the score of *King of Kings* should be acknowledged as one of Rózsa's greatest.

Recognition

King of Kings was ignored in the 1961 Oscar race, but it received favorable reviews by many critics and was one of that year's biggest box-office successes. Over the years, through repeated Christmas and Easter showings on the Turner Classic Movies channel, *King of Kings* has become recognized as a classic example of the so-called "biblical epic."

Recordings

Miklós Rózsa, *King of Kings*, Rhino Movie Music, 2002. An expanded original soundtrack, it includes the complete score, with over one hundred forty minutes of music. Excellent sound. ****
Miklós Rózsa, *King of Kings*, Sony Special Products, 1992. Transferred from 35 mm music tracks. Over seventy-five minutes of music. Good sound. ***½

Bibliography

Feltenstein, George, and Miklós Rózsa. Liner notes. *Miklós Rózsa, King of Kings Original MGM Motion Picture Soundtrack Recording.* Rhino R2 78348.
Rózsa, Miklós. *Double Life.* New York: Wynwood Press, 1989.

—LEM

KINGS ROW

(1942)

Erich Wolfgang Korngold

The Film

After several years of scoring adventure films starring Errol Flynn, Erich Wolfgang Korngold shifted direction at Warner Bros. by composing music for films with a more contemporary setting. For the film version of Henry Bellamann's novel *Kings Row*, Korngold created one of his most memorable title themes.

Bellamann's novel, which is set in the fictional midwestern town of Kings Row, spans a period from the late 1880s into the early 1900s. Despite the sign at the edge of town that describes Kings Row as "A Good Clean Town," there is a lot about the town that isn't very wholesome. Parris Mitchell (played as an adult by Robert Cummings) is raised by his grandmother (Maria Ouspenskaya), who lovingly ensures his educational progress as a medical student as well as his advancement as a pianist. Parris has long had a liking for Cassie Tower (Betty Field), the daughter of Dr. Tower (Claude Rains), whose mentally troubled wife is a virtual prisoner in the family home. While being tutored by Dr. Tower, Parris falls in love

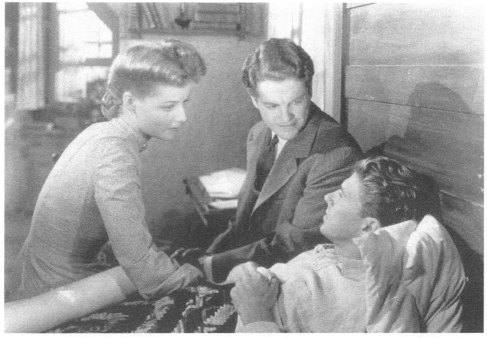

Randy Monaghan (Ann Sheridan) and Parris Mitchell (Robert Cummings) console an ailing Drake McHugh (Ronald Reagan). *Warner Bros. / Photofest © Warner Bros.*

with Cassie, but their relationship is thwarted by her instability, which leads to tragedy. The other doctor in town, Dr. Gordon (Charles Coburn), is a cruel man who performs surgeries without anesthetics. Parris's best friend, Drake (Ronald Reagan), who has a reputation as a ladies' man, becomes an unwitting victim of Gordon's cruelty.

The Music

Korngold used the leitmotivic method on several films, including *Kings Row*. Every major character in this film is represented by a signifying motif. Parris is identified with the main theme that appears in the opening titles. The Kings Row theme is filled with a sense of grandeur, with several upward leaps in its melodic line that bear an uncanny resemblance to the bold leaps in two John Williams themes that emulate Hollywood's Golden Age—the main themes of the *Star Wars* saga and the *Superman* films starring Christopher Reeve.

Although this theme is the most prominent melody in Korngold's score, there are several other motifs. Among the most prominent in the early part of the film is the sweetly lyrical theme for Parris's grandmother that has an almost chamber-music quality, with solos for both cello and violin. This theme occurs up to the point of her death, which occurs as Parris is preparing to leave for Vienna to study psychiatry.

One of the most intriguing motifs is associated with Dr. Towers's daughter, Cassie. In her moments of fearful stress, the music includes sets of descending tones with string tremolos and unusual harmonies that underscore her fragile mental state. But when she and Parris have an intimate encounter on a stormy night, the music becomes romantically charged, with dramatic thunder and lightning that heighten the passion between the two lovers.

Another noticeable motif is a fast-paced seven-tone idea for Drake. Although he is linked with several young ladies in the film, his motif is more playful than romantic. As with Cassie's motif, this idea includes a prevailingly downhill pitch pattern.

Midway through the film a new motif arrives. It is a romantic theme for strings that is associated with Randy Monaghan (Ann Sheridan), a lady from across the tracks who befriends Drake in the wake of his failed attempt to court Dr. Gordon's daughter Louise. This theme becomes very prominent in the second half of the film, in which Drake and Randy fall in love. Randy's theme is played by strings and is based on a succession of four ascending tones.

After Drake's fortune is wiped out by a bank president's theft, he takes a job working for the railroad, but an accident occurs that results in the amputation of his legs. When Randy says she will marry Drake despite his condition, a solo cello begins her theme, followed by a solo violin in an eloquent statement with soothing string sounds as accompaniment.

When Parris returns from Vienna he meets a young woman named Elise (Kaaren Verne), whose father has bought the home where Parris grew up. When Parris looks around the property the Kings Row theme returns in an eloquent slow-tempo statement played by strings.

The next scene includes a clever use of source music. After Elise plays part of Beethoven's *Pathetique* Sonata, Parris sits at the piano to give Elise some ideas about interpreting the music. After a few seconds of piano playing, the strings pick up where the piano leaves off without a break. A motif from the Beethoven sonata is then heard as part of Elise's theme.

The final appearance of the Kings Row theme is worthy of mention. After Parris tells Drake the truth about his surgery, he finds Elise and they embrace. At this point the theme swells to a high-volume level, with a chorus singing words from William Henley's poem "Invictus."

This is a very intricately designed score, with motifs that guide the viewer through almost every scene. It may lack the heroic themes that are so prominent in such Korngold scores as *The Adventures of Robin Hood* and *The Sea Hawk*, but it is still one of Korngold's best achievements as a film composer.

Recognition

Three Oscar nominations, including a nod as best picture.

Korngold was not nominated for his score, perhaps due to then-existing rules that limited Oscar consideration to a single film from each studio. That year's Warner Bros. candidate was Max Steiner's memorable music for *Now, Voyager*, which won the scoring Oscar.

Recording

Charles Gerhardt and the National Philharmonic, *Kings Row*, Varese Sarabande, 1979. Studio recording released on CD in 1985. Includes most of the film's major motifs, with good stereo sound.****

Bibliography

Korngold, George, and Tom Britton. Liner notes. *Kings Row Original Motion Picture Score.* Varèse Sarabande Records VCD 47203, 1979, CD.

—LEM

L

THE LAST OF THE MOHICANS

(1992)
Trevor Jones and Randy Edelman

The Film

Directed by Michael Mann and starring Daniel Day-Lewis, Madeleine Stowe, and Jodhi May, *The Last of the Mohicans* is an American historical drama set during the French and Indian War.

Hawkeye (Daniel Day-Lewis), an adopted son of a native, joins forces with newly arrived Britons in their fight against the French. Cora Munro (Madeleine Stowe) is part of his group, as is Alice (Jodhi May), her younger sister. After rescuing them from an ambush, Hawkeye takes them to a British fort that is under attack from the French. After a French victory and British surrender, a truce is made whereby the British agree to return home and never return, but these terms are betrayed by a war-mongering native ally of the French. The wondrous landscapes of America are shown in full splendor as the film's narrative progresses, positing the bloody battles against stunning cinematic backdrops.

The film won one Academy Award for Best Sound, was nominated for one Golden Globe, and won two of seven BAFTA nominations.

The Music

The musical score to *The Last of the Mohicans* was composed by Trevor Jones and Randy Edelman. The musical cues are split between the two composers in an unusual example of sharing a film score. The composition process for this film was not a harmonious one. Trevor Jones, in an interview with Soundtrack.net, explains: "I tend to score a particular film in the way I feel suits it best. But the fact is that if I feel I'm being asked to do something injurious to a picture, I have to say that and stick to my guns. I was asked to score parts of the picture that were under dialogue, and I didn't think required scoring. The option at the end of the day was that it was the director's prerogative to get someone else to score those

146

Hawkeye (Daniel Day-Lewis, center), Uncas (Eric Schweig), and Chingachgook (Russell Means, right) confront the British. *Morgan Creek Productions / Photofest © Morgan Creek Productions*

bits, and for me to produce a score that I felt worked for the picture. To that end, that's what happened." Jones spoke to Edelman for around ten minutes during the whole process, and while no ill feelings exist, it was far from an ideal situation. This makes it even more remarkable that, together, they composed what is now considered a classic score.

The score is well known for its intense Celtic melodies, mixed with Native American influences. This represents well the film's temporal context of the late 1700s, when European and Native cultures were beginning to clash and mix.

Opening the film is a heavily beaten drum with a dissonant string drone. The low brass perform a slowed-down version of the main theme under the title sequence. This builds up in volume and tension until the title of the film appears on the screen. At this moment, the drums stop, and the soaring, passionate main theme is heard for the first time in all its glory.

The drums reenter, the main theme dies away, and we see Hawkeye chasing a deer. The fatal gunshot that kills it also kills the music. The music gives us clues as to Hawkeye's allegiances. As Jessica Green explains, "through the unity of the strong brass title theme, the audience realizes that Hawkeye is one with Chingachgook and Uncas despite his white heritage. The music [also] draws the audience into the foreign world of pre–Revolutionary War America."

Perhaps the most powerful scene in the film is the seven-minute finale. As Magua is deciding the fate of the two sisters, Cora and Alice, the ominous drums from the start of the film are heard fading into the background. The fiddle then joins this, playing the 12/8 eight-bar phrase that is heard throughout the film, in an intensely Gaelic or Celtic style. It is hypnotic in its repetitiveness, yet strangely emotive. The fiddle motif is pulsating, fast-paced, and riddled with a sense of fate or forthcoming doom. The quick editing of the visuals here matches the fast-paced tempo. The film not only reaches its culmination narratively, but also in terms of tempo. It is hectic, frenzied, chaotic, and utterly climactic. The fiddle is joined by groups of instruments incrementally, until finally the entire orchestra brings the film ever closer to its close.

The scene reaches an emotional climax as Alice edges away from the Hurons toward a cliff edge. She has to choose between torture and a quicker death. The music is less complex here, as it is obvious that Alice has no choice. The melody is removed, and we are left only with the strings alternating between two pitches, with a thumping drum accompanying her tragic fall from the cliff. The fiddle returns as Magua turns away, not fazed by the suicide, and the film reaches its climax with Magua finally being defeated as the main melody returns.

The combined efforts of Jones and Edelman, albeit working separately, resulted in a score that admittedly may not have a great deal of variety or diversity but makes up for it in the emotional impact of the main themes. This is nowhere more powerful than in the first and final scenes of the film, where it is used as first a signifier of excitement and context and finally as a poignant underscore to tragedy, death, and hopelessness. The score deserves its place in this book, and the main theme, often heard outside the film world since 1992, deserves its place in the higher reaches of all-time memorable soundtrack melodies.

Recognition

Nominated for a Golden Globe for Best Original Score.
Nominated for a BAFTA for Best Original Score.

Recording

Trevor Jones, Randy Edelman, *The Last of the Mohicans*, Shout! Factory Records, 1992/2014. This fifty-four-minute album spread over sixteen tracks is the official release and is well recommended. ****

Bibliography

Goldwasser, Dan. "Interview: Scoring Saucy Jack" (interview with Trevor Jones). *Soundtrack.net*, October 23, 2001. https://www.soundtrack.net/content/article/?id=87.
Green, Jessica. "Understanding the Score: Film Music Communicating to and Influencing the Audience." *Journal of Aesthetic Education* 44, no. 4 (2010): 81–94.

—ML

LAURA

(1944)
David Raksin

The Film

Directed by Otto Preminger, *Laura* stars Gene Tierney, Dana Andrews, and Clifton Webb in a wartime film noir classic. The film is set in New York City and focuses on the story of Mark McPherson (Dana Andrews), an NYPD detective who is investigating the murder of Laura Hunt (Gene Tierney), a successful advertising executive. After interviewing a selection of characters, ranging from Laura's fiancé to her housekeeper, McPherson becomes too attached to the supposedly murdered woman. After falling asleep at Laura's apartment after a day investigating the case, Laura herself wakes him as she returns home. McPherson arrests Laura for the murder of a model who was wearing Laura's dress when the attack happened, but her innocence is proven when it is revealed that a newspaper columnist, infatuated with Laura, was the real killer. The columnist is shot by an NYPD officer and utters the final words "Goodbye, Laura. Goodbye, my love." The film utilizes the classic conventions of noir throughout, from the contrasts of light and dark to the use of a femme fatale to ensnare the male protagonists.

The film has been placed in the National Film Registry by the Library of Congress due to its cultural, historical, and aesthetic significance. It was nominated for several awards, but won just one: the Academy Award for Best Black and White Cinematography.

The Music

The music to *Laura* was composed by David Raksin and was his breakthrough score. The composer wrote over four hundred film and television themes in the Golden Age of cinema, and he is often referred to as the "grandfather of film music." However, he was not the first choice for this film. The director offered Alfred Newman and Bernard Herrmann the commission, but both composers refused. The former was not a fan of the director and, in any case, had too many existing commissions, while the latter was simply unimpressed with the script and refused on those grounds. *Laura* is Raksin's most well-known film score by a considerable margin, although it was only because of a change of opinion by the director, on Raksin's recommendation, that the theme music to *Laura* was written at all. Originally, Preminger wanted to use Duke Ellington's "Sophisticated Lady" or George Gershwin's "Summertime" for the main theme, but Alfred Newman, music director for 20th Century Fox, persuaded the director to allow Raksin a weekend to compose an original theme. Raksin was adamant that it should be an original composition, as he argued that the two songs were unsuitable because of "the accretion of ideas and associations that a song already so well-known would

Clifton Webb and Dana Andrews standing in front of the portrait of Laura (Gene Tierney). *20th Century Fox Film Corporation / Photofest © 20th Century Fox Film Corporation*

evoke in the audience." Preminger agreed to this, and the main theme was composed and subsequently used at frequent intervals in the film. However, the use of the song in the film is only part of the story, as a year later, lyrics were added to the melody to create a jazz standard that would go on to be recorded over four hundred times. It is one of the most recorded pieces of music in history. Raksin was suffering with writer's block during the weekend when he was to compose the theme and came across a letter from a girlfriend. He had not been able to fathom what it was saying previously but now realized it was a breakup letter. Placing it on the piano, he used the contents of the letter to improvise a melody on the piano, and thus the theme to *Laura* was composed.

The melody is a haunting, romantic theme with an air of mystery, appropriate to the film noir genre. The music somehow encapsulates the *femme fatale* nature of Laura's character along with undertones of more innocent love and romance. The music is mysterious without being sinister and seductive without being sleazy. Its chromatic melodic movement and jazzy harmony place it very firmly in a 1940s film noir context, but its durability resulted in its ongoing success and popularity. Interestingly, there is very little other music in the film except the theme and variants thereof. The characters mention a concert of Jean Sibelius music at one moment in the film, but none of his music is heard. Alfred Newman loved the theme so much that he kept encouraging the composer to return to it. Raksin replied that he didn't want to overdo it, but as he later wrote, "monothematic . . . there would be no other reiterated themes, merely needed fragments." The theme never truly resolves and is at all times mysterious. It is "a wandering ghost, musically diaphanous, shimmering, ever-changing" as the liner notes to a rereleased recording explain.

Raksin's amorous melody shines through each time it is heard, and it dominates a film that is short in duration but full of the elements that make it a 1940s film noir classic that has endured for decades.

Recognition

Surprisingly, there were over twenty nominations at various awards ceremonies for film scores in 1944, but *Laura* did not receive a single one of them.

Recordings

David Raksin, *David Raksin Conducts His Great Film Scores: Laura, Forever Amber, The Bad and the Beautiful*, RCA Red Seal, 2011. A compilation of some of Raksin's most popular film scores. A recommended purchase. ****

David Raksin, *Laura*, Kritzerland, 2013. The original 1944 soundtrack with Alfred Newman conducting. At the time of writing, this CD is out of print. The lack of variety in the film score results in a short soundtrack of thirty-eight minutes. ***

Bibliography

Hirsch, Foster. *Otto Preminger: The Man Who Would Be King*. New York: Alfred A. Knopf, 2007.

Kirgo, Julie. Liner notes. *Laura*. Available at http://www.kritzerland.com/KL_Laura_Notes.pdf.

—ML

LAWRENCE OF ARABIA
(1962)
Maurice Jarre

The Film

Directed by David Lean and starring Peter O'Toole, *Lawrence of Arabia* is considered one of cinema's most influential films.

T. E. Lawrence dies in a motorcycle crash at the age of forty-six. As he is dying, he begins to reminisce about his time serving in Cairo as an intelligence officer in 1916 during the Arab revolt against the Turks. He plays a crucial part in leading the Arabs against the Turks, and the film concludes with Lawrence helping to bring down the mighty Ottoman Empire. The film was exceptional for the size of the cast, running to over a thousand with extras included. The cinematography and narrative combined to create a true classic on an epic scale.

Lawrence of Arabia was nominated for ten Academy Awards, winning seven for Best Picture, Best Director, Best Cinematographer, Best Art Direction, Best Sound, Best Film Editing, and Best Music Score. It also received nine Golden Globe nominations, of which it won six, and five BAFTA nominations, of which it won four. It is the joint fifth-most-successful film in history in terms of Academy Award wins. Adjusted for inflation, it is comfortably in the top 100 grossing films of all time domestically, with returns of over $500 million in today's money.

The Music

The score to *Lawrence of Arabia* was composed by Maurice Jarre, a French composer who is rightly considered "one of the giants of twentieth-century film music" and was known for writing in a variety of styles, from sweeping orchestral themes to

Peter O'Toole as T. E. Lawrence. *Columbia Pictures / Photofest © Columbia Pictures*

electronic music. *Lawrence of Arabia* was Jarre's breakthrough score and earned him his first of three Academy Awards. He initially did not have any involvement with the film, but William Walton and Malcolm Arnold, the two first-choice composers, were unavailable. Jarre recalls that the director was very clear where he wanted music, which was crucial, as he was given just six weeks to complete the score. The composer stated that Lean "had clear ideas on how and where he wanted to use music. In the original script, there were very precise indications for where the music would begin and end. He wanted the music to come in, without it being heard to come in." Jarre combined military music to represent the British, with unusual instruments to represent the nomadic tribes in the film. Instruments such as the cithara and ondes Martenot were used to evoke an exotic atmosphere.

The opening theme begins with tempestuous drums, playing a tribal, irregular rhythm. This is then joined by a brass fanfare, harsh in sound. Almost instantly, we are introduced to the sweeping string melody, perhaps the most well-known theme in the film. Interestingly, the tribal drums continue to sound during this beautiful theme, contrasting not only two musical styles but also two cultures with it. The romantic theme dies down and is replaced by a march, which is one moment Arabian in style and the next moment Turkish. This represents well the two opposing sides represented during the film. The Turkish section is a variation on Kenneth Alford's march "The Voice of the Guns" (1917), which is prominently featured on the soundtrack. The director had used one of Alford's other marches, "The Colonel Bogey March," in his *Bridge on the River Kwai*, which appears elsewhere in this book.

The soundtrack matches the epic scope of the film. Jarre used a 104-piece orchestra including sixty string players, eleven percussionists, and two pianos. He also used three of the aforementioned ondes Martenot, an instrument that produces eerie electronic sounds and was used initially by French composer Olivier Messiaen. The score has been described as epic, symphonic, exotic, but also curiously "sun-scorched." This latter description is apt. There is simply something about Jarre's juxtaposition of Western European symphonic sounds and Arabian musical expression that depicts perfectly the vast, arid deserts of the film. There is little doubt that this score deserves its place in the top 100 film scores, and it might well be found in the top ten were they to be ranked in such a way. Indeed, the American Film Institute ranks *Lawrence of Arabia* third in its top twenty-five list of film scores.

Recognition

Academy Award for Best Music Score.
Nominated for Golden Globe for Best Original Score.
Nominated for a Grammy for Best Original Score.

Recordings

Maurice Jarre, *Lawrence of Arabia*, Tadlow, 2010. This two-CD edition by Nic Raine and the City of Prague Philharmonic Orchestra runs to over one hundred forty minutes across twenty-six tracks. *Lawrence of Arabia* occupies the first disc and the second contains other Jarre music. For the extra music and the other works of the composer, this is well recommended. ****

Maurice Jarre, London Symphony Orchestra, *Lawrence of Arabia*, Foyer, 2011. This is the original recording of the score rereleased, thirty-three minutes over fourteen tracks. Recommended for its authenticity. ***

Bibliography

Goodfellow, Melanie. "Jarre Mixed Ancient, Ethnic and Electronic Music: European Achievement in World Cinema." *Variety*, November 27, 2005.

McLellan, Dennis. "Maurice Jarre Dies at 84; Composer for *Lawrence of Arabia*." *Los Angeles Times*, March 31, 2009.

—ML

THE LION IN WINTER

(1968)
John Barry

The Film

By the time Peter O'Toole played King Henry II in *The Lion in Winter* he had already played this twelfth-century English monarch in the 1964 film *Becket* (discussed earlier in this book). This time out, O'Toole was made to look fifty years of age, to resemble an aging king who worries about who his successor is going to be.

The 1968 film, adapted by James Goldman from his 1966 stage play, is a fictional gathering of the English royal family in December of 1183. It is set at the English court in Chinon, in the West of France, to which King Henry has invited his three sons and his estranged wife, Eleanor of Aquitaine (Katharine Hepburn), to join him for a Christmas reunion along with King Philip of France and Henry's mistress, Alais, Philip's sister. These historical characters are all portrayed as having hidden agendas dealing with the succession to the English throne. Henry wants to place John, the youngest son, on the throne, while Eleanor favors their eldest, Richard. Meanwhile, Geoffrey, the middle son, yearns to be a power player in this politically contrived situation.

The Music

Despite its medieval setting, *The Lion in Winter* is quite modern in terms of its dialogue, which includes such witty moments as the queen's summing up of an argument with the words "What family doesn't have its ups and downs." Inspired by the anachronisms in Goldman's screenplay, John Barry created a score that includes both old and modern musical elements.

Eleanor of Aquitaine (Katharine Hepburn) and her husband, Henry II (Peter O'Toole). *MGM-United Artists / Photofest © MGM-United Artists*

A good example of this duality comes immediately in the film's opening credits, which begin musically with a loud pair of statements by trumpets and strings of a dramatic eight-note idea. The French horns and strings then repeat this idea twice. This repetitive music leads directly into a dynamic thematic statement by trumpets based on the opening idea, with rhythmic accents played by brass and strings along with repeated tones on timpani that provide a rock-music type of background. Then a melody sung by a choir is sounded above the timpani. The translation of the Latin text deals with a day of wrath and judgment, as though the music were intended for a medieval funeral mass. There is no funeral in the film, however; instead, there are numerous heated verbal exchanges concerning the royal succession.

The second major theme in the score occurs when Queen Eleanor's boat sails toward the shore where King Henry awaits her arrival. As the boat floats along, female voices introduce a chant-like melody that celebrates Eleanor as queen. Male voices join in singing this theme while strings accompany this sweet-sounding music in an emotionally lyrical and smoothly flowing way.

It is worthy of note that the selection of the Latin texts for both of these themes is the work of Denis Stevens, who at the time was the artistic director of the Accademia Monteverdiana, the choir that recorded the choral music heard in the film.

After Eleanor's arrival and the gathering of their sons and the French king, there is not much music in the first hour of the film. One exception is a short fanfare for trumpets in two-part harmony that is sounded when Henry walks with Eleanor into a dining hall for a Christmas feast.

Another exception comes at around thirty minutes in with a short piece for trombones and trumpets, which are joined with strings and soft female voices, as Richard approaches his mother's private chamber. Such music provides pleasant interludes between the moments of heated anger spouted by all of the royal family, especially the cunning queen and the conniving Geoffrey, the latter speaking with venom in almost every syllable.

The score's main theme returns a few times. A memorable occurrence comes in the latter part of the film, starting around 1:47:00, when Henry's three sons are roused from their sleep during the night by castle guards who lock them up in a dungeon. At this point dynamic brass chords, strings, and rumbling timpani accompany the action as Henry determines to leave Chinon on the spur of the moment. The melodic part of this music includes trumpets playing a variant of the score's main eight-note motif. Throughout this scene wordless voices add a repeated series of descending chords while the timpani melodically add a second variant of the film's main motif.

Other noteworthy music in the film includes "Allons gai gai gai," with French words sung by Alais to Henry in an early scene. This lilting tune comes during an interlude that precedes Henry's explanation of why he wants John on the throne. Later in the film Alais sings an unaccompanied piece called "The Christmas Wine," with words by James Goldman.

Since nothing is resolved regarding the royal succession, the film may seem rather pointless. However, John Barry's inspired music makes the film entertaining in a darkly comedic way and is a testament to his artistic ingenuity. While the film contains only a meager amount of music, what Barry composed is first rate. The dramatic main-title theme, with its insistent rhythmic drive and strongly sung Latin text, bears more than a little resemblance to the opening chorus of Carl Orff's cantata *Carmina Burana*, but Barry's melodic idea has a quality that is truly original in design. When this theme returns one last time in the final scene, the film comes to a majestic close that confirms the fact that, even without any real plot resolution, Barry's music makes the film an emotionally satisfying experience.

In summing up Barry's achievement, it is safe to say that his music is crucial to the success of *Lion in Winter*. This score represents one of his most memorable film-music creations.

Recognition

Seven Oscar nominations and winner of three, including an award for Barry's score.

Voted by New York film critics as best film of 1968.

Recording

John Barry, *The Lion in Winter*, Columbia Legacy, 1995. Original soundtrack recording, issued on CD. Excellent sound.****

Bibliography

Deutsch, Didier. Liner notes. *The Lion in Winter*. Columbia Legacy CK 66133, 1995, CD.

—LEM

THE LORD OF THE RINGS: THE FELLOWSHIP OF THE RING

(2001)
Howard Shore

The Film

In December of 2014, Peter Jackson completed a monumental task that seemed unthinkable as recently as the 1990s. Jackson and his production team had brought J. R. R. Tolkien's fantasy epics, *The Lord of the Rings* and *The Hobbit*, to life on screen over a thirteen-year period.

The films have all been commercially successful, grossing billions of dollars worldwide, with the full complement of six films finding themselves within the top-forty rankings of all time in terms of box-office earnings. Through the success of the two trilogies, Jackson established himself as a leading director, and the profiles of actors such as Elijah Wood, Sean Astin, and Andy Serkis have been raised significantly.

However, the production of the six films and the trials of translating such revered literature into the medium of the big screen brought significant protest from within the Tolkien family, as well as pressure from millions of expectant fans. Jackson needed to assemble a prestigious production team in order to do Tolkien's respected works cinematic justice. One of the greatest decisions he had to make was choosing someone who would succeed in conjuring Tolkien's world musically.

The Fellowship of the Ring received thirteen nominations for Academy Awards and won four of those: Best Score, Best Makeup, Best Visual Effects, and Best Cinematography. In total, the film received 152 nominations for awards worldwide and won 98. While not the most successful of the trilogy in terms of awards, *The Fellowship of the Ring* was still universally acclaimed. The trilogy became the most awarded film series of all time, receiving an astonishing 475 awards from 800 nominations.

Elijah Wood as Frodo Baggins. *New Line Cinema / Photofest © New Line Cinema*

The first film, highlighted in this chapter, was *The Fellowship of the Ring*, released in December 2001. It had a budget of $93 million and grossed $871 million worldwide.

The Music

Jackson chose the Canadian composer Howard Shore to underscore his six films, and Shore's music has been received with critical acclaim for both trilogies.

One of the challenges composers face when writing music for a fantasy film is to ensure the audience recalls the locations and characters across the films. The music must act as an audial anchor point to grasp the attention of the audience. Even if some audience members may not remember all the exotic names of the locations and characters, the music can at least provoke a recognition of location.

The first significant location the audience sees is the Shire, home of Bilbo and Frodo Baggins and the rest of the Hobbits of Middle-earth. The music used to represent the Shire is perhaps the most well-known from the six films. The tin whistle is used to evoke a certain Celtic atmosphere, and it is not unreasonable to make the strong link between the Shire and the United Kingdom, particularly the countryside in the midlands and southern England where Tolkien grew up. What is unique about this motif is that while starting out as a piece of music to represent a location, it transforms throughout the films into something with a far deeper meaning. The melody remains the same, but a grander, hymn-like setting emerges that begins to denote homesickness but also the resilience of the Hobbits on the road. One example of this is when Frodo Baggins and his acquaintance Samwise Gamgee have left the borders of the Shire. The same melody is heard, but it is now in strings and French horn as well as the original tin whistle. It accompanies a tender moment of reminiscing but also represents the growth in character of the two hobbits as they explore a new world.

More broadly, the landscapes of Middle-earth are represented musically in a way that immerses the audience in the expansive world Tolkien (and Jackson) created. The elves in their valley home of Rivendell presented Shore with a challenge. He must have wondered how he would attempt an underscoring of a location that is described in the book as being inconceivably beautiful, exotic, and otherworldly.

Shore creates this exoticism using harmonies that have a somewhat Eastern feel, with ethereal female voices accompanying swelling string arpeggios and chimes. Doug Adams describes the Rivendell motif as containing a "wonderful tone of opulence," and says it is "welcoming, open and gives a sense of age." The narrative, in which Elrond and Bilbo both say the name "Rivendell" as the music is heard, assists Shore by introducing a new location to the audience in the most literal fashion possible. When you isolate the clips, it might seem heavy-handed to see a character actually vocalize the name of the location followed by its musical leitmotif, but in the midst of a three-hour film, it is very useful and acts as an explicit signposting for viewers.

Howard Shore elevated himself to the highest echelons of the film composer world with his remarkable scores for all six of the Tolkien adaptations. The pressure to score such a diverse but also publicly adored fictional world might have caused some composers to crumble, but Shore approached it with enthusiasm and sincerity, immersing himself in Jackson's re-creation of Middle-earth. The music is undoubtedly a key aspect of the films and their success, and it has entered the film music canon alongside the many great scores that preceded it.

Recognition

Academy Award for Best Original Score.
Grammy for Best Soundtrack.
Nominated for Golden Globe for Best Original Score.
Nominated for BAFTA for Best Original Score.

Recordings

Howard Shore, *The Lord of the Rings: The Fellowship of the Ring—The Complete Recordings*, Reprise Records, 2001. Studio recording, rereleased in 2013. Official Soundtrack with high-quality performances and sound. ****
The London Studio Orchestra, *The Lord of the Rings: The Fellowship of the Ring*, NPL, 2010. For those on a budget, but not recommended due to electronically produced sounds. **

Bibliography

Adams, Doug. *The Music of the* Lord of the Rings *Films: A Comprehensive Account of Howard Shore's Scores*. Los Angeles: Alfred, 2011.

—ML

LOST HORIZON

(1937)
Dimitri Tiomkin

The Film

Frank Capra is probably best-known for social-commentary films set in contemporary America. But unlike *Mr. Smith Goes to Washington* and *Meet John Doe*, Capra's version of James Hilton's novel *Lost Horizon* takes viewers to a faraway place called Shangri-La. Nestled in a valley surrounded by the Himalayas, Shangri-La's mild climate helps to provide a peaceful existence for its inhabitants. It also allows them to age very slowly.

Hilton's story centers on Robert Conway (Ronald Colman), a British diplomat and humanitarian, who is first seen helping the evacuation of foreigners during a revolution in China. When Conway boards a plane with four other passengers, he does not realize that they are being hijacked. When the plane crashes on a mountainside, all but the pilot survive unharmed. They are soon aided by a rescue team led by the mysterious Chang. After a perilous mountain journey they arrive

After crash-landing in the Himalayas, Robert Conway (Ronald Colman, center), George Conway (John Howard), Alexander Lovett (Edward Everett Horton), and Henry Barnard (Thomas Mitchell) are welcomed by Chang (H. B. Warner) and his people. *Columbia Pictures / Photofest* © *Columbia Pictures*

in Shangri-La, where they are treated like royal guests. Eventually Conway, who becomes infatuated with this place, learns that his coming to Shangri-La was no accident.

The Music

Since *Lost Horizon* has an exotic Eastern setting, Capra felt that its composer should be someone other than such western Europeans as Max Steiner, Erich Wolfgang Korngold, and Franz Waxman. Thus Dimitri Tiomkin, who was born in Russia, had the ideal ethnic background for this scoring project. A second advantage was the fact that Tiomkin had refused to sign any contract that would have confined his work to a single studio. The invitation from Capra to score *Lost Horizon* was thus easy to accept.

Three distinct musical ideas are introduced at the beginning of Tiomkin's score. The opening credits begin with a bold succession of orchestral harmonies that accompany a dramatic melodic motif. This short musical fanfare leads to a lyrical melody in a waltz-like pattern that represents the film's central love theme. This music in turn leads to the credits' third melodic idea, a soaring theme that represents Shangri-La itself. The melody of this theme progresses in a steadily flowing way that lacks the resting spaces that would normally help to establish a metric pattern. This music's non-metric character is enhanced by wordless choral singing that is added to the orchestration. With a visual background of a mountain peak, the music soars higher and higher until Capra's name appears on the screen.

Music continues nonstop through a printed forward that features the love theme and concludes with a repetition of the fanfare idea as the following information is shown: "Baskul, the night of March 10, 1935."

The film begins with a chaotic scene of political unrest at the Baskul airport, where Conway is attempting to get dozens of Westerners on airplanes that will fly them to Shanghai. Highly dramatic and rhythmically propelled music continues until Conway and the last remaining fugitives are airborne.

More turbulent music can be heard when the plane lands in an unnamed place to take on more fuel. There is no music in the subsequent scene when the plane runs out of fuel and crashes on a snowy plateau in the Himalayas.

One of the film's musical highlights occurs when the rescuers approach the plane with the intention of taking the passengers to safety. At this point, a slow march-like idea begins to sound. With Tiomkin's use of the lowered seventh step of the scale, this theme resembles the modal tones of Gregorian chant melodies. There is also a repeated accompanying pattern of two chords that are a whole step apart (this parallel harmony has often been used to establish ancient settings (as in Miklós Rósza's score for *Ben-Hur*.) As the trek to Shangri-la continues, the music gets progressively more dramatic, until the travelers enter a hidden passageway that leads to the Valley of the Blue Moon, where the lamasery of Shangri-La is located. At this point, the music shifts to a lyrical choral piece that suggests the serene nature of this enchanted place.

Much choral music is heard in the Shangri-La scenes, along with several repetitions of the love theme, which accompanies Conway and Sondra (Jane Wyatt), a young school teacher.

The most memorable music in the film occurs following the death of the High Lama, who has explained to Conway the reasons for his having been brought to Shangri-La. While Conway's brother George is trying to convince him to leave Shangri-La and return to the outside world, a large contingent of musicians is heard in the Shangri-La theme, with a great number of percussion instruments added to the orchestration. During a torchlight procession to the lamasery, the music continues to sound, although it gets muffled when George closes a window so he can talk to his brother. When they depart, along with George's supposedly young female friend, Maria, and several porters, the music gains in intensity, with the love theme returning as Sondra frantically chases after them. The music builds to a grand conclusion as they reach the hidden passageway.

Tiomkin's music is hugely responsible for the exotic impact that *Lost Horizon* can have on its viewers. The funeral procession music itself remains one of the most remarkable pieces ever written for a film. This is truly one of Tiomkin's film masterworks and richly deserves inclusion in this book.

Recognition

Lost Horizon was one of 1937's most critically acclaimed films and a box-office success.

Nominated for seven Academy Awards, including citations for Best Picture and Best Score. It won in two categories: sound and art direction.

Recordings

Charles Gerhardt, National Philharmonic Orchestra, *Lost Horizon: The Classic Film Scores of Dimitri Tiomkin*, RCA, 1991. CD reissue of the 1975 vinyl recording. Includes around twenty-three minutes of Tiomkin's score. Reissued again in 2010 on the Sony label. ****

Dimitri Tiomkin, *Lost Horizon*, Soundtrack Factory, 1999. This is a limited edition, B00004T25M. Dated sound. ***

Bibliography

Palmer, Christopher. *Dimitri Tiomkin: A Portrait*. London: T. E. Books, 1984.
Sven, Kurt. Liner notes. *Lost Horizon: The Classic Film Scores of Dimitri Tiomkin*. RCA 1669-2-RG, 1991, CD.

—LEM

M

THE MAGNIFICENT SEVEN

(1960)

Elmer Bernstein

The Film

Directed by John Sturges and starring Yul Brynner, Eli Wallach, Horst Buchholz, James Coburn, Brad Dexter, Steve McQueen, Robert Vaughn, and Charles Bronson, *The Magnificent Seven* has entered the film canon of well-known American western.

Calvera (Eli Wallach) is in charge of a group of bandits who carry out raids on a Mexican village. Under attack, the villagers seek weapons from the Americans in exchange for their own goods. A gunslinger, Chris (Yul Brynner), convinces the villages that employing gunfighters would be cheaper than buying weapons, thus begins the recruitment of six other fighters—Chico, Luck, Vin, O'Reilly, Britt, and Lee—to form the Magnificent Seven. Their arrival in the village is not universally popular to begin with. They are seen eating the best food, and the women cower from them for fear of being raped. The seven eventually convince the villagers of their positive intent and train them in self-defense. The next attack by Calvera and his bandits is successfully deterred. In disguise, Chico infiltrates the bandits' camp and learns of their future plans to attack once more. The reason behind this is that the bandits are low on food. The final attack on the village results in a bloody final battle that kills Calvera and many villagers and leaves just three of the Magnificent Seven alive.

The film was nominated for one Academy Award and one Golden Globe.

The Music

The score to *The Magnificent Seven* was composed by Elmer Bernstein. He was actually the third or fourth choice for the film. The director initially wanted Dimitri Tiomkin to score it, but, the two fell out after a disagreement over *High Noon*. Aaron Copland was discussed as a possible replacement, and Alex North also allegedly watched rough cuts of the film in preparation for potentially composing a score for it. However, it was Bernstein who ultimately received the commission,

Two of the Magnificent Seven: Steve McQueen and Yul Brynner. *United Artists / Photofest* © *United Artists*

and Sturges has since called it one of the best film scores ever written. It was placed eighth on the American Film Institute's top twenty-five list of greatest all-time film scores.

The composer did not watch the film initially. He simply discussed the options with Sturges. Bernstein recalled fondly the enthusiasm the director had for music, saying that "John loved music. I think he would have happily stripped all the dialogue out of all the movies he ever made" in favor of music. After composing a few themes, Bernstein did watch the film, and he was taken aback by the plodding pace of the narrative. He decided that his compositions had to drive the film along. From this desire to have a memorable, exciting theme, the film's main melody came about. Bernstein was particularly proud of it, claiming, "Every once in a while—it doesn't happen often—you hit on something that really feels quite thrilling. The opening rhythm [. . .] was like a surge of energy." Spencer describes the main theme as marvelously rousing and exuberantly heroic, and he is correct. It is a string-dominated melody interjected by a brass countermelody, and the galloping nature of the theme ensures that it drives the film along at a fast pace whenever it appears. Its first appearance is during the opening credits, but it does not make an immediate appearance. First, there are huge chords to let the audience know the film has begun, harking back to classical and early Romantic composers and the opening to symphonies. The main theme soon enters after a string opening and a brass countermelody is heard. Then a guitar variation with woodwinds carries the melody into the opening scenes of the film, but not before the title sequence ends with one final grand rendition of the main theme.

Bernstein got the inspiration for the main theme from a long-standing desire to compose something "American," which he had not had the chance to do in his previous commissions. He knew a great deal about this style of music, as he was an ardent fan of American folk music, and he had a strong relationship with one of the other composers discussed for the film, Aaron Copland. Copland, argued Bernstein, "invented American music to a great degree," and Bernstein credited Copland with having "a certain style, a certain sound [that is] very attractive." He claimed that by the time he got the commission to compose the score to *The Magnificent Seven*, this style of American music had been in his head for many years, and it finally "had a chance to be set free." He attributes the energy and rhythmic intensity of the score to this desire to compose something typically American.

Another key musical theme was that depicting Calvera. The use of woodblocks, timpani, and strings provided the melody, which has a Mexican, flamenco-influenced feel. These percussive sounds of danger run into melodic fragments on French horn before the Spanish guitar offers a quieter mood, but one that still signifies great danger. It is a welcome respite from the galloping main theme and shows the broad palette with which Bernstein composed the score.

It is difficult to deny that Bernstein's approach to scoring *The Magnificent Seven* saw somewhat of a breakthrough for a purely American aesthetic in film scoring, moving away from the domination of European-born composers from the Golden Age of Hollywood, which was ending. The score found itself on the borderline between replicating the scores of the 1940s and 1950s and moving toward more contemporary forms of composition. It has been argued that *The Magnificent Seven* theme was the most memorable melody in film scores until *Jaws* and *Star Wars* appeared in the 1970s, and it is difficult to challenge this claim. Bernstein wrote his name into film music history with this score. It has an American, western charm that endures to this day.

Recognition

The score was nominated for an Academy Award.
Nominated for a Laurel Award for Top Musical Score (where it came in fourth).
In 1998 won the International Film Music Critics' Award for Best Re-Released Existing Score.

Recording

Elmer Bernstein, *The Magnificent Seven*, Soundtrack Factory, 2017. This is a remastered version of the original soundtrack plus four bonus tracks. ****

Bibliography

Hannan, B. *The Making of "The Magnificent Seven": Behind the Scenes of the Pivotal Western*. Jefferson, NC: McFarland, 2015.
Russell, M., and J. E. Young. *Film Music*. Vol. 1. New York: Focal Press, 2000.
Spencer, K. *Film and Television Scores, 1950–1979: A Critical Survey by Genre*. Jefferson, NC: McFarland, 2008.

—ML

THE MAN WITH THE GOLDEN ARM
(1955)
Elmer Bernstein

The Film

Otto Preminger's film adaptation of Nelson Algren's gritty novel *The Man with the Golden Arm* raised eyebrows in 1955 for its frank portrayal of heroin addiction, a subject that was taboo under Hollywood's then-existing Production Code. As with Preminger's previous film *The Moon Is Blue*, *Golden Arm* was released without the Code organization's seal of approval.

In the film Frank Sinatra portrays Frankie Machine, a recovering heroin addict whose life is complicated by his supposedly crippled wife, Zosh (Eleanor Parker). She has a clinging dependency on her husband and wants him to return to his former job as a poker game dealer, but he wants to turn his life around by becoming a drummer in a big band.

With the help of Molly (Kim Novak), a former girlfriend who lives downstairs and encourages him to improve his drumming skills, Frankie tries to stay clean and pass an important musical audition, but an unscrupulous drug dealer has other plans for him.

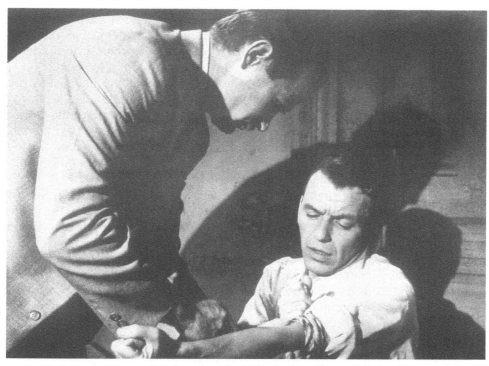

Louie (Darren McGavin) watches as the heroin-addicted Frankie (Frank Sinatra) prepares to shoot up. *United Artists / Photofest © United Artists*

The Music

Elmer Bernstein's music for *Golden Arm* features a groundbreaking score in its vivid use of the jazz idiom. Although there are some noteworthy predecessors in the use of jazz scoring in film, especially *A Streetcar Named Desire* (1951) and *On the Waterfront* (1954), *Golden Arm* is unique because, with its uptown Chicago setting, jazz sounds are front and center in the score.

The most important musical idea comes at the very beginning of the film, when the credits are accompanied by an up-tempo theme that starts with steady-driven rhythmic patterns on cymbals that alternate with a low-pitched riff for trombones. This music is followed by a rhythmically driven idea for trumpets in a minor key that features a number of trombone riffs between the melodic trumpet phrases. Enhancing the dynamic quality of this theme is a repeated five-note bass pattern that drives the theme forward. Built on top of this bass, the trumpets introduce another segment of the theme that contains a repeated use of descending two-note melodic figures. The brash trumpet motifs, together with the repeated bass pattern and an energetic swirling accompaniment provided by strings, combine to produce a theme that is distinctively jazzy in character.

This theme shows up many times during the film. One of its more noteworthy appearances occurs in an early scene in a bar where Frankie hangs out along with a rather slow-witted friend named Sparrow (Arnold Stang), who follows Frankie around like a pet dog. When Frankie first shows up at the bar after getting out of rehab, the main theme sounds like a live performance inside the bar, but from an unseen band. When Frankie and Sparrow leave the bar, the music suddenly subsides in volume but continues softly in the background for a moment.

Several scenes include bits of the main-title idea, including one in which a drug dealer named Louie tries to coax Frankie to get a heroin injection. High-pitched trills on a piano lead to phrases of the main theme featuring muted trumpets with a low pizzicato riff on string bass. This music is incorporated along with eerie, high-pitched violin and flute tones and drums that continue to sound during Louie's persistent urging that Frankie give in to his addiction. Bernstein's multi-layered music expresses Frankie's physical craving for the drug.

A strong repetition of this theme occurs when Frankie finds Louie in the bar and follows him across the street to his apartment. At this point bits of the main-title idea played by brass, strings, and drums are heard. High-pitched vibrato sounds of an organ along with stabbing brass chords and percussive piano chords are heard as Louie prepares his needle. Then the music becomes gradually more dynamic as the injection takes place.

Not all of the score is in the jazz vein. Frankie's scenes with his wife, Zosh, feature a soft string accompaniment that suggests the fragile state of their marriage. A romantic-style love theme is introduced when Molly returns from work to her apartment where Frankie is practicing on his drum pad (his drumming gives Zosh a headache, so he practices downstairs while Molly is away). A lyrical theme for strings with several violin, clarinet, and flute solos suggests their mutual affection. As they talk, bits of the main-title theme are interjected. An especially intriguing musical moment in this scene occurs when Molly falls asleep. As Frankie drapes a coat over her a tender piano version of the theme is heard, followed by an unaccompanied solo flute. The cue then comes to a quiet ending with the addition of a second flute.

There is considerable jazz used as source music in the film. When Frankie shows up in frail condition for his audition, a big band is already rehearsing. Notable in this scene is the appearance of real-life jazz musicians, including Shelley Mann on drums and Shorty Rogers as the band leader. Rogers also served as arranger for the jazz numbers played in the film.

Man with the Golden Arm is noteworthy for its groundbreaking portrayal of drug addiction and for its extensive use of jazz. It paved the way for many other films that featured jazz, including Johnny Mandel's score for *I Want to Live* (1958) and Duke Ellington's music for *Anatomy of a Murder* (1959). On its own terms, *Golden Arm* features a main-title theme that remains one of the most significant musical creations of Elmer Bernstein, a composer who was at the start of a fifty-year-long career when he scored Preminger's film. This score remains one of Bernstein's most memorable works and thus deserves to be included in this book.

Recognition

Three Oscar nominations, including Art Direction, Best Actor (Sinatra), and Best Original Score, which was Elmer Bernstein's first nomination.

Predecessor of many films with jazz scores, several by Bernstein, including *Sweet Smell of Success* (1957) and *The Rat Race* (1960).

Recording

Elmer Bernstein, *Man with the Golden Arm*, Spectrum Music, 2001, CD. This is an import release of the original soundtrack on the 1955 Decca recording. Good mono sound. ***1/2

Bibliography

Bernstein, Elmer. Liner notes. *The Man with the Golden Arm*. Spectrum Music 544 627-2, 2001, CD.

—LEM

THE MISSION
(1986)
Ennio Morricone

The Film

A list of movies about the missionary work of Catholic priests should include Bruce Beresford's *Black Robe* (1991) and Martin Scorsese's *Silence* (2016). A third film in this rare genre is Roland Joffé's *The Mission*, which concerns a group of Jesuit priests who try to convert members of the Guarani tribe in a remote region bordering on Argentina, Paraguay, and Brazil in the mid-1700s. Joffé's film is particularly worth examining because of Ennio Morricone's score.

Screenwriter Robert Bolt based *The Mission* on historical documents about the conflict between Spain and Portugal over territorial boundaries and the enslaving of captured Guarani tribesmen. The film primarily concerns two men, Father Gabriel (Jeremy Irons), and a penitent former slave trader, Rodrigo Mendoza (Robert De Niro), who joins the Jesuit society in an effort to build a chapel in a Guarani village. When Catholic Church officials order the mission of San Carlos to be closed, the lives of the Jesuits and their native converts are endangered by the intrusion of soldiers who have been commissioned to shut down the mission by any means necessary.

The Music

The film begins without music as the preliminary production credits are shown. An ongoing narration begins with the dictating of a letter to the pope drafted by Cardinal Altamirano (Ray McAnally) concerning the forced closing of the San Carlos mission.

Father Gabriel (Jeremy Irons, center) among South American tribesmen. *Warner Bros. / Photofest © Warner Bros.*

The first music in Morricone's score features both traditional string instruments and native drums as an eerie background for a scene in which several Guarani tribe members bear a wooden cross to which a missionary priest has been tied. Once the cross is tossed into a river the music stops and the only subsequent sounds are those of the water, which becomes increasingly turbulent as the cross plunges over a waterfall.

In the next moment, during which the film's title is shown, soft harp sounds are heard as the cardinal's narration explains the work by Jesuit priests in converting the Guarani. As the screen reveals shots of Iguaçu Falls, the score's first prominent theme arrives with a repeated series of four tones, as in the pitch pattern C-B-G-B. This motif, which stays within a pitch range of only four tones, is associated with the Jesuits throughout the film.

The score's second motif begins as source music when Fr. Gabriel hopes to win the confidence of the Guarani by playing an oboe that he carries with him on his perilous climb to a high plateau where the tribe lives. The music that he plays is a lilting melody that echoes through the jungle. After one of the natives breaks the oboe, other tribal members feel sympathy for Gabriel and lead him to their village. As they walk along, the oboe melody (called "Gabriel's Oboe" on the soundtrack recording) is developed into a smoothly flowing cue for oboe and strings.

A third musical motif is a tune for the Guarani that, like the Jesuit theme, stays within a range of four scale steps. This motif, which includes a metrical pattern of three beats, with two longer tones followed by two shorter ones, first occurs when Rodrigo and his men bring a number of captured Guarani to the city of Asunción for sale to the local governor and slave trader Don Cabeza. The breathy sounds of the Andean flute are heard in this motif, while turbulent string sounds add a sinister accompaniment.

Several noteworthy musical cues occur in the sequence where Gabriel gives Rodrigo an unusual penance as atonement for having killed his brother in a jealous rage. In the next scene Gabriel and four other Jesuits accompany Rodrigo in a treacherous climb up the side of a cliff behind a waterfall, with Rodrigo pulling along a large assortment of swords and pieces of armor that have been roped together to weigh them down. At one point in the climb, the score includes the Jesuit motif with discordant low woodwind tones. After the arduous journey, Rodrigo joins the priests and Guarani people in building the mission. The extended cue in this scene features Gabriel's theme combined with a rhythmic pattern of native drum sounds, along with the Guarani theme that is chanted by choral voices.

This ingenious intermixing of themes, which also includes the simultaneous use of different rhythmic meters, occurs several times. When the cardinal inspects the San Carlos mission that he has been asked to close, Morricone's musical ideas contribute an uplifting feeling. In the later raid on the village by Spanish and Portuguese soldiers, several motifs are heard, along with discordant harmonies. A final juxtaposition of these themes occurs during the closing credits.

Scattered about the film are musical ideas used as source music, including a festive piece heard during a celebration, in which Rodrigo fatally duels with his brother. There is also considerable religious vocal music, including choral renditions of the chant melody "Ave Maria" as sung by the Guarani, who have been musically trained by the Jesuits.

With its simultaneous combination of multiple melodic and rhythmic ideas, this score is one of Morricone's most musically ingenious creations and richly deserves to be discussed in this book.

Recognition

Winner of the Palme d'or at the 1984 Cannes Film Festival.
Seven Oscar nominations, including Best Picture and Original Score. Winner of the Oscar for Chris Menges's cinematography.

Recordings

Ennio Morricone, *Cinema Paradiso: The Classic Film Music of Ennio Morricone,* Silva Screen, 1996, CD, SSD 1057. This is one of the best of many recordings of themes from this film. Includes five tracks from *The Mission.* Excellent sound. ****
Ennio Morricone, *The Mission,* Virgin, 1992, CD. Excellent sound. ****

Bibliography

Hickman, Roger. *Reel Music: Exploring 100 Years of Film Music.* New York: W. W. Norton, 2006.
MacDonald, Laurence E. *The Invisible Art of Film Music: A Comprehensive History.* Second edition. Lanham, MD: Scarecrow Press, 2013.

—LEM

N

THE NATURAL

(1984)
Randy Newman

The Film

Films set in the world of professional baseball have been around since the silent era. Some, like *Pride of the Yankees* (1942) and *The Babe* (2004), have been biographical in nature, while such others as *Bull Durham* (1987) and *Major League* (1989) have been based on fictional stories. Barry Levinson's *The Natural* belongs in the latter category.

Levinson's film, which is based on Bernard Malamud's 1952 novel, is the story of Roy Hobbs (Robert Redford), a former pitcher who has missed several years of potential playing time as the result of a gunshot wound inflicted by a mentally unstable woman. Sixteen years later Roy is signed by the New York Knights and gets a second chance at baseball fame. When Roy's home run hitting makes him an overnight celebrity, several lives are altered by his athletic prowess.

The Music

When Randy Newman became the composer of *The Natural* he had scored only two previous films, the 1971 satire *Cold Turkey* and the 1981 period film *Ragtime*. But he obviously came to Levinson's film with a high degree of creative energy, because the score to *The Natural* is filled with both tuneful and heroic themes.

There is no music during the opening credits, in which the only sounds are those of an oncoming train. Once Roy boards the train, music accompanies a flashback sequence in which he remembers his teen years, when he was coached by his father on the family farm, and his early twenties, when he was the pitching protégé of an old-time baseball scout.

The flashback includes several melodic ideas, beginning with a horn motif based on consecutive pairs of rising pitches. The second idea, for flute and strings, accompanies Roy getting pitching advice from his father while his childhood friend Iris looks on. This lilting idea is later associated with Roy and Iris (played

Roy Hobbs (Robert Redford, left), Red (Richard Farnsworth), and Pop Fisher (Wilford Brimley, right). *Tri-Star / Photofest © Tri-Star*

as an adult by Glenn Close). Also included is a theme for brass and strings that utilizes the pentatonic scale. This theme, which is the film's most heroic musical idea, is first heard when Roy carves a baseball bat out of wood from a tree that is struck by lightning during a thunderstorm that follows the fatal heart attack of Roy's father. As the bat is shown in close-up with the name "Wonderboy" inscribed on it, the horns are featured in a dramatic version of the heroic theme, which includes a six-tone extension with a boldly rising melodic jump.

Another part of the flashback with several notable musical motifs occurs when Roy gets off a Chicago-bound train that makes a water stop near the site of a carnival. When Roy's baseball-scout companion makes a bet with Max Mercy (Robert Duvall), a prominent sports reporter, that Roy can strike out a prominent slugger known as the Whammer (a fictional character that resembles Babe Ruth), the music starts as Roy goes into his windup for the third pitch. At this point the previously heard horn motif begins softly, but as the pitched ball is shown flying through the air in slow motion, the music gains momentum. When the Whammer swings and misses, the score includes a rhythmic trumpet idea that brings to mind the music of Aaron Copland with its repeated use of rising tones that employ the pentatonic scale. Adding to the Coplandesque flavor of this music are syncopated accents and periodic silent spaces that are similar to rhythmic patterns in Copland's ballet scores *Billy the Kid* and *Rodeo*.

A few scenes have no scoring. A good example is the end of the flashback, when Roy is shot at close range by the deranged Harriet Bird. The preliminary quietness of the scene makes the unexpected gunshot all the more startling.

Newman's music enhances several later scenes in the film. One exceptional musical moment occurs when Roy, now a member of the Knights ballclub but assigned by the team's manager to sit in the dugout during their games, finally gets a chance to bat during an approaching storm. Accompanied by rumbles of thunder, Roy takes his Wonderboy bat, approaches the plate, and hits the ball so hard that it becomes unstrung in midair. As rain begins Roy crosses the plate and scores the winning run.

Two themes from the earlier flashback sequence are heard in this scene. The first idea, which sounds like an altered version of the earlier horn motif, begins as Roy approaches the plate. The second idea, which is based on the flashback's heroic theme, now features French horns and trumpets in a soaring arrangement of the six-note extension motif. This music accompanies Roy's swing and the unraveling ball's flight to the outfield. When Roy finishes rounding the bases the music features the pentatonic first part of the heroic theme. The music fades down as Roy lingers at home plate while the rain falls and everyone else heads for cover.

Another noteworthy melody is introduced when Roy is reunited with Iris and learns that she has a teenage son. After Roy leaves her apartment, the flute intones a six-note idea that ascends boldly in pitch. It is heard again in a heroic statement during the film's climactic scene when Roy's game-winning homer clinches a victory for the Knights in the pennant race.

In addition to the aforementioned musical themes, there is an often-used motif of four sustained chords that punctuate many of the film's most memorably emotional moments.

Newman's score also includes swing-style music that accompanies montage sequences that reveal the baseball heroics of Roy Hobbs as the sports world's latest sensation.

Randy Newman's music creates an aura of heroic fantasy that, along with Caleb Deschanel's atmospheric photography, helps to make *The Natural* a memorable film. Newman's richly atmospheric musical accompaniment definitely deserves a place among the scores discussed in this book.

Recognition

The Natural won favorable reviews from many critics who praised the film's strong performances, beautiful photography, and memorable music.
Four Oscar nominations, including one for Randy Newman's music.

Recording

Randy Newman, *The Natural*, Reprise, 1990. CD. Original soundtrack with most of the film's main themes. Excellent sound. ****

Bibliography

Hickman, Roger. *Reel Music: Exploring 100 Years of Film Music*. New York: W. W. Norton, 2006.
The Natural. Insert notes. TriStar DVD, # 04609.

—LEM

NORTH BY NORTHWEST

(1959)
Bernard Herrmann

The Film

North by Northwest is widely regarded as one of the finest films ever produced. It is one of seven Hitchcock films to feature the music of Bernard Herrmann. Unusually for the period, it also features kinetic typography (or moving text) in the opening credits, designed by graphic designer Saul Bass. Some have called it the first James Bond film, with the suspense, action, and thrills of Hitchcock's film easily comparable to the Bond films that would begin to appear three years later. Starring Cary Grant as Roger Thornhill, the victim of mistaken identity, the film takes the audience on an exhilarating journey across the northern United States from New York to Chicago, before culminating in a memorable finale atop Mount Rushmore. The film was nominated for three Academy Awards, for Best Film Editing, Best Art Direction—Set Decoration (Color), and Best Original Screenplay

Roger O. Thornhill (Cary Grant) and Eve Kendall (Eva Marie Saint) are pursued on Mount Rushmore. *MGM / Photofest © MGM*

(Ernest Lehman), but lost out to *Ben-Hur* and *Pillow Talk*. As of 2016, it is one of seven hundred films added to the National Film Registry for preservation in the Library of Congress.

The Music

The score by Bernard Herrmann played a significant role in generating the excitement and thrills of the film's narrative. Two musical themes in particular reoccur throughout the film and represent the espionage story arc of Thornhill and an unforeseen romance respectively.

The first musical theme, heard immediately over the opening credits, is in a vigorous 3/8 time signature, with syncopation every third bar giving the feel of two bars of 6 followed by one bar of 3. Percussion, led by the timpani, provides the introduction, with the string section, high woodwinds, and low brass entering with the rousing, disorientating main theme. The repetitiveness of the music, and its consistent use in the film, holds an almost hypnotic quality, and its use at the very opening of the film provides a sense of power and complexity, highlighting the impact of film music at its most potent. Tonally, the constant shift between minor and major harmonies offers an unusual and striking musical accompaniment to the drama that is set to unfold. The soundscape is similar to that used by Herrmann in *Vertigo*, which is unsurprising given that there was only a year between the two films. The theme recurs at several key moments in the film and becomes the leitmotif for Cary Grant's character. Its use is extensive and varied. For example, it is used for dramatic yet comedic effect when Thornhill drives in a drunken state at the start of the film, sounding somewhat incongruous when combined with Grant's humorous facial expressions. On the other hand, it accompanies the film's white-knuckle finale on Mount Rushmore, with Herrmann's music acting as a backdrop to precipitous drops and gun battles.

The second predominant theme found in the score is a luscious love theme, depicting the unlikely and volatile romance between Thornhill and Eve Kendall (Eva Marie Saint). The two meet on the 20th Century Limited train as it winds its way up the Hudson River valley. After a romantic encounter overnight, Thornhill thinks that he discovers that Kendall is working with his enemies, but it transpires that she is a government agent and that Thornhill is her cover. The love theme depicting their romance is one of Herrmann's most beautiful and has been compared to Richard Wagner's *Tristan und Isolde* in its use of cascading string suspensions and chromaticism. While the musical theme and visuals that accompany some of the most romantic moments may appear hackneyed and overbearing to modern-day audiences, there is no denying that these moments epitomize the Golden Age of Hollywood. The theme develops as the film progresses, with the theme being relatively restrained during Thornhill and Kendall's first meeting in the refreshment car aboard the train but becoming ever more romanticized and impassioned during the kissing scenes in Kendall's compartment.

Finally, and interestingly, the famous crop-dusting sequence, an image of which adorns the front cover of almost all commercial DVD and VHS releases, is not accompanied by music. Herrmann and Hitchcock were astute at deciding when music was not required, and despite it being the defining scene in the film, the sound effects of the plane and bullets were deemed to be sufficient without Herrmann providing further drama.

Recognition

Perhaps surprisingly, the score was not nominated for any major awards. It was however a nominated entry on the American Film Institute's lineup of greatest film scores, but missed out on the final list. However, two of Herrmann's other scores, *Pyscho* and *Vertigo*, did make the top twenty-five.
Earned three Oscar nominations. Won for Best Original Score.

Recordings

Bernard Herrmann, *North by Northwest*, Sony, 2010. This remastered original 1959 recording, performed by the MGM Studio Orchestra, is still definitive. The liner notes make mention of some sound deterioration due to damaged master tapes, but these are never a major issue. Rating: ***½

Laurie Johnson, London Studio Symphony Orchestra, *North by Northwest*, Varese Sarabande, 1991. This recording is from 1979. The sound quality is superior compared with the original remastered version, having been pressed in Japan. There are certain idiosyncrasies of Herrmann missing, but it is still a worthwhile recording to discover. ***

—ML

NOW, VOYAGER

(1942)
Max Steiner

The Film

From her Oscar-winning performance in *Jezebel* (1938) to her scenery-chewing role in *What Ever Happened to Baby Jane?* (1962), Bette Davis dominated the screen as few other actresses ever have. And in many of her most memorable films, including *Now, Voyager*, her screen portrayals were accompanied by the music of Max Steiner.

Now, Voyager, adapted from a best-selling novel by the veteran screenwriter Casey Robinson, features Davis as Charlotte Vale, the repressed daughter of a prominent Boston widow. At the start of the film, Charlotte is on the verge of a nervous breakdown, largely stemming from her unloving mother's domineering ways. After a stint in the Cascade sanitarium under the tender care of Dr. Jaquith (Claude Rains), Charlotte begins to come out of her shell. But her newfound sense of freedom becomes a source of resentment to her mother, who cannot accept the independent person Charlotte has become.

On a cruise to South America, Jerry Durrance (Paul Henreid) meets transformed spinster Charlotte Vale (Bette Davis). *Warner Bros. / Photofest © Warner Bros.*

The Music

Max Steiner's score is based on three principal melodic ideas, the first of which is introduced during the opening credits. This theme, which features a soaring idea pronounced by strings with accompanying French horns, is based on a melodic line that skips up and down the scale in meandering fashion. Along with the unusual nature of this melody is the harmony's unpredictable chordal movement. In this theme, Steiner musically suggests that Charlotte, although she is totally submissive to her mother's ironclad will, inwardly desires to escape from this domination. This music hints at a sense of freedom that Charlotte begins to experience, once Dr. Jaquith is able to rescue her from her "ugly duckling" life in her mother's upscale Boston home.

While this theme periodically returns, a second idea of less optimistic character is introduced early in the film to suggest the controlled nature of Charlotte's upbringing. This second idea, a slow-moving melody based on a descending pair of adjacent scale tones, stays within a small range of only four pitches. Here the limited tonal space and repetitive rhythmic flow convey the dull and monotonous nature of Charlotte's sheltered day-to-day existence.

When the "new" Charlotte appears after months of therapy and weight loss, along with changes of wardrobe, hairstyle, and makeup, the music takes on a more optimistic demeanor. A love theme connects Charlotte with Jerry Durrance

(Paul Henreid), an unhappily married man she meets on a South American cruise. This melody is based on a repeated motif of seven tones. Curiously, both this theme and the film's opening idea share a common characteristic—the sustained sound of the first tone, followed by six tones that move in a smoothly flowing pattern. Although more conventional in design than the film's melodically adventurous opening theme, this idea adds a romantic ambiance as these two troubled people quickly sense a mutual attraction.

When Charlotte and Jerry get stranded on Sugarloaf Mountain near Rio, the strings add a soaring version of the love theme as Jerry kisses Charlotte while she sleeps by a makeshift campfire. A lovely version of this theme is heard during the next sequence when the two spend several days in Rio. At one point, when Jerry lights two cigarettes and hands one to Charlotte, this wordless gesture is accompanied by the sounds of a solo cello followed by a single violin that adds great expressiveness to the orchestration of the love theme. This lighting of cigarettes recurs several times; in each occurrence, the love theme adds wonderfully romantic sounds.

One additional thematic idea is associated with Jerry's daughter, Tina, whom Charlotte meets at the Cascade sanitarium, to which Charlotte has returned following her mother's death. Tina, unwanted by her own mother, is musically accompanied by an idea that borrows the repeated use of a descending pair of tones from Charlotte's theme. As Tina finds in Charlotte a substitute for the motherly love she cannot have elsewhere, Steiner's score cleverly intertwines bits of both the Charlotte and Tina themes.

In the film's final segment, when Charlotte hosts a party with Tina as a special guest, the love theme is heard again as Charlotte and Jerry share cigarettes and vow to keep Tina as their mutual child. As the strings begin to soar, Steiner's melody confirms their love one more time.

Other music in the film includes a Latin-style theme for the scenes set in South America. There is also the clever use of a theme from Tchaikovsky's *Pathetique* Symphony, which begins as Charlotte sits in a concert hall with Jerry on her right and her fiancé, Elliot, on her left. This theme continues to sound as underscoring during the subsequent scene when Charlotte tells Elliot that they should not marry.

Since *Now, Voyager* is much more than a conventional love story, Steiner incorporated his music into the film in a uniquely emotional manner. His love theme expresses great depths of feeling and provides the awareness that, although Charlotte and Jerry may never actually wind up together, their love is unstoppable. Steiner's score is memorable, and so is the way in which his melodic ideas become storytelling elements. This is a truly exceptional score and one that is highly worthy of being represented in this book.

Recognition

Placed on the National Film Registry by the Library of Congress in 2007 as "culturally, historically, and theatrically significant."

Selected by the AFI as number twenty-three on its list "100 Years . . . 100 Passions" as one of the great love stories in American cinema.

The love theme, with words by Kim Gannon, was adapted into the song "It Can't Be Wrong," which became a chart-topping hit in 1943.

Recording

Charles Gerhardt, National Philharmonic Orchestra, *Now, Voyager: The Classic Film Scores of Max Steiner*, RCA, 1991, rereleased on Sony, 2011. No original soundtrack exists, and there is no studio recording of the complete score. This disc includes six minutes of the score. Excellent sound.****

Bibliography

Thomas, Tony. *The Films of the Forties*. New York: Citadel Press, 1975.

—LEM

O

THE OMEN

(1976)
Jerry Goldsmith

The Film

Directed by Richard Donner and starring Gregory Peck, Lee Remick, David Warner, Harvey Spencer Stephens, Billie Whitelaw, Patrick Troughton, Martin Benson, and Leo McKern, *The Omen* is the first in a series of supernatural horror films.

Robert Thorn (Gregory Peck), a high-ranking ambassador, and his wife, Katherine (Lee Remick), become parents to a stillborn baby, but Katherine was not made aware that her child did not survive. Her husband immediately adopts an orphan without his wife's knowledge, seemingly bringing the child up as their own. The family is beset by disturbing events while the child, named Damien, grows up. It is revealed that Damien may not be human—a warning that a priest (Patrick Troughton) delivers to the Thorns after discovering the baby's mysterious past. Robert and Katherine are ultimately killed, and Damien is brought up by the US president.

The film was nominated for two Academy Awards, of which it won one for Best Original Score. It also received a Golden Globe and BAFTA nomination.

The Music

The score to *The Omen* was composed by Jerry Goldsmith. Of eighteen career Academy Award nominations, the award for Best Original Score for this film was his only win. Goldsmith was commissioned to write the score when the director, Richard Donner, and some of the production team attended a concert of his film music. Immediately afterward, they offered Goldsmith the job.

The film opens with a lush love theme, which goes against the very nature of the story about to unfold. The love between Peck and Remick's characters was scored beautifully by Goldsmith, and this emotive melody would ensure that the later events of the narrative were all the more horrifying and poignant. Goldsmith was keen to incorporate a love theme, as he thought it was ultimately a love story gone wrong. He wanted to portray the love between husband and wife, but also

Robert Thorn (Gregory Peck) grapples with the devil's emissary Mrs. Baylock (Billie Whitelaw).
20th Century Fox Film Corporation / Photofest © 20th Century Fox Film Corporation

between them and the child, who they do not immediately realize is the devil or antichrist. The poignancy of Robert Thorn first losing his wife and then the child he has grown to love is heightened by Goldsmith's established love theme. It is evidence that horror movies are most successful when a balance is struck and something wonderful is established before being ripped away from the audience and on-screen characters. As Spencer describes it, "as the darker aspects of the story unfold, Goldsmith's love theme adds an emotionally involving sentiment that accentuates the dramatic conflict and maintains a human dimension even as the supernatural elements take control of the story."

Perhaps the most famous musical cue from the film is the song "Ave Satani," sung in Latin, which also received an Academy Award nomination for Best Original Song. It is based on Gregorian chant and has a demonic, horrifying sound. Indeed, it is a sound that has been mimicked in horror movies in the decades following *The Omen*. The song was orchestrated by an old friend of Goldsmith's, Arthur Morton, and the composer gives much of the credit to him for its success. Goldsmith said, "I hadn't written that much chorus in the previous 25 years and I admit I was somewhat rusty. He made a tremendous contribution in that area alone. Arthur arranged at least 65 per cent of the choral writing and he opened it up in a way that sounded much better than the way I wrote it."

The director was initially unsure about the Gregorian chant aspect of the score. When Goldsmith told him he wanted to write something liturgical in style, claiming that he could "see and hear a choral group," Donner was hesitant. However, at a recording session in London, the director recalls hearing a "guttural deep breathing" when the choir and orchestra were performing together. He claimed he got the shivers and that the hairs stood up on the back of his neck. The music is in the form of the Gregorian chant, but with words praising Satan. The choirmaster Goldsmith collaborated with was fluent in Latin, and with his help, they wrote disturbing lyrics for "Ave Satani," which he described as a kind of black mass.

The other aspect of the score can, according to Goldsmith, barely be called music. He recalls that he "did some very interesting things with the chorus" during a scene where a pack of Rottweilers attacks one of the characters. He asked the chorus to not sing but to make grunt and groan sounds and strange noises that "are not necessarily musical." The director, in a documentary from 2000, stated enthusiastically that when the dogs attack, he asked Goldsmith to remove the music in favor of these breathy "antichristo, antichristo" chants from the choir. He stated that the score "kicked the movie over the top" and that it was a deeply troubling musical accompaniment. It is without question one of the reasons why the film was so successful and why it resulted in an Academy Award. The demonic sounds were used in scenes where there was seemingly no peril, which cleverly hinted to the audience that something was certainly amiss. It is this Gregorian chant score, surely the only one to be found in this book, that makes Goldsmith's terrifying score worthy of a place in the top 100 soundtracks of all time. It was revolutionary and ultimately inspirational for many horror scores that would follow, but it remains perhaps the scariest of them all.

Recognition

Academy Award for Best Original Score.
Nominated for Academy Award for Best Original Song.
Nominated for Grammy for Best Album of Original Score.

Recording

Jerry Goldsmith, *The Omen*, Varese Sarabande, 1990. The original soundtrack, conducted by Lionel Newman. ***

Bibliography

Goldsmith, Jerry. Interview in the documentary *The Omen Revealed*, 20th Century Fox, 2000.

Spencer, K. *Film and Television Scores, 1950–1979: A Critical Survey by Genre*. Jefferson, NC: McFarland, 2008.

—ML

ON GOLDEN POND

(1981)
Dave Grusin

The Film

Directed by Mark Rydell and starring Henry Fonda and Katharine Hepburn, *On Golden Pond* deals with old age in a poignant, touching fashion.

Ethel (Katharine Hepburn) and Norman (Henry Fonda) are an elderly couple who enjoy an annual summer trip to an idyllic lake, Golden Pond, in New England. The film tackles the difficult relationship between Norman, who is beginning to lose his memory, and his daughter, Chelsea, who visits the couple one summer with her fiancé, Bill, and his son, Billy. Chelsea reveals to her mother than she feels like Norman is overbearing and controlling, even from many miles away. While Chelsea and Bill visit Europe, Norman and Ethel look after Billy, who enjoys fishing with his grandfather. Upon her return from Europe, Chelsea reconciles with her father after noticing how ill he is becoming.

As the couple prepares to leave the lake and return home, Norman collapses with what appears to be a heart attack. The film ends in a bittersweet fashion, with the couple knowing deep down that it was one of the final times they would visit the lake together. The film was praised for approaching challenging subjects like family feuds, empty nest syndrome, and existentialism. The fear of becoming old is represented in a sensitive way without becoming cinematically clichéd or kitschy and will resonate with many viewers who have lost parents or grandparents to old age. The shots of the scenic lake add a feeling of tranquillity as the Thayers' family problems are satisfyingly resolved.

The film was nominated for ten Academy Awards, of which it won three: Best Actor, Best Actress, and Best Writing. It also won three out of six Golden Globe nominations and one of six BAFTA nominations.

In their twilight: Norman Thayer Jr. (Henry Fonda) and Ethel Thayer (Katharine Hepburn). *Universal Pictures / Photofest © Universal Pictures*

The Music

The music to *On Golden Pond* was composed by Dave Grusin. The score was placed at number twenty-four in the American Film Institute's list of top film scores. The composer was pleased with the slow pace of the narrative, saying that "there was space in the picture for music, and there was space for it to breathe in the sense of having a comfortable home for a score."

The main theme to *On Golden Pond* is simple but moving. It underscores scenes of the tranquil lake, accompanied by the soft sounds of loons. The birds had an important part in the narrative and are placed in the score to reflect this. The theme opens with a solo piano, playing dissonant but comforting rubato melodic fragments in the higher octaves of the instrument. The left and right hand of the piano move together much of the time, creating an almost hymn-like atmosphere. The entry of the lower bass notes of the piano is truly one of the music moments that gives one goose bumps. The strings then enter with a subtle accompaniment as the piano melody becomes more frantic, but never harsh or sinister. A flute then joins the ensemble to perform the second musical theme in a minor key, adding a harp and some simple percussion. The original theme returns in piano, with the strings swelling to a climax, but never overpowering the piano. The most human of instruments, the oboe, then enters very briefly with a heartbreaking cue, only for the music to die away to the sounds of the loon. The main theme to *On Golden Pond* is beautiful. There are few other words that could do it justice. Grusin actually picked up on the idea that the music sounds hymn-like, and he was concerned. He stated that his score "might be too simple or sound too churchy," but that it was intentional, reflecting on the New England landscape and its Protestant hymns.

The score uses this main theme for most of its other cues, cutting, altering, and varying it to suit the scene. There is a playful respite from this in the shape of the "New Hampshire Hornpipe," which accompanies Billy's first fishing trip on the lake. It is a musical cue of youthful exuberance, which contrasts keenly with the gentler, sentimental theme that accompanies the elderly couple.

The score is beautifully evocative, and despite this, the composer is coy and humble about its success, saying, "It wasn't planned to be an important part of the film. It's just that the nature of the story dictated the areas where music could help." The music did help the film. The narrative itself was already melancholic but gentle, and the music only added to this feeling of lost youth and concerns about the onset of old age, poor health, and death. Never does Grusin's score become dark or depressing, though. It retains the sentimental loveliness that the main theme introduces at the very beginning of the film. It is one of the finest examples of how a simple theme, with relatively simplistic orchestration, can have a significant emotional impact on a film's audience. The score is certainly capable of extracting tears, one of the reasons for its resounding success.

Recognition

Nominated for an Academy Award for Best Original Score.
Nominated for a Grammy for Best Original Score.

Recording

Dave Grusin, *On Golden Pond*, Varese Sarabande, 2017. This is an unusual album in that it includes dialog from the film as well as all of Grusin's main musical themes, including "New Hampshire Hornpipe." Despite this, it runs to only eleven tracks, but is still recommended for the main theme alone. ***

Bibliography

"Music for the Screen: *On Golden Pond*." *Dave Grusin Archive*. Accessed November 24, 2017. http://www.grusin.net/on_golden_pond.htm.
Sikoryak, J. "The AFI's Top 25." *Film Score Monthly* 10, no. 6 (2005): 32–33.

—ML

ON THE WATERFRONT

(1954)
Leonard Bernstein

The Film

Many noteworthy films from the mid-1950s reflect the growing trend for wide-screen productions shot in color. Elia Kazan's *On the Waterfront* bucked that trend by being filmed with neither a widescreen process nor color cinematography, yet it remains one of the most memorable films of all time.

Screenwriter Budd Schulberg based his script on a 1949 Pulitzer-Prize-winning series of articles by *New York Sun* reporter Malcolm Johnson that exposed corruption in a longshoremen's union that represented New York–area dockworkers. In the film, which takes place on the New Jersey side of the East River, Marlon Brando plays Terry Malloy, an ex-boxer who works on the docks. His life is complicated by his brother Charley's involvement with the local union and its ruthless boss, Johnny Friendly (Lee J. Cobb). Unknowingly, Terry sets up the killing of a dockworker who was about to testify to federal investigators about corrupt labor practices by union leaders. His life gets even more

Father Barry (Karl Malden, left) tends to the badly beaten Terry Malloy (Marlon Brando), with his distressed girlfriend, Edie (Eva Marie Saint), at his side. *Columbia Pictures / Photofest © Columbia Pictures*

complicated when he falls in love with the dead worker's sister and puts his life at risk when he defies the union by agreeing to testify at a federal hearing.

The Music

On the Waterfront represents Leonard Bernstein's only film score. As with his earlier music for the Broadway musical *On the Town*, Bernstein's score is a mixture of musical genres, with jazz-inflected rhythms combined with music in a more traditional style.

The score is based on four principal themes, the first of which appears during the opening credits. This music is quite unusual because it lacks the orchestral main-title scoring that was typical of American films of that era. Instead, the opening theme begins softly with a pattern of slow-tempo ascending tones played by an unaccompanied French horn. This melody, which is Terry's theme, is repeated by woodwinds and then by flutes with a muted trumpet echoing the flute phrases in the form of a canon (also known as a round).

The film's opening scene, which is set on the docks, establishes the strong-armed rule by union boss Johnny Friendly, who is musically represented by the score's second idea, the union theme. It begins with rhythmically driven drum sounds that lead to a jazz-flavored melody played by an alto saxophone. This idea, which is based on repeated pairs of descending pitches, musically defines the brash character of Friendly and of his gang of thugs that help him maintain his domination over the workers.

This music occurs again after Fr. Barry, a local priest, assembles dockworkers in his church to discuss the problems they are having with their union. When church windows are smashed, a rhythmically charged variation of the union theme accompanies multiple beatings inflicted on the fleeing workers by Friendly's men, who are armed with baseball bats.

The score's most romantic theme begins after Terry rescues Edie from the churchyard and decides to escort her home. As they walk through a park, a solo flute introduces a lyrical melody that frequently includes the interval of an ascending seventh.

This love theme returns in a later scene where Terry shows Edie the pigeons on the roof of the building where her brother kept his coop. First a cello sounds the love theme, then several string instruments play it, followed by a trumpet as the music begins to grow in intensity. This music continues as Edie, who at this point is unaware of Terry's role in her brother's death, agrees to go out with Terry.

Another theme of significance to the plot consists of slow-moving string tones that add a somber mood. This music is prominently featured in the scene where Terry and Edie discover Charley's body hanging on a meat hook. This cue, which is based on a slow-moving repeated pattern of four tones, is one of the most emotionally charged moments in the entire score.

The union theme and Terry's theme are both heard in the film's final sequence in which Terry, after having testified, now confronts Friendly and is badly beaten by Friendly's thugs. During the fight, brass instruments play Friendly's theme with pounding drums as background. When Fr. Barry helps Terry to get on his feet, a solo harp begins Terry's theme, then a vibraphone sounds it. As Terry staggers toward the dock, muted trumpets are added. Finally a big brass statement occurs, as Friendly is snubbed and the workers follow Terry through a sliding door. As the door comes down the film ends with several powerfully accented chords.

A flaw in the scoring occurs in the presentation of the love theme, which is too strongly orchestrated for the scene where Terry simply wants Edie to go out with him. Still, this is a major score and the love theme is one of Bernstein's most romantic creations. Additionally, Terry's theme, especially as it highlights the drama of the film's final scene, is one of the composer's most inspired creations. As a musical means of highlighting Terry's triumph over the corruption that has surrounded him, this final musical cue provides a singularly powerful conclusion to the film. This sequence alone warrants Bernstein's music to have a place among the greatest film scores of all time, and it richly deserves to be included in this book.

Recognition

Ranked number twenty-two on the AFI's list of twenty-five greatest film scores.
Twelve Oscar nominations, including Best Score. Strangely, Bernstein lost but the film did win eight, the most since *Gone with the Wind* in 1939.

Recording

Leonard Bernstein, *On the Waterfront Symphonic Suite*, CBS Masterworks, 1986. Conducted by Bernstein, this was released on vinyl in 1961 and rereleased several more times on the Sony label. No original soundtrack exists.

Bibliography

Hickman, Roger. *Reel Music: Exploring 100 Years of Film Music.* New York: W. W. Norton, 2006.
Secrest, Meryle. *Leonard Bernstein: A Life.* New York: Alfred A. Knopf, 1994.

—LEM

ONCE UPON A TIME IN THE WEST

(1989)
Ennio Morricone

The Film

Directed by Sergio Leone and starring Henry Fonda, Charles Bronson, and Claudia Cardinale, *Once Upon a Time in the West* is a spaghetti western, which, while not being as popular as earlier Leone films, has become a cult classic among film lovers around the globe.

In the violent fictional town of Flagstone in the Wild West, a husband is joined by his new wife, a prostitute. Unfortunately, she finds him murdered upon arrival and enlists the help of a mysterious man to help solve the crime. This man, both a marksman and harmonica player, sets out to find the unknown murderer. It is revealed that a man by the name of Frank is the suspected killer, and the man with the harmonica, along with the outlaw Cheyenne, search for him in pursuit of justice. The film was not nominated for any major awards; a fact that seems inconceivable given its reception and cult status since its release.

Harmonica (Charles Bronson) in a showdown. *Paramount Pictures / Photofest © Paramount Pictures*

The Music

As harmonica man places his harmonica into the mouth of Frank, who moments later lies dead, the nine-minute finale, with very little dialogue or action, is over. The defining factor between tedium and genius? Ennio Morricone's score.

Morricone was a longtime collaborator of Leone's. Unusually, Morricone completed the score before filming had even commenced, using Leone's in-depth direction to guide his musical ideas. Leone then played the music to the characters on set, to inspire their performances and to assist them in getting into character for each shoot.

The music is crucial to the film's success and is widely considered one of Morricone's finest scores. For an epic film of such length, the score is sparse. Morricone wrote only forty minutes of music. However, one of the reasons for the film's critical acclaim was the prominence of the score. While film music's traditional position of importance in a film might be below that of the visual and dialogue, in *Once Upon a Time in the West*, slow, panoramic shots with no dialogue give Morricone's music a chance to shine, and the music is foregrounded. For that reason, it may receive more attention and praise from an audience than a score that is constantly "hidden" below the action or dialogue. The fact that his musical themes are so memorable adds weight to this justification of the praise awarded to his score. Each character in the film has a musical cue, or leitmotif. The Italian singer Edda Dell'Orso provides the theme for Claudia Cardinale's character, using wordless vocals to create an evocative theme for the prostitute.

The film begins without music, using sound effects instead. The sound of a train, grasshoppers in the desert, and a wheel turning softly in the breeze create an atmospheric opening for the audience. Only when harmonica man is introduced do we hear an on-screen harmonica, which is then followed by the musical cue for Frank. From this moment on, the musical cues for each character continue to appear during their respective appearances on screen.

Three musical themes dominate the film. The aforementioned wordless vocals of Dell'Orso; the theme for harmonica man, which is played, not surprisingly, on the harmonica; and a theme performed on banjo for the outlaw Cheyenne. The Dell'Orso vocals are most effective at the start of the film as the camera follows Cardinale's character through the train station into the new town. The music reaches a crescendo and it is clear that the Morricone score will be a key component in the film to come.

Sometimes the solo harmonica plays the theme for harmonica man, but at high points in the film the full orchestra and choir take it. The combination of these themes with cues for more minor characters not mentioned here results in a classic Morricone score that is considered one of his finest. The cue "The Man with the Harmonica" has found its way into popular culture and music, with many films trying to emulate this iconic musical cue to varying degrees of success. The British rock band Muse have sometimes finished their set with the bassist, Christopher Wolstenholme, performing the theme on a harmonica before tossing it into the crowd, further evidence that film music can exist outside the confines of a narrative. This is especially the case for such memorable themes as composed by the gifted hand of Ennio Morricone.

Recognition

As highlighted earlier, the film did not receive any nominations for major awards. However, the score did receive a nomination for an Italian National Syndicate of Film Journalists Award for Best Score.

Recordings

Ennio Morricone, *Once Upon a Time in the West*, Sony Legacy, 1989. This is the official soundtrack and the only one recommended for the full score. Thirteen short but memorable tracks, for a total running time of thirty-four minutes. ****

Ennio Morricone, *Once Upon a Time in the West Soundtrack*, Disky Communications, 1999. This is a compilation album that includes some of Morricone's other film music. Not the complete soundtrack to *Once Upon a Time in the West*, but recommended if some variety is preferred. **

Bibliography

Kehr, Dave. *"Once Upon a Time in the West" When Movies Mattered: Reviews from a Transformative Decade*. Chicago: University of Chicago Press.

—ML

OUT OF AFRICA
(1985)
John Barry

The Film

Directed by Sydney Pollack and starring Robert Redford and Meryl Streep, *Out of Africa* was an outstandingly popular film on its release and retains that enduring acclaim to this day.

The story recounts the life of Karen Blixen (Streep) as she recalls her life in Africa. In 1913 she moves to Nairobi to complete a marriage of convenience. En route to Nairobi, Blixen meets Denys Finch Hatton (Redford), a local big-game hunter. After her marriage of convenience takes a turn for the worse over the subsequent months and ends in divorce, Karen and Denys fall for each other and start living together. However, Denys does not believe in marriage, and despite proclaiming his love to her, he moves out.

A fire at Karen's farm puts her future at risk, and she starts preparing to leave for Denmark. At a sale of her possessions, Denys appears and agrees to fly her to Mombasa, with Karen continuing on to Denmark. Denys's plane crashes, and he dies. After the funeral, Karen becomes an author, writing about her time in Africa.

The film was nominated for eleven Academy Awards, of which it won seven, making it the joint fifth-most-successful film of all time by wins. The winning categories were Best Picture, Best Director, Best Writing, Best Cinematography, Best Art Direction, Best Sound, and Best Music. It was also nominated for six Golden Globes, winning three, and seven BAFTAs, also winning three.

The Music

The score to *Out of Africa* was composed by John Barry. The director praised Barry's score in a BBC documentary, claiming that the music "gave the picture more size than it really had. It gave the picture some kind of real romantic resonance."

The main theme of the film begins with a string crescendo before the famous majestic French horn melody enters for the first time. Barry was a keen user of the

Karen Blixen (Meryl Streep) and Denys Finch Hatton (Robert Redford). *MCA Universal / Photofest © MCA Universal*

French horn in film scores, and it is nowhere more evident than in his two "Africa" films *Born Free* and *Out of Africa.* The horns seem to glide above the strings, before the strings reassert themselves by taking on the second section of the main melody. The horns become an instrument of counterpoint, interjecting the main melody with a beautiful, searching countermelody.

Perhaps the most memorable scene in the film takes inspiration from the main theme, but also adapts it to great effect in the first instance. As Redford and Streep fly over Africa in a small biplane, a bittersweet, romantic, but curiously melancholic theme accompanies them. In a scene that has been described quite simply as "gorgeous," the expected heroic, exhilarating music does not materialize. It is elegiac. The beauty of the scene is almost too overwhelming to provide happiness and acts as a foreshadowing of mourning for the lost landscape as well as the death that will later occur. Barry has even been described as the third actor in this scene. It "enriches the visuals" and "exults in a moment and mourns in its fleetingness." It is the sort of scene that moves an audience deeply, but without causing tears, a scene where the actors long for the moment to last forever, but the music reveals that it will not. Barry's score shows restraint and refrains from "an emotional bloodbath" as the director referred to it. "John," the director continued, "found a wonderful way to be unashamed of the emotion, but controlled it." It is a big, epic score, but not in a clichéd or extravagantly emotional fashion. It is guarded against excessive sentimentality and offers just the right amount of poignancy to have a deep impact on the audience without pushing it at us. Barry compared his work on *Out of Africa* to his James Bond film work, claiming that in Bond films, the music follows the action and is more bombastic and in-your-face. In *Out of Africa*, he explains, he wanted to "capture the love story [. . .] the feeling between those two people—that's what I write about. And when they go in that plane and she puts her hand back, to me it was a golden moment, when it was just the communication between them. I mean, that broke my heart. That is what the whole movie is about." Barry acknowledges that he enjoys writing sad music, claiming that it's a wonderful thing to break people's hearts with instrumental music. With *Out of Africa*, and that one scene in particular, I think we can safely say mission accomplished. Barry's heartbreaking score is fully worthy of its Academy Award and its place in this book as one of the 100 greatest film scores of all time.

Recognition

Academy Award for Best Original Score.
Golden Globe for Best Original Score.
Nominated for a BAFTA for Best Score.
Voted fifteenth in the American Film Institute's top twenty-five film scores of all
     time.

Recording

John Barry, *Out of Africa*, Varese Sarabande, 1997/2013. This eighteen-track studio
     recording by the Royal Scottish National Orchestra is heartily recommended. A
     score that deserves to be listened to over and over again. ****

Bibliography

Handy, Bruce. "The Man Who Knew the Score." *Vanity Fair*, February 2009. Accessed November 24, 2017. https://www.vanityfair.com/culture/2009/02/john-barry200902.

—ML

P

THE PIANO

(1993)
Michael Nyman

The Film

Directed by Jane Campion and starring Holly Hunter, Harvey Keitel, Sam Neill, and Anna Paquin, *The Piano* is a dramatic film set in New Zealand during the nineteenth century.

Ada (Hunter) and her daughter, Flora (Paquin), along with all their belongings, including a piano, are deposited on a New Zealand beach after Ada is sold into a marriage to Alisdair Stewart (Neill). Ada is a mute Scottish woman who expresses herself through her piano playing and through sign language. Alisdair tells Ada that there is no room in his house for the piano and leaves it on the beach. Later he agrees to trade it to his friend Baines (Keitel) for some land. Ada is enraged, but a deal is struck where Ada can earn her piano back at a rate of one piano key per "lesson." She agrees, but negotiates for a number of lessons equal to only the number of black keys. Baines tries to seduce Ada during the lessons, but she is reluctant and only allows small increases in intimacy in exchange for more black keys. Baines finally gives up and returns the piano to Ada. Ada finds, however, that she misses Baines and ends up entering into an intimate relationship with him. Alisdair discovers this and cuts off Ada's index finger to stop her playing the piano. But after he hears what he believes to be Ada's voice in his head, Alisdair decides to end the marriage and send Ada and Flora away with Baines.

The film was nominated for eight Academy Awards, winning three for Best Actress in a Leading Role, Best Actress in a Supporting Role, and Best Original Screenplay. It also won one of six Golden Globe nominations and three of ten BAFTA nominations.

The Music

The score to *The Piano* was composed by Michael Nyman. The director asked Nyman for something different from his usual string scores, which stunned the composer, as they were considered his signature. Campion discussed the difficul-

The mute Ada (Holly Hunter) and her daughter Flora (Anna Paquin). *Miramax / Photofest* © *Miramax*

ties of explaining to a composer what was desired, especially when directors often have little music knowledge. She recalls that "when composers discuss music with someone as primitive as myself, they have to talk about it in terms of senses and emotion, rather than keys and tempo. When I wrote the screenplay, even though the piano is an integral character, I heard no music in my head at all." Campion let Nyman work and then asked if he could make a certain cue happier or sadder. After much deliberation, Nyman decided that Scottish folk songs would be a good inspiration, given that Ada was arriving from Scotland.

The music was written with lead actress Holly Hunter in mind. She had not played piano since she was sixteen years old and was considered an amateur at the time of filming. The composer jokes that she was "good at playing slow music and she wasn't good at playing Michael Nyman," so the composer wrote some very slow music especially for Hunter. Every time the piano plays in the film, it is Hunter, not Nyman, who is performing. Because of this, when Nyman is performing his score in public, he makes a conscious effort to perform it as Hunter, to remain authentic to the film. Nyman found it challenging to write a score that was lacking in real energy and tempo, as was his usual style. The composer explains that because Ada communicated through music, he had to consciously alter his style from a twentieth-century male minimalist composer, to a nineteenth-century female performer of emotions.

At all times during the script, the director would ask, "If Ada could speak, what would she be saying?" Nyman then had to write a piece of music that reflected this. The composer would receive an annotated list of scenes, with the emotion required by Campion. This was the moment where Nyman decided that Ada would express herself through Scottish folk music, having heard it at home before travelling to New Zealand. He spent time in London transcribing songs and arranging them for piano or using them for inspiration. The resulting pieces were a type of nineteenth-century salon music, but inflected with minimalist techniques more common to Nyman's usual style of composition. This music worked so well for the character of Ada, that Hunter thanked Nyman when receiving her Academy Award, claiming that it helped her get into character.

The main theme to the film, "The Heart Asks Pleasure First," has become phenomenally popular. It is one of the more minimalist pieces in the film, but it has a flowing, lilting, mesmerizing melody that soars over the top of a relentless ostinato. It is based on the Scottish folk song "Gloomy Winter's Noo Awa."

In summarizing how scoring *The Piano* has affected his career, Nyman claims that it is very much a "pre-Piano" and "post-Piano" split. When receiving commissions, he is sometimes asked for "The Piano sound," which reinforces the impact of this score on the film world, but also the composer himself. As a self-professed minimalist, Nyman claims that scoring this film opened him up to the world of lyricism and melody.

Despite perhaps being one of the simpler scores in this book, *The Piano* has a deserved place among the other ninety-nine scores simply because it is not only musically beautiful but also uniquely functions as a character's voice. The piano, as an instrument, is Ada, and through this, so is Nyman's music, performed by Holly. The music replaces Ada's voice, and so Nyman and Hunter are effectively actors in the film, providing dialogue, albeit in the form of music.

Recognition

Nominated for a Golden Globe for Best Original Score.
Nominated for a BAFTA for Best Score.

Recording

Michael Nyman, *The Piano*, Venture, 1993, 2012. This twenty-track recording has a duration of just over one hour. Recommended as the only official soundtrack release. ****

Bibliography

Tims, A. "How We Made: Michael Nyman and Jane Campion on *The Piano*." *Guardian*, July 30, 2012. Accessed November 24, 2017. https://www.theguardian.com/film/2012/jul/30/how-we-made-the-piano.

—ML

THE PINK PANTHER
(1963)
Henry Mancini

The Film

Directed by Blake Edwards and starring David Niven, Peter Sellers, Robert Wagner, Capucine, and Claudia Cardinale, *The Pink Panther* is an American comedy film that was a hit.

The Pink Panther, the largest diamond on the planet, is given to child princess Dala (portrayed as an adult by Claudia Cardinale) by her father. The film flashes forward twenty years, where British thief Sir Charles Lytton (David Niven) aims to take the diamond from the vacationing Dala. In a comedic twist, Lytton's nephew, George (Robert Wagner), is also within reach of Dala, eyeing up the diamond for himself. After stealing it, he intends to place the blame on the mysterious thief, the "Phantom," unbeknownst to him that the Phantom is in fact his uncle, Lytton. Adding yet more humor to the film is the hopeless French police offer Jacques Clouseau (Peter Sellers), who, in yet another twist, does not realize that his wife Simone (Capucine) is the lover of Lytton. Clouseau tries and fails spectacularly to stop the attempted thefts, and the film evolves into a cat-and-mouse, cloak-and-dagger story line whereby each character is avoiding the next, not realizing the amount of double crossing and betrayal that is occurring. After Lytton and George are eventually caught, a final twist reveals that Dala stole the Pink Panther from her own safe, leaving Lytton, George, and Simone to escape unreprimanded.

The film was nominated for an Academy Award for Best Original Score, and Peter Sellers was nominated for a Golden Globe and BAFTA for Best Actor.

The Music

The score to *The Pink Panther* was composed by Henry Mancini, a highly successful film composer who earned four Academy Awards, a Golden Globe, and twenty Grammys in his lifetime. The main theme to the film (and the subsequent sequels and spin-offs) is known worldwide and has been described as "the ultimate in big screen crime jazz." The theme "oozes danger and intrigue" as it kicks in on piano, bass, and vibraphone. The saxophone is smoky, the music is bluesy, and it has a charming, comedic sleaze factor that contributes toward the silky-smoothness of the film's characters. It is sly and witty to the extreme.

That Mancini chose to write in such a way is intriguing. Rather than score the film as a pure thriller, a glamour show, or a comedy, he saw it "as a series of separate scenes to be charmed by isolated jazz-pop melodies." The way David Niven's character sneaked in and out of hotel rooms, safecracking, and seducing women (in a proto-James Bond role, it could be said) inspired the jazzy theme in E minor so familiar to audiences today. His saxophone-playing colleague Plas

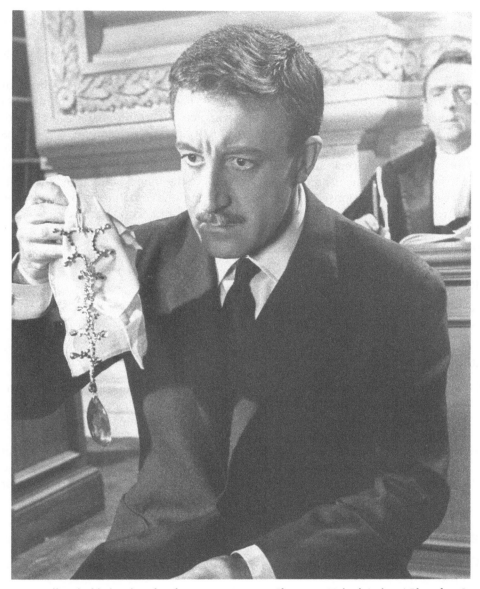

Peter Sellers in his iconic role of Inspector Jacques Clouseau. *United Artists / Photofest* © *United Artists*

Johnson provided the "throaty" sounds for the main theme, a result of Mancini "seeing scores in sounds" and writing the score with particular performers in mind. Mancini was adamant that he did not want a "funny" score for a funny film. On the surface, this might seem illogical, but the composer saw funny scores as redundant and even destructive to the visual comedy. Instead, Mancini wrote a witty theme, but not one that is a joke; a unique theme, but not purely a novelty number. It is a "seriously swinging piece of jazz-pop with an invigorating sense of fun and sophistication." For this reason, the comedy is not doubled up. The music is there to add a smooth commentary to the already funny narrative. The actors are doing the funny business, and the music is buttering the proverbial bread.

The opening sequence introduces us to the theme, which is the subject of variations and adaptations as the film goes on. The now famous ascending bass line underscores an animated opening sequence, where the actor's names are accompanied by the guttural sounds of Plas Johnson's saxophone. As well as the main theme being adapted throughout the film, the other half of Mancini's score uses "generic cocktail Muzak" to move along the narrative. This almost inconsequential music is nonetheless essential to the mood of the film, and it offers restraint when opposed to the ubiquitous and unavoidable main jazz theme. The two combine to create a truly memorable score and one that deserves its twentieth position in the American Film Institute's top twenty-five film scores of all time list.

Recognition

Nominated for Academy Award for Best Original Score.
Nominated for Grammy for Best Original Score.

Recordings

Henry Mancini, *The Pink Panther*, Diamond Records, 2016. This recording contains twelve tracks with just over a half hour of music. Some reviewers claim the quality is not as high as some older recordings, but as the most up-to-date official soundtrack album, it is still recommended. ***
Henry Mancini, *Ultimate Pink Panther*, SBME, 2004. This compilation album of several Pink Panther movie scores is one to recommend for the collector who wishes to hear more than just the 1963 score. Twenty-four tracks spread over seventy-one minutes. ***

Bibliography

Caps, J. *Henry Mancini: Reinventing Film Music*. Urbana: University of Illinois Press, 2012.
Spencer, K. *Film and Television Scores, 1950–1979: A Critical Survey by Genre*. Jefferson, NC: McFarland, 2008.

—ML

PIRATES OF THE CARIBBEAN: THE CURSE OF THE BLACK PEARL

(2003)
Hans Zimmer and Klaus Badelt

The Film

The first in a long-running, successful series of films, *Pirates of the Caribbean: The Curse of the Black Pearl* is unique in cinema history for being the only film to be inspired by a theme park ride, rather than vice versa. Directed by Gore Verbinski, it introduced the world to the swashbuckling, permanently drunk, slightly perverse character of Captain Jack Sparrow (Johnny Depp).

Set in the early 1700s, Sparrow meets Elizabeth Swann (Keira Knightley), who is destined to be married to Commodore James Norrington. Sparrow encounters Will Turner (Orlando Bloom) for the first time, and they duel. Jack is captured and imprisoned. The same night the *Black Pearl*, a pirate ship, attacks the town, and its captain (Geoffrey Rush) takes Elizabeth prisoner.

Elizabeth learns that after the *Black Pearl*'s crew stole cursed treasure, they were forced to bear the curse of undeath, appearing as decomposed corpses in the

Johnny Depp as Jack Sparrow and Orlando Bloom as Will Turner. *Walt Disney Pictures / Photofest © Walt Disney Pictures*

moonlight. To lift the curse, they need to return all the treasure, with a medallion owned by Elizabeth being the final piece. Meanwhile, Jack and Will form a tenuous alliance to rescue Elizabeth. The remainder of the film sees a love triangle developing between Jack, Will, and Elizabeth and the eventual lifting of the curse from the crew of the *Black Pearl*. Jack escapes execution by sailing off on the *Black Pearl*, with Norrington pledging to pursue him as the film draws to a close.

The film was expected to be a flop, but after a relatively slow start at the box office, it eventually grossed well over $600 million worldwide, placing it just outside the list of the 100 highest-grossing films of all time. Importantly, it prompted a host of sequels, which performed even better, three being among the top forty highest-grossing films and the other comfortably in the top seventy-five. The film was also responsible for propelling Johnny Depp into the mainstream, as he had been a mainstay of cult films before his role as Jack Sparrow.

The film was nominated for five Academy Awards, a Golden Globe, and five BAFTAs, of which it won one for Best Makeup and Hair.

The Music

The score to the first in the *Pirates of the Caribbean* series was composed by Hans Zimmer and Klaus Badelt. Alan Silvestri was originally commissioned to write the score, but left the project due to creative differences with producer Jerry Bruckheimer. Hans Zimmer declined composing the majority of the score, as he was contracted to do another film at the time. He recommended Klaus Badelt to the film's producers. For one reason or another, Zimmer actually did write most of the primary themes, and did so in one night. He recalls, "Well, it is a pirate movie, so [. . .] I spent a day and a half writing tunes, Klaus Badelt wrote a lot of stuff, and we rolled up our sleeves, got drunk, behaved in a debauched way, and produced a score!" Due to time constraints, a team of composers (including Ramin Djawadi, later of *Game of Thrones* fame) was brought in to orchestrate Zimmer's melodies. Zimmer described the process as "very collaborative and a great panic, because it was a last-minute rescore."

Unusually for a score in this book, it was heavily criticized. Described as a "schizophrenic pastiche of Hollywood excess" by one review, the chaotic, swashbuckling, relentless smorgasbord of sound is, it could be argued, one of the reasons the score is so highly regarded. Another review claims it is "brainless film music" of "brute masculinity," and accuses Zimmer of "imbecilic regurgitation" of his other music. While these reviews have to be acknowledged, it is perhaps an overly critical assessment of music for a film based on an amusement park ride that parodies a genre of films produced in the previous century. The music is sometimes Korngoldian in style (see *The Sea Hawk*) when depicting the pirate narrative, but in fact,where Badelt and Zimmer's score excels is in its variety. It is undoubtedly a fun romp through the life of a drunken pirate, but the lighter, more tender moments reveal a much different musical palette. The bombastically excessive "He's a Pirate" theme gives way to cues such as "The Underwater March," which has achingly beautiful harmonic progressions and a feeling of real poignancy.

The score to *Pirates of the Caribbean* will not, and did not, please everybody, but it is difficult to deny that the music played an essential role in the film's extraordinary success and deserves a place in the top 100 film scores. Korngold may hold the crown for a more consciously Romantic approach to underscoring piracy on the high seas, but Badelt and Zimmer certainly conjure up the joviality and grandiloquence that a resurrection of the genre inspires and that is more in tune with the sensibilities of twenty-first-century audiences. It does the score a disservice to claim the main theme is a "tepid little thirty-second jig," as posited by one reviewer.

Recognition

ASCAP Film and Television Music Awards: Top Box Office Films (Klaus Badelt).
Nominated for Online Film Critics Society Award for Best Original Score.
Nominated for a Saturday Award for Best Music.
Nominated for World Soundtrack Award for Best Original Soundtrack of the
    Year.

Recording

Hans Zimmer, *Pirates of the Caribbean: The Curse of the Black Pearl / Dead Man's Chest*, EMI, 2011. This combines the first two films in the series into one recording. Slightly cheap casing, but the recording is recommended. ***

Bibliography

Filmtracks. "Editorial Review: *Pirates of the Caribbean: The Curse of the Black Pearl*." July 22, 2003. http://www.filmtracks.com/titles/pirates_caribbean.html.
Goldwasser, Dan. "Breaking the Rules with Hans Zimmer." *Soundtrack.net*, September 6, 2006. https://www.soundtrack.net/content/article/?id=205.
Goldwasser, Dan. "The Honor of Composing." *Soundtrack.net*, December 17, 2003. https://www.soundtrack.net/content/article/?id=112.

—ML

PLANET OF THE APES

(1968)
Jerry Goldsmith

The Film

Directed by Franklin J. Schaffner and starring Charlton Heston and Roddy McDowall, *Planet of the Apes* is the first in the series of nine films (at the time of writing), consisting of either sequels or remakes. The screenplay was loosely based on the 1963 novel *La Planète des Singes* by Pierre Boulle.

Almost two millennia in the future, a spaceship originating from Earth crashes on an alien planet. The crew members remark on its similarities to their own planet, seemingly lightyears away. The inhabitants, an ape-like species, kill one of the crew, and the others are taken captive and sent to the ape city for trial. One of the surviving crew befriends a female ape, and they escape the city together, only to find a destroyed Statue of Liberty on a beach, leading to the famous plot twist that they have actually returned to a future Earth, with humans ostensibly extinct.

The film was nominated for two Academy Awards, for Best Costume Design and Best Original Score. It also won an honorary award for John Chambers for his work on the film's extraordinary makeup.

Human George Taylor (Charlton Heston, center) is on trial, while in the foreground Zira (Kim Hunter) and Cornelius (Roddy McDowall) plead his case. *20th Century Fox Film Corporation / Photofest © 20th Century Fox Film Corporation*

The Music

The score was composed by Jerry Goldsmith. Goldsmith chose the bold and brave course of creating an avant-garde score for the film, which later turned out to be a monumentally successful decision. As Fitzgerald and Hayward explain, "Goldsmith opted for a score that incorporated numerous challenges to what film audiences might typically have considered musically 'normal.' In place of tonal harmony is dissonance and atonality; instead of traditionally countered melodies, there are unpredictable, angular melodic ideas. The score avoids regular beats and rhythms (apart from times when a rhythm pattern provides emphasis to a dramatic orchestration), and the orchestration is characterized by unusual textures and timbres." This unusual approach to scoring added to the otherworldliness and uneasiness experienced not only by the on-screen characters, but also by the audiences. Indeed, Goldsmith remains one of the very few film composers to risk adopting serialism (a twentieth-century avant-garde compositional technique) to film music. Even today it would be seen as completely out of the ordinary to hear such a score.

The foregrounding of the score at times resulted in the audience being challenged by the unique sound. For many, it would have been their first time hearing such dissonant and ostensibly nonsensical music. In fact, it is fairly well-known that Goldsmith used kitchen crockery as instruments as well as unusual techniques on traditional instruments, such as blowing through the mouthpiece of a French horn without the horn attached. Goldsmith also raided the sound effects instrument collection of an old friend who worked at Disney on cartoons. He used them to create unusual percussive sounds. The opening scenes of the film, showing the landscape of the strange planet for the first time, have almost no dialogue and rely on music and sound effects to provide the audial element of the film. The music is consciously placed at the forefront of the sound world to encourage the audience to feel a certain way about the uncertainty of the exploration. To avoid the music being too alien to the audiences, Goldsmith decided against the use of electronics, which were at this time becoming more popular in film composition and the popular music world. Instead, he worked to "ingeniously mix futurism and primitivism," to create a score that, according to Jeff Bond, "seems to emerge quite naturally out of the alien but strangely recognizable simian world." The only electronics used were to provide some slight echo on string lines to add an ominous feel to a few musical cues. Otherwise, it was a traditionally recorded score on acoustic instruments.

In a film fairly saturated with music, it is particularly interesting to note the decision not to score the final scene or the end credits, at the shocking revelation that the planet is actually Earth. The composer explains: "It was such a dramatic moment, and one had to have faith in the drama that was on the screen. The audience didn't need to be pushed any more—it worked, and it worked beautifully. Heston was very dramatic there, a little bit over-the-top maybe, maybe not; I don't know . . . but anything more would have been adding too much to it, so we just decided to play with just the sound effects, and let sound effects play over the credits, and it worked very well."

On a commentary accompanying the DVD of the film, Goldsmith says, "People ask me why I haven't written something like that again, and it's because they haven't made that kind of picture. I haven't been presented with this kind of a film." The unique aesthetic of *Planet of the Apes* resulted in one of the most unusual scores in this book, but there are few scores more deserving of a place in the top 100 than this. It threw out the rulebook of film scoring and was overwhelmingly successful in doing so.

Recognition

Nominated for an Academy Award for Best Original Score.

Recording

Jerry Goldsmith, *Planet of the Apes*, Varese Sarabande, 1997. This rerelease of the original official album is worth the purchase, simply to revel in the eighteen tracks of Goldsmith's quite unique score. ****

Bibliography

Bond, J. "Comment of the Apes: Jerry Speaks, We Listen." *Film Score Monthly* 9, no. 4 (2004): 10–13.
Fitzgerald, Jon, and Philip Hayward. "The Sound of an Upside-Down World: Jerry Goldsmith's Landmark Score for Planet of the Apes (1968)." *Music and the Moving Image* 6, no. 2 (2013): 32–43.

—ML

THE PRISONER OF ZENDA

(1937)
Alfred Newman

The Film

The most acclaimed adaptation of Anthony Hope's novel *The Prisoner of Zenda* is David O. Selznick's 1937 film in which Ronald Colman appears as both Rudolf V of Ruritania and his British look-alike cousin, Rudolf Rassendyll. By sheer coincidence the British cousin is vacationing in Ruritania on the eve of the royal coronation. When the monarch hosts a party in his royal hunting lodge at Zenda and suddenly becomes indisposed, his two loyal companions persuade their English guest to impersonate the prince at the impending coronation.

Rassendyll manages to fool everyone except the prince's half-brother, Michael, who has hired the roguish Rupert of Hentzau to drug the prince and thus help Michael to become king. Meanwhile, Princess Flavia (Madeleine Carroll) wonders why the newly crowned monarch seems so unlike the royal cousin to whom she is betrothed. When Rassendyll learns that the rightful heir has been kidnapped, he is persuaded to continue the pretense indefinitely.

The Music

Selznick expected Max Steiner to score *Zenda*, but since Steiner had just signed a contract with Warner Bros., he was unavailable. Through Steiner's recommendation, Alfred Newman inherited the project and also composed a logo motif for

Major Rudolph Rassendyll (Ronald Colman) poses as royalty with Princess Flavia (Madeleine Carroll). *MGM / Photofest © MGM*

Selznick's newly formed company that consists of a dramatic series of chime tones and orchestral chords.

Following this motif the film's title appears onscreen along with a military formation of over thirty uniformed trumpeters sounding a rousing fanfare accompanied by dramatic snare-drum rolls. This fanfare, which recurs throughout the film, leads into the remaining credits, accompanied by the Zenda theme, a lively idea for strings (plus a hint of the trumpet fanfare). The film's lilting love theme is played by strings, French horns, and harp, with a seven-note motif comprised of mostly descending tones, then continues softly during the explanatory crawl.

Following the crawl, the Zenda theme returns as a map of Europe appears to reveal the location of the fictional country of Ruritania somewhere east of Austria.

In the film's opening scene, when Rassendyll arrives by train at Strelsau, the country's capital, people are stunned by his appearance (since he looks so like the monarch). The trumpet fanfare returns briefly as he leaves the station, and the camera zooms in on a wall poster of Rudolf V that clearly reveals Rassendyll's physical resemblance to the monarch.

When Colonel Zapt and Captain Fritz von Tarlenheim, the monarch's trusty companions, find Rassendyll napping under a tree while fishing, strings softly introduce another theme, a march idea that figures prominently in later scenes.

One of the film's musical highlights occurs in the coronation scene, which includes a veritable smorgasbord of musical ideas, starting with the trumpet fanfare that is heard when the "prince" arrives at the cathedral. The ceremony itself begins with soft organ music followed by a piece borrowed from Handel, the chorus "See, the Conquering Hero Comes," from the oratorio *Judas Maccabaeus*. As the crowning takes place the march theme is sounded by an organ, followed by a repetition of the trumpet fanfare. When Flavia steps forward to pledge her loyalty, there is a lovely unaccompanied piece for a wordless choir of female voices. The scene concludes with a joyous short choral piece and another triumphant sounding of the fanfare.

A musically noteworthy scene occurs soon after the ceremony, when the Zenda theme underscores Flavia's reminiscence to the "king" about their previous meetings. As they talk behind closed doors, the love theme returns in a lovely arrangement for strings with a solo violin that adds a lilting countermelody. This theme especially enhances the moment when the "king" and Flavia begin to show signs of mutual affection.

The march returns in ceremonial style at the beginning of the grand ball when the royal couple walk down a long staircase. As they proceed, the camera backs away until the massive ballroom comes into full view, with the march adding a regal musical accompaniment.

The ballroom scene prominently features "Artist's Life," a waltz by Johann Strauss Jr., which is begun four times but is never concluded, because each time the music starts the "king" stops dancing in order to talk with Flavia, who explains to him that when the monarch stops dancing the music halts.

One of the film's most romantic moments occurs in the next scene as the royal couple walk onto the terrace. When they kiss, the love theme provides a lyrical background that includes the sweet melodic tones of a solo violin.

The score is somewhat motivic, with a playful woodwind idea associated with Rupert and a sweet motif for violins connected with Antoinette de Mauban, Michael's devoted lover, who begs him to stop trying to seize the throne. Michael is musically represented by an ominous variation of the fanfare played by low brass.

Newman's score, with its many grandiose and romantic themes, makes a huge contribution to *Prisoner of Zenda*. As one of the composer's most melodiously inspired works, his music clearly deserves a place of distinction in this book.

Recognition

Two Oscar nominations, including one for Newman's score.
Admiration for the film resulted in MGM's 1952 remake, a virtual scene-for-scene makeover using basically the same script along with the recycled Alfred Newman score.

Recordings

Richard Kaufman, New Zealand Symphony Orchestra, *Wuthering Heights: A Tribute to Alfred Newman*, Koch International Classics, 1997. This CD includes a rerecorded seven-minute suite from *Zenda*. Good sound. ***½
Alfred Newman, *The Prisoner of Zenda*, Film Score Monthly, 2005. This CD is the soundtrack of the 1952 remake, with Newman's music updated by Conrad Sa-

linger. No soundtrack exists from the 1937 film. Good sound, but no match for the original interpretations by Newman himself. ***

Bibliography

Thomas, Tony. *The Great Adventure Films*. Secaucus, NJ: Citadel Press, 1976.

—LEM

PSYCHO

(1960)
Bernard Herrmann

The Film

Directed by Alfred Hitchcock and starring Anthony Perkins and Janet Leigh, *Psycho* is regarded as one of the finest horror films ever produced and one of prolific director Hitchcock's more effective films. Indeed, Hitchcock is often referred to as a director of horror films, despite most of his creative output not falling in this genre.

Marion Crane (Janet Leigh) and Sam Loomis (John Gavin) are having a passionate affair but are unable to marry for financial reasons. When Marion is handed $40,000 in cash to take to the bank for her employer, she runs away with the intention of marrying Loomis in California. As the weather on her long journey becomes treacherous, she decides to stay in a motel for the night. The Bates Motel, run by namesake Norman Bates (Anthony Perkins), is the scene of the memorably disturbing shower murder scene—one of cinema's most iconic moments. It is revealed, after many suspects are interrogated, that Norman murdered Marion while suffering from an alternate personality disorder. The film was nominated for four Academy Awards, and Janet Leigh won a Golden Globe for Best Supporting Actress. Adjusted for inflation, it is approximately the 150th highest-grossing film in American film history.

The Music

The score to *Psycho* was written by Hitchcock's longtime collaborator, Bernard Herrmann. The composer and director had a close, trusting, sometimes tempestuous relationship, and the composition process for this film was no different. The score is considered "perhaps Herrmann's most spectacular Hitchcock achievement." The film had a low budget, but Herrmann refused to lower his fee. Instead, he opted for fewer musicians. Rather than write a jazz score, which Hitchcock had requested, Herrmann decided on a string-only ensemble. The composer wanted to complement the black-and-white photography with a "black-and-white score." The fact that the more brutal aspects of the score were produced only by strings, without the usual backup of the forceful brass or percussion, makes Herrmann's

Just taking a shower: Janet Leigh as Marion Crane. *Paramount Pictures / Photofest © Paramount Pictures*

score even more astounding. Composer Fred Steiner understood Herrmann's "black-and-white score" analogy, stating, "When the expressive range of the strings orchestration is compared to that of black-and-white photography, Herrmann's analogy becomes perfectly clear. Both have the capability within the limits of one basic colour of delivering an enormous range of expression and of producing a great variety of dramatic and emotional effects."

The score to *Psycho* almost did not exist. Hitchcock was adamant that he did not want music in the film, but Herrmann's persuasiveness eventually altered the director's viewpoint. The most famous scene in the film was also originally intended to be musically silent. Such was the impact of Herrmann persuading Hitchcock to use music that it saved the film. The director was on the verge of giving up on the film and dividing it up into television episodes, but Herrmann's music for the shower scene made him change his mind. "Do what you like," said Hitchcock to Herrmann before the Christmas vacation, "but only one thing I ask of you: please write nothing for the murder in the shower. That must be without music." Herrmann was astonished and promptly ignored Hitchcock's request. When the two returned in the new year, Herrmann played the scene to Hitchcock without any music and then said, "I really do have something composed for it, and now that you've seen it your way, let's try mine." After hearing it Hitchcock replied, "Of course, that's the one we'll use." When the composer reminded him that he had absolutely requested no music, the director dryly replied, "improper suggestion, my boy, improper suggestion."

The stabbing, percussive sound of the strings in the shower scene has been described as representing "terror" and "primordial dread," and is now undoubtedly one of the most famous musical cues in the history of cinema. The music is the film, and the film is the music. One cannot exist without the other. It reiterates the point that Herrmann's stubbornness and Hitchcock's rare willingness to back down and admit he was wrong saved the film. The cue has been described as having undertones of Bartok or Stravinsky and representing for audiences in 1960 bleak terror, "icy modernity," and nightmarish apprehension.

The score takes the audience on a "stomach-churning roller-coaster ride" of emotions, as it slashes its way through dissonance and upsets musical conventions by foregrounding string music not as lush, romantic melodies, but as grim violence. It is anti-Romantic. It is a constant bad mood represented in musical form.

The success of Herrmann's score has produced numerous pastiches and parodies, from *The Simpsons* to a disco remix. While these homages are undoubtedly compliments to Herrmann's music, perhaps the biggest compliment the composer could receive was from Hitchcock himself, who claimed that a third of the film's power came from music. From a traditionally stubborn director with very concrete views on how his films should look and sound, this admission of the effect of music in film is praise indeed.

Recognition

Remarkably, Herrmann's score was not nominated for any major or minor awards.

Recording

Bernard Herrmann, *Psycho*, Varese Sarabande, 1997/2013. This forty-track, one-hour album is a comprehensive collection of the musical cues from the film. The Royal Scottish National Orchestra perform wonderfully. Well recommended. ****

Bibliography

Palmer, Christopher. *The Composer in Hollywood*. London: Marion Boyars, 1990.
Sullivan, Jack. *Hitchcock's Music*. New Haven, CT: Yale University Press, 2006.

—ML

Q

QUO VADIS

(1951)
Miklós Rózsa

The Film

Eight years before the widescreen remake of *Ben-Hur*, MGM made another grandiose epic based on an acclaimed literary work, namely *Quo Vadis*, which relates the conflict between imperial Rome and the early Christian converts in the first century AD.

The film's plot involves Marcus Vinicius (Robert Taylor), a Roman commander whose military conquests earn him the admiration of Emperor Nero (Peter Ustinov). But when Marcus becomes infatuated with a Christian woman named Lygia (Deborah Kerr), he risks his position as a Roman soldier by attempting to rescue her and her family from the fire that Nero has capriciously ordered so that he can carry out his architectural plan for a new Rome. The burning of the city leads to the persecution of the Christians, who have been made scapegoats for Nero's deadly conflagration. Ultimately, Marcus must choose between his loyalty to Rome and his love for a woman whose faith is totally foreign to his pagan beliefs.

The Music

Rózsa's score is a skillful combination of musical styles. According to the writer of the film's souvenir booklet, Rózsa used music with a Greek influence for scenes with Nero, while old Hebraic melodies inspired the chanting heard in the Christian rituals. Music based on Greek and Sicilian sources was also used in creating the melodic ideas for the film's military processions.

To create a musical spectrum that would reflect the film's ancient setting, Rózsa chose to set his principal thematic ideas in old church modes, especially the Dorian mode (equivalent to the scale of D minor with the all-natural pitches of D-E-F-G-A-B-C-D). Rózsa also used parallelism in the harmony to reflect the story's ancient setting.

Roman commander Marcus Vinicius (Robert Taylor) has fallen in love with Lygia (Deborah Kerr), a devout Christian. *MGM / Photofest © MGM*

The first Dorian idea appears in the opening credits, where a trumpet fanfare is followed by a dramatic sounding of a five-note motif that is associated with the Romans. This is soon followed by the choral singing of the words "Quo vadis, Domine," which is based on a six-note motif that reflects the Christian element in the film.

The Roman motif is heard in one of the film's first scenes when an angered Marcus rides in his chariot to the royal palace to protest Nero's edict that Marcus's soldiers must remain encamped outside the city until the other armies arrive.

These two motifs are incorporated into a score that also includes a love theme that is introduced when Marcus first meets Lygia, the daughter of an enslaved king, who lives with a retired Roman general's family that offers hospitality to Marcus while he awaits a formal military entry into Rome. At Marcus's first sighting of Lygia the strings play a lyrical melody based on four ascending tones. This melodic idea recurs whenever this handsome couple is seen together.

This love theme is heard during their second meeting, when Marcus observes Lygia drawing a fish (a secret symbol used among the early Christians). As they talk, a solo violin adds a lilting quality to this theme, especially when she admits her attraction for Marcus, despite her strong rejection of Rome's policy of military conquest.

Music of a celebratory nature is heard in several scenes, including a moment when the vestal virgins sing a song of praise to Nero. This is soon followed by a rousing minor-key march theme that accompanies Marcus and his legion of soldiers. At the high point of the procession the Roman motif is sounded by brass.

A second love theme in the score is associated with Nero's loyal adviser Petronius, whose servant, Eunice, proclaims her love for him and stays loyally by his side as his relationship with Nero deteriorates over the emperor's plan to rebuild Rome. The strings add a lyrical sound to this theme whenever it occurs.

When Marcus hears that Rome is ablaze, the Roman motif dramatically recurs as he speeds off in a chariot to find Lygia. During the subsequent chase, when two charioteers are ordered to stop Marcus from going into Rome, the music becomes very turbulent, with brass sounding the Roman motif while drums and swirling woodwinds add to the excitement.

The fire scene, while a truly spectacular segment of the film, is devoid of music due to the screaming of victims and the sounds of the fire and the destruction that it causes.

Scenes set in a Roman arena include singing by Christian prisoners who seem to joyfully accept their impending deaths. This vocal music, which is devoid of orchestral accompaniment, is melodically consistent with the modal instrumental motifs in the film.

One further theme is heard when Nero realizes the Roman citizens have turned against him. Built on a variation of the Roman motif, the horns sound a dramatic idea in a march-like style that leads to the moment when he strangles his wife. This is followed by a melody for strings built in melodic thirds that occurs when Nero's faithful slave Acte assists him in plunging a dagger into his heart.

In addition to the music heard in the film, Rózsa created an overture and exit music for the film. The overture includes a dynamic version of the Roman motif, while the exit music features a soaring version of the Marcus and Lygia love theme.

Coming early in Rózsa's career at MGM, the score of *Quo Vadis* helped to establish him as the leading composer for films set in the past, including such epics as *Ivanhoe* and *Knights of the Round Table*. Rózsa's painstaking research into ancient musical idioms ultimately led to the Oscar-winning music of *Ben-Hur* (also discussed in this book). With its inspired pageantry and drama, the music of *Quo Vadis* clearly stands as one of Rózsa's finest achievements.

Recognition

Eight Oscar nominations, including Best Picture and Best Original Score.
Highest-grossing film of 1951.
Score included on the AFI list of 100 years of film scores.

Recordings

Miklós Rózsa, *Quo Vadis*, Decca, 1977, Studio Recording with Rózsa conducting the Royal Philharmonic, issued on CD in 1985. Excellent sound. ****
Miklós Rózsa, *Quo Vadis*, Silva Screen. 2012. Recording by Nic Raine and the City of Prague Philharmonic Orchestra and Chorus. Excellent sound. ****

Bibliography

Quo Vadis Souvenir Booklet. New York: Al Greenstone, 1951.

—LEM

R

RAIDERS OF THE LOST ARK

(1981)
John Williams

The Film

Directed by Steven Spielberg and starring Harrison Ford, *Raiders of the Lost Ark* is the first film in the Indiana Jones series, based on a screenplay by George Lucas. In 1936, after just escaping a temple in Peru on an expedition, archaeologist Indiana Jones (Harrison Ford) returns to the less dangerous career of a teacher in a New England college. The Nazis, having been in power for three years, are looking for Jones's old mentor, Abner Ravenwood. Jones concludes that the Nazis are searching for the Ark of the Covenant, which will, according to their beliefs, render their armies invincible. Jones travels to Nepal to search out Abner Ravenwood. There he finds his ex-lover Marion Ravenwood (Karen Allen), his old mentor's daughter, who has in her possession a headpiece that is crucial to the locating of the Ark. It is revealed that her father Abner has died. After Marion refuses to sell the headpiece to Indiana, he leaves, but the Nazis are not far behind and try to forcibly take it from Marion. She and Indiana escape, and the two decide to work together to locate the Ark before the Nazis do. Jones and Marion travel to Cairo, Egypt, not far from the ancient city of Tanis, an area Abner Ravenwood was an expert on, hence the Nazi interest in him.

After finding the Ark in Cairo, Indiana and Marion are ambushed by Colonel Dietrich (Wolf Kahler), who throws them both down a well and seals it up. Managing to escape, they eventually seize the Ark back from the Nazis after much fighting. While sailing back to the United Kingdom, the ship that Indiana, Marion, and the Ark are on is attacked by a Nazi U-Boat, and the Ark is taken to a secret island location in the Aegean Sea with the intention of testing it before it is presented to Adolf Hitler. Jones and Marion follow the Ark, are discovered by the Nazis, and are forced to watch as it is opened. A vortex of flame shoots fire into the Nazi soldiers, killing them instantly. Only Indiana and Marion survive the inferno. The lid seals the Ark shut, and it is sent to Washington, DC, in a crate, where it is to be analysed alongside many other identical specimens.

The film was nominated for nine Academy Awards, winning five of them for Best Art Direction, Best Sound, Best Film Editing, Best Effects, and Sound Effects Editing (special award). It also received one Golden Globe nomination and won two of seven BAFTA nominations.

Harrison Ford as the iconic Indiana Jones in an early scene from *Raiders of the Lost Ark*. Paramount Pictures / Photofest © Paramount Pictures

The Music

The score to *Raiders of the Lost Ark* was composed by John Williams, one of many collaborations he would eventually have with Steven Spielberg. The score was performed by the London Symphony Orchestra and conducted by the composer. Williams's score is considered one of the finest neoclassical film scores, partly because of how it harks back to the Hollywood film scores of the 1930s and 1940s, but also for the inspiration it takes from music of the Romantic period. It was a conscious decision by Williams to take a nostalgic approach to the score, steeped in the aesthetic of the 1930s without becoming an homage. The composer stated, "To discern a 30s mood and express it isn't like doing a pastiche. A pastiche is not that difficult. What is not easy is taking it a stage further and doing the real thing, with some sincerity." In other words, Williams wanted to compose a 1930s film score in 1981, but did not want it to be clichéd, stereotypical, or parodic of actual 1930s scores. He wanted to transfer the stylistic approach to his film scoring. The resulting score is successful because it shows Williams's fondness for earlier works, while still giving the music his own signature sound. The score helped him to cement his place in the film music canon as a natural successor to Max Steiner, one of the Golden Age greats of Hollywood film scoring.

The main theme, and the film's most famous, is the "Raiders March." This theme represents Indiana Jones not only in this film but in the sequels. Williams perceived the heroic march as being a musical theme the viewers would connect with the protagonist. He described it as "a heroic theme that swells when things are going well for our hero, the kind of music that makes the audience want to cheer."

The second key musical theme in the film is "Marion's Theme," often considered the film's love theme. This too recalls the great love themes of the Golden Age of Hollywood, which once more was a conscious decision by the composer. Williams reminisces: "I used to love those old romantic themes in Warner Bros. films like *Now, Voyager*. For the love story between Indiana Jones and Marion I thought that the music could be like one of those '30s themes and that would contrast well with the humor and silliness, even if it is inappropriate emotionally." The use of allegedly "feminine" instruments such as the strings and upper woodwinds helped to create a deeply "feminine" musical theme, and this contrasted heavily with the "masculine," grandiose "Raiders March." Williams also created an eerie theme for the Ark of the Covenant, which is by far the most sinister music found in the film. It is dissonant and harsh and represents well the danger associated with it.

Williams's score to this film, as well as the sequels that followed, contributed significantly to its success. Many of his collaborations with Stephen Spielberg were likewise successful, some of which are also featured in this book.

Recognition

Grammy for Best Original Score.
Nominated for Academy Award for Best Original Score.
Nominated for a BAFTA for Best Original Score.

Recording

John Williams, *Raiders of the Lost Ark*, Concord Records, 1981/2017. This is the official soundtrack release, conducted by John Williams and performed by the London Symphony Orchestra. It is seventy-three minutes in length, spanning twenty-two tracks. ***

Bibliography

Audissino, E. *John Williams's Film Music: Jaws, Star Wars, Raiders of the Lost Ark, and the Return of the Classical Hollywood Music Style*. Madison: University of Wisconsin Press, 2014.
Williams, John. *The Music of Indiana Jones* (DVD). Paramount Pictures, 2003.

—ML

THE RED PONY

(1949)
Aaron Copland

The Film

Many noteworthy films have been scored by composers who are recognized for works other than film music. Among these composers is Aaron Copland, who famously wrote symphonies, concertos, ballet scores, and even operas. He also wrote music for seven films, including Lewis Milestone's *The Red Pony*, the music of which has become one of Copland's most frequently recorded works.

The plot of the film, which John Steinbeck adapted from his own short novel, takes place on a California ranch in the early twentieth century, where young Tommy (Peter Miles) has been promised a colt when the family's mare, Rosie, gives birth. His parents, Alice and Fred Tiflin (Myrna Loy and Shepherd Strudwick) try to raise him to be a rancher, but Tommy is a daydreamer who can imagine himself as a knight in shining armor or a circus performer. Ranch foreman Billy Buck (Robert Mitchum) encourages Tommy's sense of adventure when he shows the boy newspaper accounts of his rodeo exploits. Tommy soon learns that raising a horse is much more difficult than he could have imagined.

From left: Billy Buck (Robert Mitchum), Tom Tiflin (Peter Miles), and Tom's grandfather (Louis Calhern). *Republic Pictures / Photofest © Republic Pictures*

The Music

The film opens with a fanfare-like idea for brass that accompanies the Republic studio logo. This motif, based on a descending pattern of seven notes, leads to a lyrical idea for woodwinds and strings that accompanies a spoken narration about farming in California's Salinas Valley, where the film takes place. This music leads to a repetition of the fanfare, as the cover of the Steinbeck novel comes into view.

The ensuing credits are accompanied by the score's main theme, a lively tune for trumpets based on the tones of a major triad (as in C-E-G), which are repeatedly sounded in an ascending pattern. This music is harmonically repetitive, with only two alternating chords predominating in the background. This theme is purposefully rather childlike and also musically reminiscent of "Jingle Bells," with sleigh-bell sounds sometimes included as percussion effects. The theme continues as morning begins on the Tiflin ranch with Billy brushing down the pregnant horse while Alice prepares breakfast. The music begins to fade, with flutes softly repeating the first tones of the main theme as the family gathers.

A significant secondary theme is a lively motif that accompanies Billy and Tommy as they walk to the bunkhouse where Billy opens a trunk containing his rodeo-riding medals and also a newspaper clipping that he lets Tommy borrow to show his young friends. The downhill progression of the melodic tones, plus the rhythmic syncopation and quintuple meter of this idea are elements of Copland's music that those familiar with his work will recognize as similar in style to themes of his scores for the ballets *Billy the Kid* and *Rodeo*.

Two cues that occur early in the film reveal Tommy's penchant for daydreaming. In the first of these, as Tommy is walking to school he picks up a stick and starts tapping it on his metal lunch pail. At this point snare drum sounds become synchronized with Tommy's tapping. As Tommy turns and walks backwards, he imagines himself and Billy Buck astride horses and wearing suits of armor, with a castle in the distance. The music for this daydream is a pompous-sounding march played by brass, with the metallic tapping sounds continuing throughout the cue.

When Tommy, back from school, stacks logs in the wood box, the main theme returns briefly. Shortly thereafter, while feeding chickens in the coop, Tommy imagines himself as a ringmaster and the chickens as horses in a circus act. The circus music is set in triple meter, with raucous woodwind sounds accompanying a lively theme for brass and drums.

A later scene with noteworthy music occurs after the colt is born and Billy helps Tommy train the young pony, called Gabilan. As the horse gallops around the corral, fast-sounding strings and syncopated harmonies add an energetic western-style music to the scene.

A later scene mirrors an earlier one when Tommy and Billy walk to the stable in the rain, where Gabilan has what appears to be a cold. The bunkhouse theme is now played by flute and strings in a slower tempo that foreshadows the tragic events that lie ahead.

The most dramatic moment in the film arrives when Tommy discovers the body of his beloved pony with vultures attacking the carcass. When Tommy tries to grab a vulture, loud stabbing strings create high intensity as the bird continually pecks at Tommy's face and arms.

Copland's film scores contain some of his finest music. While he won an Oscar for *The Heiress*, also from 1949, *Red Pony* remains Copland's most memorable film composition. This score, which influenced the western scores of Elmer Bernstein, Jerry Goldsmith, and Jerome Moross in the 1950s and 1960s remains a masterful achievement and worthy of being included in this book.

Recognition

Leonard Maltin's *2015 Movie Guide* praises Steinbeck's screenplay and Copland's music.
The *Allmovie* website calls *Pony* "one of the most acclaimed films to emerge from Republic studios."

Recordings

Aaron Copland, New Philharmonia Orchestra, *The Red Pony Suite*, CBS Master-works, 1972. Compilation issued on CD in 1988. Leisurely performed, good sound. ***
Leonard Slatkin, Saint Louis Symphony, *Copland: Music for Films*, RCA Red Seal, 1994. Excellent sound and performance. ****
John Williams and the Boston Pops, *Music for Stage and Screen*, Sony Classical, 1994. Includes *The Red Pony Suite*. Good sound. ***½

Bibliography

MacDonald, Laurence E. *The Invisible Art of Film Music: A Comprehensive History.* Second edition. Lanham, MD: Scarecrow Press, 2013.
Tibbetts, John C., and James M. Welsh. *The Encyclopedia of Novels into Film.* New York: Facts on File, 1998.

—LEM

THE RED VIOLIN

(1999)
John Corigliano

The Film

There have been a few films about inanimate objects. One example is *Winchester '73* (1950), about a stolen rifle; another is *The Yellow Rolls-Royce* (1964), about a deluxe automobile. *The Red Violin* is a unique film in which the principal "character" is a musical instrument.

François Girard's film concerns a violin made in Cremona in 1681 by Nicolo Bussotti (Carlo Cecchi), who crafts it as a gift for his unborn child, but after the

Carlo Cecchi as Nicolo and Irene Grazioli as Anna. *Lions Gate Films, Inc. / Photofest © Lions Gate Films, Inc.*

baby and mother both die in childbirth, Bussotti donates the violin to monks who run an orphanage in Vienna. After many years, roaming gypsies acquire the instrument but eventually trade it to a famous English violinist. After the violinist's suicide, the violin is taken to China and placed in a Shanghai music shop. The violin survives Mao's ban on foreign music and musical instruments by being smuggled out of China. It finally winds up in Montreal, where it becomes the most prized item in an auction of musical instruments. The film covers three hundred years in the life of this priceless violin.

The Music

Excluding a documentary named *A Williamsburg Sampler* (1974), *Red Violin* represents the third feature film scored by renowned composer John Corigliano. As with Aaron Copland, who composed film scores periodically during his career, Corigliano has turned to film work very infrequently. But *Red Violin*'s director Girard explicitly sought Corigliano as the film's composer. His approach to the score was explained in his liner notes to a 2007 recording based on the film's music. In his own words:

> My father John Corigliano (I was a Jr.) was a great solo violinist and the concertmaster of the New York Philharmonic for more than a quarter of a century. My childhood years were punctuated by snatches of the great concertos being practiced by my father, as well as scales and technical exercises. . . . The story of *The Red Violin* . . . spans three centuries in the life of a magnificent but haunted violin in its travels through time and space. A story this episodic needed to be tied together with a single musical idea. For this purpose I used the Baroque device of a chaconne, a repeated pattern of chords upon which the music is built.

The younger Corigliano was obviously well suited to create the voice of the violin in his score, and the resulting music was written expressly for Joshua Bell. The strings are the most featured instruments in the score, with Bell's solo sounds as the "voice" of the red violin.

The chaconne is heard at the very beginning of the film, where a pattern of eight slow-moving chords is played softly, then repeated four more times with increasing volume, until the violin maker Bussotti shows his pregnant wife, Anna (Irene Grazioli) his latest creation, which is not yet shellacked. At this point Anna's theme is introduced by violins, which play a seven-note idea that includes stepwise motion at first, before leaping up a fifth. The pattern of tones, which is based on the Dorian mode, is as follows: D-E—, D-E-F-C-B—. The pauses after the second and seventh tones are characteristic of this motif's rhythmic design throughout the film, and the ascending fifth becomes a significant part of the theme's melodic contour.

This motif appears again when Bussotti observes his wife singing to their unborn child. The motif is then transferred to the violin. The violin that Bussotti has made for his child will haunt those who hear it played over the course of the next three hundred years. It isn't just the motif but the soulful expressiveness of Bell's playing that helps to convey the idea of music so emotionally moving that it haunts those who hear it.

The scenes with the red violin being played feature melodic variations on Anna's motif. This includes scenes in which the violin is played alone and also when an orchestra joins the violin.

The scales and technical etudes to which Corigliano refers in his notes are featured in the second section of the film when a prodigiously talented child named Kaspar Weiss is playing with other boys in an orphans' orchestra in Vienna. A particularly memorable moment occurs when Kaspar's teacher shows him a new gadget he calls a "chronometer," with a pendulum that ticks out the rhythmic beat, like the modern metronome. As the teacher speeds up the ticking sounds, the playing by Kaspar also speeds up and becomes very impressive.

Another memorable moment comes when Frederick Pope, the English violinist who acquires the instrument from gypsies who loiter on his estate, appears in concert and, instead of the scheduled piece with orchestra, plays a solo piece of his own composition, which happens to be one of many variations heard in the film that are based on Anna's motif.

One additional comment concerns the red violin after it is donated to the monks; it is played by one talented youngster after another in a scene edited to suggest the passing of time, with the same players in the background but with different boy soloists in front. Throughout this clever scene, the music continues without interruption in a style suggestive of Antonio Vivaldi's works, but actually conceived by Corigliano to resemble a piece from the eighteenth century.

With the episodic nature of the film and five languages being spoken, Corigliano's music ingeniously unifies the film. The score is basically a single set of musical ideas, but with several melodic variants introduced through the course of the violin's travels. In short, Corigliano's music stands at the pinnacle of film scoring.

Recognition

Several awards won in Canada, where the film was produced.
Oscar for Best Original Score, 1999.

Recordings

Joshua Bell with Marin Alsop and the Baltimore Symphony, *Corigliano: The Red Violin Concerto*, Sony, 2007. The concerto is an expansion of the film's music into a four-movement work. Excellent sound. ****
John Corigliano, Joshua Bell, *The Red Violin*, Sony, 1999. Excellent sound. ****

Bibliography

Bell, Joshua, with Marin Alsop and the Baltimore Symphony. Liner notes. *Corigliano: The Red Violin Concerto*. Sony 82876-88060-2, 2007, CD.

—LEM

THE ROBE
(1953)
Alfred Newman

The Film

Many films have been adapted from best-selling novels, but in the case of *The Robe*, the screen version of Lloyd C. Douglas's book was based on a genuine publishing phenomenon. The hardcover novel topped the charts in 1942 and remained a best seller for the next three years, with the reissue becoming the number-one book again in 1953 when the film was released.

The 20th Century Fox adaptation of *The Robe* became the first widescreen film since the debut of the groundbreaking travelogue film called *This Is Cinerama*, which premiered in specially equipped movie theaters in 1952. *The Robe* was not only the first film released in CinemaScope, but also the first widescreen film to include a narrative storyline.

Douglas's story, set in the first century, concerns a Roman tribune named Marcellus Gallio (Richard Burton), the son of a Roman senator, who is assigned

Diana (Jean Simmons) and tormented tribune Marcellus Gallio (Richard Burton). *20th Century Fox Film Corporation / Photofest © 20th Century Fox Film Corporation*

to Judea, where Jesus of Nazareth is an itinerant preacher and healer. It is Marcellus's fate to not only supervise Jesus's crucifixion but to win the robe, Jesus's outer garment, in a dice game. The robe becomes the source of great torment for Marcellus, whose Greek slave, Demetrius (Victor Mature), disappears with the garment. The film portrays Marcellus's anguish for having put Jesus to death and his bitter conflict with Caligula, the heir to the throne as Rome's next emperor.

The Music

As with Miklós Rózsa's music for MGM's *Quo Vadis* and the 1959 version of *Ben-Hur*, Newman's score for *The Robe* includes brass fanfares that help to establish the ancient setting of the story, which takes place during the Roman occupation of Judea (called Palestine in the film). A dramatic piece for brass and wordless choir sets the context immediately during the opening credits. This solemn music (the robe theme) begins with a melodic motif that consists of a single tone that is sounded five times and followed by a sixth tone of higher pitch.

Several significant themes are introduced in the film's opening slave-market scene in which Marcellus offends Caligula by outbidding the future monarch for ownership of Demetrius. A seven-note motif for trumpets associated with Marcellus is repeatedly sounded during his narration at the beginning of this scene. The next theme starts with the arrival of Caligula, who is musically represented by a march theme for brass and drums that begins with a fanfare-like six-note idea. The motifs for Marcellus and Caligula return many times later in the film.

When Marcellus sees Diana (Jean Simmons), a young woman he remembers from their childhood, the score's most lyrical music (the Diana theme) is introduced by oboe and harp. Other woodwinds, including English horn and flutes, join in sounding this theme, which begins with a seven-note motif that is mostly descending in pitch and rhythmically smooth-flowing.

A musically memorable scene occurs when Marcellus prepares to embark for Judea, thanks to Caligula's decree that reassigns him to the region across the Mediterranean where Jewish patriots are in revolt against the Romans. When Diana appears at the waterfront to say farewell to Marcellus, her theme begins softly with oboe and harp and then evolves into a lyrical statement for strings. The "Newman sound," which is noticeable by the sweetly resonant quality of the high-pitched violins, lends emotional depth to this music. A moment featuring a solo cello also adds a poignant ambience to the cue, which concludes with an intensely romantic version of the theme for strings and French horns, plus the Marcellus motif woven into the orchestration.

Another noteworthy musical moment occurs at around 23:00 into the film, when Marcellus arrives in Judea and witnesses a procession in which a large crowd is following Jesus of Nazareth, who is riding on a donkey toward Jerusalem. A lively choral piece that includes the repeated singing of the word "Hosanna" is heard with an accompaniment that prominently features tambourine and harp and a short trumpet motif in the background. This joyful theme is in striking contrast with the music that comes next.

In the following sequence, when Jesus is bearing a cross through the streets of Jerusalem the music becomes extremely dramatic, with echoes of the robe theme heard during the procession. For the next ten minutes there is virtually nonstop music as Jesus, on the cross, forgives those who put him there, and Marcellus wins Jesus's robe. At this point the music becomes extremely dynamic, with high violins and wordless voices added to the orchestral mix. Moments later, when Demetrius scorns his master and runs off with the robe, the wearing of which results in Marcellus experiencing great anguish, long-held brass chords and a French-horn variant of the robe theme bring the crucifixion scene to a dramatic conclusion.

The Diana theme, which returns several times, is especially noticeable in a scene where the mentally tortured Marcellus is reunited with Diana. Soon thereafter, subdued music with a gentle orchestration occurs when Marcellus is commissioned by Emperor Tiberius to seek out and destroy the robe. In the village of Cana, Marcellus meets a weaver named Justus, and a lilting theme for woodwinds is heard when local merchants are instructed by Justus to return money to Marcellus, who has nonchalantly agreed to overpay for his purchases.

A lyrical piece of source music occurs in the Cana scene when a disabled woman named Miriam sings for the villagers a song about Jesus, with Marcellus overhearing it. The song's accompaniment consists solely of plucked tones on a handheld harp. The melody of this song is then heard in a soft cue for woodwinds and strings when Marcellus learns more about Miriam.

The Robe includes an abundance of musically inspired themes that rank among the best work of Alfred Newman's entire Hollywood career, and therefore this score richly deserves a place in this book.

Recognition

The Robe was a big box-office hit, largely due to the novelty of the CinemaScope widescreen process.

Five Oscar nominations, including Best Picture and Best Actor (Burton). Newman was not nominated, which caused a backlash among Motion Picture Academy members.

Two Oscar wins, for Art Direction and Costume Design.

Inspired a sequel, *Demetrius and the Gladiators*, with Victor Mature reprising his role.

Recordings

Alfred Newman, *The Robe*, Fox Film Scores, 1993. This CD is based on an original stereo soundtrack recording. Regrettably lacks Crucifixion music. Good sound. ***½

Alfred Newman, *The Robe*, Varése Sarabande, 1991. The 1953 studio recording by Newman. Acceptable monaural sound. ***

Bibliography

Sackett, Susan. *The Hollywood Reporter Book of Box Office Hits*. New York: Billboard Books, 1990.

Thomas, Tony. Liner notes. *The Robe*. Fox Film Scores 07822-11011-2, 1993, CD.

—LEM

S

SCHINDLER'S LIST

(1993)
John Williams

The Film

Schindler's List, released in 1993, was a game changer for the Holocaust genre of films. Aside from the hugely influential American television series *Holocaust* (1978), the cataclysmic event had rarely been represented in a commercially successful film. Many films did exist prior to Spielberg's epic tale of redemption and survival, but they did not achieve the same worldwide exposure.

Oskar Schindler is a wealthy businessman, basking in the early successes of the Nazi war effort. Sensing a business opportunity, but also moved by the expulsion of the Jews to ghettos across Poland, Schindler sets up a factory and hires Jews as cheap labor. After witnessing the sadistic ways of the notorious Amon Goeth in the Plaszów labor camp, Schindler's motive moves away from his business and toward a realization that he can use his fortune to buy Jews, thus saving them. The film concludes with Schindler breaking down in tears, regretful that he did not save more Jews.

The film was nominated for twelve Academy Awards and won seven for Best Picture, Best Director, Best Adapted Screenplay, Best Cinematography, Best Art Direction, Best Film Editing, and Best Music. It also won three of six Golden Globe nominations and seven of thirteen BAFTA nominations.

The Music

"You need a better composer than I for this film." "I know, but they're all dead!"

This exchange between John Williams and Steven Spielberg occurred when the esteemed composer was shown the script to Spielberg's new Holocaust film in the early 1990s. The difficulty of the subject material prompted Williams to doubt himself and, more surprisingly, to dissuade him from attempting to score what would become one of Spielberg's most critically acclaimed films.

Itzhak Stern (Ben Kingsley) and Oskar Schindler (Liam Neeson) compiling their list. *Universal Pictures / Photofest © Universal Pictures*

Sometimes film music by itself is as recognizable and revered as the film it accompanies. John Williams's heartrending solo violin theme to *Schindler's List* is arguably one such piece. Performed by the Israeli-American violinist Itzhak Perlman, the evocative melody was undoubtedly the key contributing factor to Williams winning his fifth (and, at the time of writing, latest) Academy Award for Best Original Score. The theme has been appropriated in a number of ways, including by figure skaters for their routines, such is the prominence of the melody in wider society.

However, any acclaimed score owes its success to the sum of its many parts, and the soundtrack of *Schindler's List* should not be defined by one violin theme alone. The inclusion of a wide variety of musical styles and forms benefitted the film, with the audience hearing an eclectic range of music from tango, to German folk songs, to J. S. Bach suites. One of the most effective and poignant musical moments in the film occurs during the liquidation of the Kraków ghetto. Schindler and his girlfriend witness the harrowing scenes from a nearby hill, and the famous "Girl in the Red Coat" is seen for the first time, seeking shelter from the Nazi oppressors. The music used to accompany this scene is the Yiddish folk song "Oyfn Pripetshik." This is a well-known Jewish popular song, with lyrics telling of a Rabbi teaching young children the alphabet. It has a personal significance to the director too, as Spielberg's grandmother frequently sang the song to her grandchildren. The instrumentation of a young children's choir in *Schindler's List* offers a tragic marrying of destructive visuals and childlike innocence in the music.

A further example of the emotional impact of Williams's score is in a scene that depicts the burning of hundreds of Jewish bodies in the labor camp. As the smoke rises and ash falls, Williams underscores the visuals with a piece entitled "Immolation (With Our Lives, We Give Life)." This choral and orchestral piece, which has a religious hymn-like quality, offers an emotive accompaniment to a scene of unimaginable tragedy. The success of Williams's score at moments such as this is that it avoids expansive Hollywood orchestration and the sentimentality and clichés that can sometimes infuse it. Instead, the often understated score provides an emotional, dramatic, yet appropriately sensitive accompaniment to a challenging and distressing narrative. There is no defiance, heroism, or triumph in Williams's score, but instead, a simplistic beauty that is seldom matched in his other film music.

John Williams may be better known for the bombastic scores he created for Hollywood blockbusters such as *Star Wars*, *Jurassic Park*, and *E.T.*, but his most solemn, reflective score is arguably one of his most successful. Despite Williams showing some reluctance to compose for the film, and suggesting that he would find it difficult to score films based on such dark subject matter on a regular basis, Spielberg must have had no doubt that Williams would create a musical score to remember.

Recognition

1993 Academy Award for Best Original Score.
1993 BAFTA Award for Best Film Music.
1995 Grammy Award for Best Score Soundtrack.
1993 Golden Globe nomination for Best Original Score.

Recordings

City of Prague Philharmonic, *100 Greatest Film Themes*, Silva Screen, 2007. Collection of film themes, including *Schindler's List*. ***

John Williams, Boston Symphony Orchestra, Itzhak Perlman, *Schindler's List*, MCA, 1993. The official soundtrack recording, also featuring the Li-Ron Herzeliya Children's Choir. Recorded partly at Symphony Hall in Boston, it remains the unrivalled recording on which to hear the complete soundtrack. ****

John Williams, Pittsburgh Symphony Orchestra, *John Williams: Greatest Hits 1969–1999*, Sony Classical, 1999.***

—ML

SCOTT OF THE ANTARCTIC

(1948)
Ralph Vaughan Williams

The Film

The British *Scott of the Antarctic* may by one of the more obscure films to be featured in this book, but it is indispensible to any thorough study of great film music due to its inclusion of a masterful score by renowned English composer Ralph Vaughan Williams.

This meticulously produced film recreates the ill-fated attempt by British naval commander Robert Falcon Scott (John Mills) to be the first man to reach the South Pole.

The film documents the origin of the expedition, which begins in 1910 when Scott first attempts to raise the funds necessary for the journey. Once he and scientist Edward Wilson (Harold Warrender) procure the financial backing for the expedition, Scott approaches the other men that he needs to assist him in making the historic journey possible.

Captain R. F. Scott (John Mills, with goggles) and P. O. "Taff" Evans (James Robertson Justice).
Eagle-Lion Classics / Photofest © Eagle-Lion Classics

Most of the film is devoted to scenes of the arduous journey by Scott and his twelve-man team that sets sail for the Antarctic continent and then proceeds on land for the last nine hundred miles to reach the southernmost point on the planet. The journey is fraught with unexpected perils, including the breakdown of equipment and the deaths of their horses. Nothing ultimately stops Scott and four of his men from achieving their goal, but unexpectedly turbulent conditions endanger their lives on the way back.

The Music

By the time Ralph Vaughan Williams was asked to score this film, he was a highly accomplished composer of symphonies, operas, and many other types of concert music. He had also created a few film scores, the first of which was composed for *49th Parallel* in 1941. The idea of creating music for the Scott expedition greatly stimulated his musical imagination, and the finished score requires a full symphony orchestra, plus a solo soprano and a small women's choir.

The main theme, which is introduced in the opening credits, consists of a six-note motif that moves up the scale and then back down in a limited pitch range of four tones. This melodic idea prominently features brass instruments that play in a solemn march-like style, with rumbling timpani in the background.

The score's second theme musically invokes the desolate yet impressively beautiful Antarctic landscape, which is seen shortly after the opening credits. Panoramic views of snow and ice are accompanied by an eerie melody that is based on the last part of the opening theme's motif. This theme is sung wordlessly by a solo soprano accompanied by a small group of female voices. The gently descending melodic pattern of this theme seems to suggest that this barren continent is best appreciated from a distance, and woe to anyone who actually attempts to go there.

One of the most dramatic of the early cues accompanies the sighting of the Great Ice Barrier by Scott and his team from the deck of their ship as it proceeds south. Tremolo strings, along with various woodwinds and melodic percussion including the xylophone are heard in this cue. When the barrier is seen in close-up shots, a dramatic series of brass chords and harp glissandos adds a sense of awe to the scene.

At about thirty minutes into the film there is an amusing scene in which penguins are seen cavorting on the ice. Staccato woodwind chords accompany the waddling moves of several penguins; when they begin to slide downhill, tremolo strings suggest the birds' smoothly gliding moves.

Most of the cues in the first hour of the film are extremely brief. The longest one occurs around 56:10 when Scott and his team, now moving on foot, start to climb up a great glacier that separates them from the region closest to the South Pole. As they near the top of this formidably icy formation, the main theme returns with gradually ascending chordal sounds and increasing volume; the scene culminates in a glorious brass statement with rumbling timpani and a final long-held climactic orchestral chord.

A short musical cue accompanies the moment when the team reaches the South Pole. It does not convey a happy sense of accomplishment because of the Norwegian flag that has already been placed at the pole by Roald Amundsen's team. The music conveys a sense of both disappointment and frustration that Scott's team has been unsuccessful in reaching the pole ahead of their rivals.

The later cues are also less optimistic than the earlier ones, since Scott and his fellow adventurers begin to succumb to the effects of dangerously cold weather as they attempt to return from the Pole. The main theme returns several times in later scenes, where it is accompanied by brass chords that have a plodding sameness that reflects the men's increasing difficulty in continuing their return journey.

At the end of the film, when a rescue team finds Scott's journal, confirming his death and that of four members of his team, the main theme is stated triumphantly, with major-key harmonies that celebrate the heroic endeavor of reaching the South Pole, even at the cost of five lives.

Vaughan Williams's score contributes a sense of both adventure and awe to Scott's mission. Instead of concentrating on the human tragedy of the journey, the music underscores the bravery of these men who accomplish what few others have ever dared to attempt. The music ultimately honors their victory in reaching the South Pole and is a testament to the collective courage of Scott and the members of his expedition. Few other film scores have attempted to achieve this degree of musical resonance. This is the finest of Vaughan Williams's eleven film scores and worthy of inclusion in this book.

Recognition

Nominated in 1949 by BAFTA as best picture of 1948.
Third-most-popular film at British box office in 1949.

Recordings

Kees Bakels, Bournemouth Symphony, *Sinfonia Antartica*, Naxos, 1998. Based on the film score. Excellent sound. ****
Rumon Gamba, BBC Philharmonic, *The Film Music of Ralph Vaughn Williams: Scott of the Antarctic, The People's Land, Coastal Command*, Chandos Movies, 2002. Excellent sound. ****

Bibliography

Thomas, Tony. *The Great Adventure Films*. New York: Citadel Press, 1976.

—LEM

THE SEA HAWK

(1940)
Erich Wolfgang Korngold

The Film

Directed by Michael Curtiz and starring Errol Flynn, *The Sea Hawk* was critically acclaimed as a welcome, swashbuckling distraction from the dark realities of the Second World War. *Time* magazine described it as "1940's lustiest assault on the double feature, [with] Errol Flynn and 3,000 other cinemactors performing every imaginable feat of spectacular derring-do." The same review continues by proclaiming it a "handsome, shipshape picture." This was Curtiz and Flynn's tenth collaboration, as they continued to forge a healthy, profitable working relationship in cinema.

The plot sees King Philip II of Spain declaring his intention to destroy England en route to world conquest. On the way to England, the ship carrying Philip's ambassador is ambushed by the pirate ship *Albatross* and her captain, Geoffrey Thorpe (Flynn). Perhaps unsurprisingly, Thorpe falls in love with the ambas-

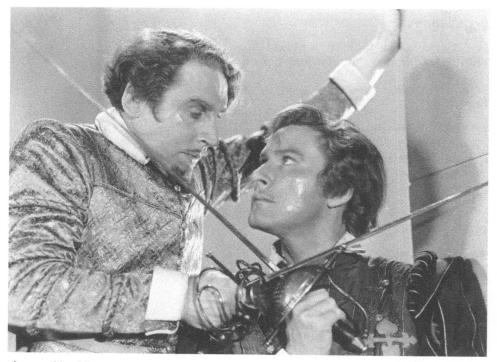

The swashbuckling Errol Flynn (right) as Geoffrey Thorpe takes on Lord Wolfingham. *Warner Bros. / Photofest © Warner Bros.*

sador's niece when they transport the captives to England. Thorpe, along with privateers, known as "sea hawks," plan to sail to the New World to seize Spanish gold. This plot is foiled when they are ambushed and driven into a swamp. Thorpe and other survivors are taken to Spain and sentenced to a life in slavery. Eventually Thorpe escapes, makes it back to England, and reveals the plan for the Spanish invasion to Queen Elizabeth. The Queen knights Thorpe and sets to work building a naval fleet to oppose the Spanish.

The film was nominated for four Academy Awards but did not win any.

The Music

The score to *The Sea Hawk* was composed by Erich Wolfgang Korngold, one of many European-born film composers of the Golden Age of Hollywood who harked back to the Romantic period for musical inspiration. Often considered one of his finest film scores, the soundtrack of *The Sea Hawk* excels in every department. It is in some ways more thrilling than the film it accompanies, but when the two are combined, it only helps to reinforce *The Sea Hawk* as a classic of the 1940s. The score saturates the film—one of the longest he ever worked on, running over two hours—with all but approximately fifteen minutes of the film being underscored by Korngold's music.

The opening to the film, in the guise of an overture as was often the case in the 1940s, introduces Korngold's key themes. A riotous fanfare that opens the overture leaves the audience in no doubt as to the nature of the adventurous, exciting narrative that is to follow. This segues into a flowing, luscious string theme that hints at the love story between Thorpe and the ambassador's niece. Dissonant brass and soaring French horns then lead the listener into an exotic-sounding descending string passage, denoting the journey to Panama and the New World. We are then led into Erroll Flynn's swashbuckling theme, which surely inspired countless films in similar genres that followed.

The music is cleverly integrated into the sound world of the film. In one scene, when the Spanish ship carrying the ambassador approaches the English Channel at the start of the film, the slave oarsmen row in time to a beating drum (seen on screen), but are also underscored by a monotonous, lethargic dirge in Korngold's underscore in the same tempo. This synchronization occurs again in the two cues "Thorpe Enters the Castle" and "Duel," where Korngold expertly underscores two examples of swordfighting and coordinates his music to exactly match the choreography of the dueling.

The love theme in *The Sea Hawk* contains the string-laden pathos and romanticism to be expected from a film of this period. While arguably sounding excessive to modern cinematic tastes, soaring melodies were a staple of the Golden Age of Hollywood and fit the aesthetic of the film well. Remarkably, Korngold changes key with each new musical phrase in the love theme, only making the links back to the great composers of the Romantic period more explicit.

Korngold dealt with scene and mood transitions very effectively. The shift from one visual and musical theme to the next was accomplished in an almost operatic manner, much like Wagner might have done in one of his epic music dramas. Rather than a fade to silence and a fade back in to the next scene, Korngold modu-

lated, adapted, and transitioned his music smoothly and professionally throughout the film. It is undoubtedly one of his most complex and immersive works for
film and shows clearly his classical training and European influence, which he
brought to the United States as an immigrant composer. Like Franz Waxman and
others before him, the Western European music tradition found its place through
Korngold' influence in the classic films of the Golden Age of Hollywood.

Recognition

Nominated for the Academy Award for Best Score but missed out to *Tin Pan Alley*
    by Alfred Newman.

Recording

Erich Wolfgang Korngold, *The Sea Hawk, Deception*, Naxos, 2007. This recording
    performed by the Moscow Symphony Orchestra and Choir combines two of
    Korngold's films from a similar period. While *The Sea Hawk* is considered the
    finer score, *Deception* is as close to film noir as his writing ever came, so it is
    worth listening to for that reason. A fine recording that comes with high recom-
    mendation. ****

Bibliography

"Cinema: The New Pictures." *Time*, August 19, 1940.

—ML

THE 7TH *VOYAGE OF SINBAD*

(1958)
Bernard Herrmann

The Film

Fantasy films inspired by the Arabian Nights stories have been around since the
silent era. In 1958, producer Charles Schneer introduced Sinbad the sailor to a
younger generation of filmgoers by making *The 7th Voyage of Sinbad*, with special
effects by Ray Harryhausen, who utilized "Dynamation," a stop-motion photo-
graphic process in which miniature lifelike figures appear as enormous creatures
on the movie screen.

In *7th Voyage*, Sinbad (Kerwin Mathews) sails to the island of Colossa in order
to break a spell that has been cast on his fiancée, Parisa (Kathryn Grant), by the
evil wizard Sokurah (Torin Thatcher). Parisa, magically reduced to the size of a
mouse, accompanies Sinbad on the voyage that is imperiled by encounters with
such giant monsters as a cyclops, a dragon, and a roc (a two-headed bird), an

Kerwin Mathews (as Sinbad) battles a reanimated skeleton, thanks to the stop-motion magic of special effects master Ray Harryhausen. *Columbia Pictures / Photofest © Columbia Pictures*

eggshell from which is needed to restore Parisa to human size. There is also a human skeleton that Sokurah magically brings to life as a means of killing Sinbad in a climactic sword fight.

The Music

Bernard Herrmann's score is filled with ingenious musical ideas from the very beginning of the opening credits, which are accompanied by a boisterous theme in a minor key that immediately establishes a fantasy atmosphere. This theme is based on a nine-note idea that begins with three repeated tones that are followed by notes that move stepwise within a small pitch range. This theme's clever instrumentation includes brass sounds for the repeated three tones, then a combination of instruments including strings and woodwinds for the rest of the motif. During the credits this motivic idea is heard a total of five times, with the second and fourth soundings being a variation on the motif with strings and harp in a more romantic style and short trills added to certain melodic tones. After this back-and-forth alternation, the credits end with several strongly accented orchestral chords.

A second prominent theme, which is associated with Sinbad and Parisa, is first heard in the opening scene when Sinbad is bringing his bride-to-be to Baghdad aboard a sailing ship. When Sinbad comes into her cabin, a sweet melody starts to sound that begins with a rising fifth. High strings add a sense of sweetness to this idea, which serves as a love theme throughout the film.

The wizard Sokurah is musically accompanied by a repeated motif of four rapid-sounding rising pitches that are menacingly sounded by brass with tremolo strings in the background. This motif is not developed into an actual theme but serves as a musical alert whenever Sokurah prepares to implement his sinister magic schemes.

In the scene where Parisa's transformation is revealed to her father and Sinbad, the love theme is transformed into a dramatic idea played by high trumpets and low woodwinds. When Sinbad sees his betrothed turned into a tiny creature, the strings sound a rather melancholy version of this theme, with very high-pitched violins adding a soulful quality to the melody.

There are many other scenes in which Sokurah's magical feats are musically accompanied by Herrmann's musical ingenuity. An early example occurs at the Baghdad court when Sokurah uses Parisa's servant Sadi as a volunteer for a magic trick in which Sadi becomes transformed into a giant cobra with a human head. The music is designed as a dance-like piece with a rapid-paced woodwind idea accompanied by a number of colorful percussion sounds.

The latter part of the film is filled with action scenes on the island of Colossa where Sinbad and his men go in search of the giant roc's egg and are confronted by the cyclops again. The music for these scenes and the later ones featuring the roc and a fire-breathing dragon are accompanied by a panoply of high-pitched flute and low-tone brass and contrabassoon sounds accompanied by lots of timpani rumbles, crashing cymbals, and bell tones provided by chimes and orchestra bells, along with other percussion effects.

One of the most ingenious musical moments in Herrmann's score comes late in the film when Sinbad, who has already been betrayed by Sokurah several times, is reunited with Parisa, now restored to human size. As they try to exit a cave, Sinbad is forced to duel with the skeleton that Sokurah has magically activated. Herrmann's music features an ascending scale-like idea for trumpets and other brass accompanied by fast-repeated xylophone tones that represent the skeleton's brittle bones. During the struggle, percussion sounds help to keep this lively piece going in a steady rhythm that resembles a weird type of dance as Sinbad fights to subdue the skeleton until it finally tumbles to the bottom of the cave and breaks into pieces.

The music punctuates almost every moment of the action scenes that take place as Sokurah tries to retrieve a magic lamp and kill Sinbad in the process. By the end of the film, after the mortally wounded dragon collapses and crushes Sokurah, the music soothingly restates the love theme as Sinbad and Parisa are once again reunited. As the ship sets sail, there is a final closing statement of the lively nine-note motif with which the film began.

The clever inventiveness of Herrmann's score enhances this unusually creative film at every turn and goes along perfectly with Harryhausen's ingenious visual effects. Three other Charles Schneer productions with Harryhausen's stop-motion creatures came in the wake of the *Sinbad* film, including *The 3 Worlds of Gulliver*, *Mysterious Island*, and *Jason and the Argonauts*, all of which include Herrmann's highly creative music. *The 7th Voyage of Sinbad* remains one of the best examples of fantasy filmmaking and also one of Bernard Herrmann's most musically exotic scoring accomplishments.

Recognition

Placed on National Film Registry by the Library of Congress in 2008.
Received 100 percent approval rating on the film review website *Rotten Tomatoes*.

Recordings

Bernard Herrmann, *The 7th Voyage of Sinbad*, Varése Sarabande, 1998. Studio recording by John Debney and Royal Scottish Orchestra. Great stereo sound. ****
Bernard Herrmann, *The 7th Voyage of Sinbad: Original soundtrack*, Varése Sarabande, 1980. Good mono sound. ***½

Bibliography

Rovin, Jeff. *Fabulous Fantasy Films*. South Brunswick, NJ: A. S. Barnes, 1977.

—LEM

THE SHAWSHANK REDEMPTION
(1994)
Thomas Newman

The Film

Directed by Frank Darabont and starring Tim Robbins and Morgan Freeman, *The Shawshank Redemption* is often praised as one of the greatest films of all time. The popular website IMDB places the film in joint first position, sharing an average score of 9.2 out of 10 (based on 1.8 million votes) with *The Godfather*. Much of this acclaim was retrospective, however, and it was not particularly successful at the box office during its first run.

In early post–World War II America, Andy Dufresne (Tim Robbins) is sentenced to two consecutive life sentences for the murder of his wife and her lover. He is interned at the Shawshank State Penitentiary, where he makes friends with Ellis "Red" Redding (Morgan Freeman), who is also serving a life sentence. Red is the prison's contraband smuggler. Andy becomes popular with some inmates, but not so much with the guards, and earns himself time in solitary confinement for taking a recording of The Marriage of Figaro by Mozart and playing it over the prison's loudspeaker system, a poignant and humanizing moment in the film.

After almost twenty years has passed of Andy's time in prison, a new arrival reveals that a prisoner elsewhere claimed responsibility for the murder of Andy's wife and lover. It is revealed that over the course of nineteen years, Andy had been digging a hole in his cell wall behind a poster of sex siren Rita Hayworth, and he finally escapes through the prison's sewage system. Before escaping, Andy tells Red of his dreams of living on the Mexican coast. Red makes him a promise that if he is released, he will retrieve a package in a specific hayfield that Andy had buried there. After forty years, Red is finally paroled, and he keeps his promise. He digs up the cache of money and a letter, and as the camera looks on from a distance, he meets Andy on the beach in Mexico in an emotional climax to one of the most noteworthy films.

The film was nominated for seven Academy Awards and two Golden Globes, but has no major award victories to its name.

Andy Dufresne (Tim Robbins) and Ellis Boyd "Red" Redding (Morgan Freeman) enjoy a game of checkers in the prison yard. *Columbia Pictures / Photofest © Columbia Pictures*

The Music

The score to *The Shawshank Redemption* was composed by Thomas Newman, the youngest son of esteemed film composer Alfred Newman. This relationship is the only father-son pairing found in this book, although Randy Newman is Alfred's nephew. Newman was still an up-and-coming composer in 1994, but had been working in film and television for some time, with John Williams, who was friendly with his father, inviting him to help orchestrate Darth Vader's death scene in *The Return of the Jedi* in 1983.

Newman was so affected by the emotional intensity of *The Shawshank Redemption* that he found it difficult to write music that would elevate these feelings further without stepping into the territory of the overly sentimental. For this reason, the score is understated. It is emotional, without a doubt, and the main theme is a beautiful, gentle melody that revolves around the undying hope that the two main characters possess, but there are no triumphant, heroic gestures from Newman. The escape theme for Andy Dufresne was toned down from three notes to one note, on the request of the director. Simplicity, according to Darabont, was paramount to the success of the scene, and Newman's one-note motif adds just enough to the already triumphant visuals. The director is very guarded against overly sentimental music, claiming that he is "very sensitive to when a score crosses that line between enhancing the emotion and impact of a scene, and when it clobbers the viewer over the head by doing too much—which can actually be a very fine line." This style of subtle composition became Newman's trademark. The composer stated that he likes to compose pieces that "do very little but tend to pack a punch," adding, "When you have such emotion coming off a screen, how can you add to that emotion without overpowering a scene?"

The cue "So Was Red," heard in the film after his release from prison, became one of the composer's favorite cues. Originally written for solo oboe, the director persuaded a reluctant Newman to add a harmonica. The harmonica player Tommy Morgan "casually delivered something dead-on perfect for the first take," according to Darabont, and this is the take heard in the finished film.

Interestingly, the subtle approach to scoring was reflected in the visuals at the climax of the film. Rather than a close-up of Red and Dufresne embracing on the beach, the camera pans back, and to the sounds of Newman's score, they embrace in the distance. No dialogue is heard. The only sound is that of the crashing waves and the music, which segues into the final credits.

Recognition

Nominated for Academy Award for Best Original Score.
Nominated for Grammy for Best Instrumental Composition.

Recording

Thomas Newman, *The Shawshank Redemption*, Epic Soundtrax, 1994/2009. This fifty-three-minute, twenty-one-track album contains the major cues from the film, including the *Marriage of Figaro* duet. The quality is good, and as the only official recording, this is to be recommended. ****

Bibliography

Adams, Russell. "How Thomas Newman Scored *The Shawshank Redemption*." *Wall Street Journal*, June 20, 2014.
Chua, D. K. "Listening to the Self: *The Shawshank Redemption* and the Technology of Music." *19th-Century Music* 34, no. 3 (2011): 341–55.

—ML

SOMEWHERE IN TIME

(1980)
John Barry

The Film

If filmgoers were polled to select the most romantic films of all time, *Casablanca* would certainly make the list. Another film that would undoubtedly be listed is *Somewhere in Time*, which has gained a cult following and has inspired an annual festival at the Grand Hotel on Mackinac Island, where much of the film was shot.

Jeannot Szwarc's film, based on Richard Matheson's novel *Bid Time Return*, concerns a successful playwright, Richard Collier (Christopher Reeve), who has become so enchanted with a portrait of a once-famous actress named Elise McKenna (Jane Seymour) that he uses self-hypnosis to travel back through time to the Grand Hotel in the summer of 1912, where the actress was then performing.

Richard succeeds in finding Elise and they fall in love almost instantly, but like Rick and Ilse in *Casablanca*, huge obstacles stand in the way of a lasting relationship.

Christopher Reeve gazes upon Jane Seymour's portrait. *Universal Pictures / Photofest © Universal Pictures*

The Music

John Barry, who became famous as the composer for James Bond films in the 1960s and 1970s, had no lack of creative imagination, but until *Somewhere in Time*, his film work did not generally display such a romantic idiom.

At the heart of this film is a love theme of flowing eloquence that musically connects two people from different historical eras and indicates to the viewer early on that they will somehow meet and fall in love.

There is no scoring in the film's opening credits. Instead there is background music with a rock beat, presumably emanating from an unseen recording device that provides party music for a reception following the premiere of Richard's new play at Millfield College in 1972. Crowd noises subside as the elderly Elise slowly approaches Richard and puts a gold watch and chain in his hands and says "Come back to me." At this point, a lyrical traveling theme for violin and strings begins to sound. It continues as she is driven from the theater to the Grand Hotel, where she is staying with Miss Roberts (Teresa Wright), her faithful companion.

When Elise sequesters herself in her room at the hotel, she turns on a record player and the sounds of the eighteenth variation from Rachmaninoff's *Rhapsody on a Theme of Paganini* begin to fill the room. This music continues as Elise looks out a window and then sits down to caress the printed program of Richard's play. Without a break in the music, the scene shifts ahead eight years to Chicago, where Richard, who is having difficulty finishing his latest play, views the skyline from his office window. When he shuts off his record player, the Rachmaninoff music suddenly stops.

In the following scene, when Richard drives out of Chicago toward an unknown destination, the lyrical traveling theme is heard again. After spontaneously checking into the Grand Hotel, he discovers a portrait of Elise that was taken during her appearances in a play at the hotel's theater back in 1912. As he looks around the portrait gallery the Rachmaninoff theme starts sounding softly; when he sees Elise's portrait, the music increases in volume.

When Richard returns repeatedly to the gallery to study the portrait, a lyrical melody for strings beginning with an ascending pattern of four tones clearly indicates his growing infatuation. This is the film's central love theme.

When Richard learns that Elise is deceased but is the same woman who gave him the watch back in 1972, he becomes obsessed with the idea of traveling back in time to find her. After he interviews his former college professor about time travel, he dons a suit from an earlier era and starts to hypnotize himself into believing that it is 1912. At this point, Barry's music creates a dark atmosphere with long-sustained string tones accompanied by repeated piano tones and rumbling timpani, along with some somber brass chords. When he awakens to find himself in June of 1912, the music becomes more serene, with lyrical major-key string harmonies instead of the previous minor-key ones.

When he finds Elise near a lake, the love theme begins softly with solo harp tones followed by strings. The music contributes a thoroughly romantic atmosphere as she notices him. Later, when he eludes the stubborn interference of her manager and spends an afternoon with her, a new up-tempo theme for strings is introduced as they drive off in a horse-drawn carriage. The love theme returns in a lilting arrangement for flute and harp as they travel by rowboat to a picturesque lighthouse. Again strings add lyricism to this sequence.

One of the most prominent appearances of the love theme occurs when Richard and Elise are alone in a hotel room. Here a solo piano begins the theme, with flute and strings then softly repeating the melody during the consummation of their relationship.

Coming after the rousing score to Disney's *The Black Hole* (1979) and shortly before his epic music for *Raise the Titanic*, Barry's score for *Somewhere in Time* came at a point when he could take otherwise mediocre films and add to them a high degree of dramatic impact. While *Somewhere in Time* was neither a critically acclaimed film nor a box-office success, John Barry's music has helped this film become a cult favorite. This score surpasses in emotional depth many other film scores of the 1980s and thus well deserves inclusion in this book.

Recognition

International Network of *Somewhere in Time* Enthusiasts fan club founded in 1980. Among their activities: an annual festival held each October on Mackinac Island, with showings of the film at the Grand Hotel.

Included on American Film Institute's list "100 Years . . . 100 Passions" among America's greatest love stories.

Recordings

John Barry, *Somewhere in Time*, MCA, 1987, CD. This is the original motion picture soundtrack. Excellent sound. ****

John Barry, *Somewhere in Time*, Varése Sarabande, 1998. Rerecording of the score by John Debney and the Royal Scottish Orchestra. Excellent sound but sluggish tempos on many tracks. ***

Bibliography

Leonard, Geoff, Pete Walker, and Gareth Bramley. *John Barry: The Man with the Midas Touch*. Bristol, UK: Redcliffe Press, 2008.

MacDonald, Laurence E. *The Invisible Art of Film Music: A Comprehensive History*. Second edition. Lanham, MD: Scarecrow Press, 2013.

—LEM

THE SONG OF BERNADETTE

(1943)

Alfred Newman

The Film

Many acclaimed films have been based on popular books. One good example is Henry King's version of Franz Werfel's *The Song of Bernadette*, which was the number-one fiction best seller of 1942. After producer Darryl Zanuck purchased the film rights, *Song of Bernadette* became a box-office hit and a leading contender for Academy Awards.

Werfel's book is a fictionalized account of miraculous events that took place in the small French town of Lourdes in the late 1850s. A teenage girl named Bernadette Soubirous (Jennifer Jones) claimed that a "beautiful lady" appeared to her several times, despite the fact that no one else could see this vision. Bernadette never claimed that she saw the Blessed Mother, but when amazing cures started happening to those who came to the cave where the visions took place, people became convinced that the "beautiful lady" that Bernadette alone saw and spoke with was actually the Mother of Jesus. The initial skepticism of Bernadette's family and the local clergy, plus her subsequent tribulations, are all vividly depicted in the film.

The Music

Although Alfred Newman was probably best known in Hollywood as an arranger of songs and dance numbers for musical films, he frequently took upon himself the task of composing original music. For *Song of Bernadette* Newman composed over one hundred minutes of underscoring and used an eighty-piece orchestra plus a large choir to record his work.

At the start of the film, a brass fanfare is heard while the 20th Century Fox logo is displayed. As the credits begin to appear Newman's music features a string arrangement of Bernadette's motif, which consists of a rising four-note motif that utilizes a pair of ascending fourths, as in D-G-A-D (think of the first eight notes of "La Marseillaise" without repetition of the same pitches). After this motif is heard several times, the music shifts to the vision motif, which features mostly ascending tones and is sounded while an explanatory note appears onscreen. Both of these motifs figure prominently in subsequent cues.

Music continues without a break into the film's opening scene, which takes place before dawn at the humble Soubirous home. Bernadette's out-of-work father is awakened by her mother with the understanding that if he goes out early, he might be able to find employment. As her parents get dressed for the day, another motif is heard. This one features a rather somber idea consisting of two pairs of descending tones. As Soubirous leaves the house, Newman's dour music sums up the direness of the family's situation. When the local baker suggests that

Jennifer Jones in her Academy Award–winning role of Bernadette Soubirous. *20th Century Fox Film Corporation / Photofest © 20th Century Fox Film Corporation*

workers are needed at the nearby hospital, the mood suddenly shifts to a more upbeat style. But when Soubirous is hired to take contaminated linens by a hand-pulled cart to a local dumping ground, the music shifts to an even more somber atmosphere than before. This lengthy cue ends at about 7:15 into the film, when the scene changes to a schoolroom where Bernadette is scolded for failing to understand her catechism assignment.

Music returns when Bernadette, her sister, and a female friend are sent out to gather firewood. Newman accompanies their walking with a playful use of staccato woodwinds and pizzicato strings. When the other two girls leave Bernadette behind, she stands near the grotto of Massabielle next to the trash site where her father had earlier dumped the soiled linens. Newman's score for this scene is filled with musical imagery. When a breeze begins, fluttery flutes suggest swirling leaves and oboes imitate bird calls while a choir adds a mysterious sound as Bernadette begins to look around. When she sees the lady who she later reports is wearing white and blue with roses at her feet, the vision motif is sounded emotionally by strings with ethereal voices in the background.

There is much noteworthy music later in the film, including a scene that occurs at around 1:14:00 when a large crowd assembled at the grotto laughs at Bernadette when she says she has been instructed to wash her face and hands with water, but there is only dirt. When the crowd begins to depart, Antoine, a neighborhood friend of Bernadette, sits disconsolately on a rock. At this point, the cue begins with the same rustling sounds that were heard when Bernadette had her first vision. Suddenly, as Antoine sees a stream of water coming under his feet, the music begins to soar with a choir singing Newman's setting of the "Hail Mary" prayer beginning with the Latin words "Sancta Maria." When Antoine calls out to the crowd the music becomes very dramatic, with church bells, voices, and full-orchestra chords.

Another noteworthy scene is a montage sequence that begins around 1:26:00 when newspaper headlines display news of Bernadette's visions and the cures that have occurred at Massabielle. As short film clips reveal a chapel being built under the supervision of a stonecutter whose sight has been restored, the music features strings, brass, and bells that collectively provide a highly emotional atmosphere.

In creating this film score, Newman may have accepted Werfel's idea that the visions were just those of a beautiful lady, but his finished product supports the concept that Bernadette has conversed with the Blessed Mother herself.

During his career Newman scored many films of an inspirational nature, including *The Robe* (also included in this book), but rarely has his music had the emotional intensity found in *Song of Bernadette*. This is one of Newman's masterworks and deserves to be listed among the greatest film scores.

Recognition

Nominated for twelve Academy Awards.
Four Oscars, including Best Actress for Jennifer Jones and Best Original Score for Newman.
Newman's music is listed on AFI's 100 Years of Film Scores.

Recording

Alfred Newman, *Song of Bernadette*, Varése Sarabande, 1999. A two-disc set. Good restoration of dated 1943 score materials. ***½

Bibliography

Burlingame, Jon. Liner notes. *Song of Bernadette*. Varése Sarabande VSD2-6025, 1999, CD.
Korda, Michael. *Making the List: A Cultural History of the American Bestseller 1900–1999*. New York: Barnes & Noble, 2001.

—LEM

SPARTACUS
(1960)
Alex North

The Film

Directed by Stanley Kubrick and starring Kirk Douglas, Laurence Olivier, and Peter Ustinov, *Spartacus* was Universal Studios' most successful film financially until *Airport* was released ten years later.

Set against a power struggle between Marcus Licinius Crassus and Gracchus in the Roman senate, the protagonist Spartacus (Kirk Douglas) is born into slavery but grows up to be a strong and likeable person. He and other slaves are taught at gladiator school and are then sold for profit. Spartacus escapes and vows never to kill another slave, even if he comes up against one in the gladiator arena. As the de facto leader of all slaves, he vows to free them all. The film does not end happily, as both Crassus and Gracchus hear of his plan to acquire a fleet of ships from pirates. They travel to meet Spartacus's slave army, ambush them, and kill thousands before crucifying Spartacus himself. In a beautifully bittersweet moment, his newborn son, born free of slavery, is shown to him as he dies on the cross.

The film was nominated for six Academy Awards, winning four for Best Supporting Actor, Best Cinematography, Best Art Direction, and Best Costume Design. It also won one of six Golden Globe nominations.

The Music

The score to *Spartacus* was composed by Alex North. As was the norm for feature-length epic films, an extensive musical score was composed. The nature of epic historical films, with the grand scale of their panoramic landscapes, movements of armies, elaborate ceremonies, and so forth, requires music to maintain drama. *Spartacus*, just over three hours long, is accompanied by a score of two hours and fifteen minutes. There are seventy-four separate musical cues, and North reports

Spartacus (Kirk Douglas) leads the revolt against the Romans. *Universal International Pictures / Photofest © Universal International Pictures*

that he threw away more pages of music than ever before. It was a genuine challenge and a labor of love for the talented composer. North had been more accustomed to composing jazz scores, so *Spartacus*, with its epic scale, was a challenge. The composer re-created the sounds of Rome not by resorting to musical clichés, but by writing in a contemporary, modern style that would enable him to experiment with exotic instruments. These instruments included a sarrusophone, Israeli recorder, Chinese oboe, lute, mandolin, Yugoslav flute, kythara, dulcimer, and bagpipes. These instruments were not necessarily from that time period or location, but they provided the exoticism and otherworldliness that the composer desired. This was, according to North, an interpretation of the past in terms of the present. The score is very much a product of opposites. As Henderson explains in a wonderful analysis of the score, it contains "martial battle music vs. lyrical romantic music, symphonic vs. chamber orchestration, brass vs. strings, tonal vs. modal," and so on. This contrast in such a lengthy score gives North's creation an operatic scale.

There are several defined musical themes in the score, including the triumphant music underscoring the rebellion of the slaves led by Spartacus. This contrasts heavily with the powerful music that accompanies the antagonists, the Roman army. North uses these two themes and many more that are introduced through the lengthy film, and, making another comparison to opera, particularly Wagner, uses the leitmotif technique to represent each character or situation musically.

The overture presents these themes or motifs in turn, but this was cut from four minutes, with only a two-minute musical medley remaining, of triumphant, fanfare-like pomposity. This fanfare is the basis for the entire score. It is simple but militaristic and ceremonial, and it is adapted throughout the film to suit different moods surrounding slavery or freedom.

The score, despite being symphonic and operatic in nature, flirts with atonality and avant-garde tonality. Keys are rarely established in the main themes, and it is a daring endeavor to write over two hours of music without the usual tonal stability expected of film scores. The exception to this is the love theme for Spartacus and Varinia, which is typically lush. Swelling strings produce a melody redolent with emotion and desire, as well as longing and sadness. It is the epitome of a successful Hollywood love theme, tonally stable, dynamically diverse, and making use of the highest registers of the violins to soar to love-induced heights. Another highly emotive moment in the film is the cue "Blue Shadows and Purple Hills." Here, North underscores the reading of a poem about going home with variations on the love theme. It is an unexpected but welcome respite from the harshness of the gladiator, Roman army, and slave themes. The instrumentation consists of tender instruments, such as the harp, lute, guitar, and solo viola. It is a truly beautiful, standout moment in the score and film, and it highlights almost perfectly how the visuals, dialogue, and music can combine to create immensely powerful moments for the audience.

Alex North did not receive any awards, but the score lives on as one of the all-time greatest for an epic film. Over two hours of music shifts and morphs as the narrative does, and North has a musical answer for every character, every scene, and every situation. *Spartacus* is sometimes a love story, sometimes a story of hope, and sometime a story of death and despair, and Alex North ensures that the music takes us on all of these journeys from start to bitter end.

Recognition

Nominated for Academy Award for Best Original Score.
Nominated for Golden Globe for Best Original Score.

Recording

Alex North, *Spartacus*, Soundtrack Factory, 2017. An imported album that covers a stupendous sixty-five tracks on two CDs. This is highly recommended simply because of the extensive nature of the recording. There is very little music from the film that did not make it onto this recording. ****

Bibliography

Burt, G. *The Art of Film Music: Special Emphasis on Hugo Friedhofer, Alex North, David Raksin, Leonard Rosenman*. Boston: Northeastern University Press, 1994.

Henderson, S. S. *Alex North, Film Composer: A Biography, with Musical Analyses of A Streetcar Named Desire, Spartacus, The Misfits, Under the Volcano, and Prizzi's Honor*. Jefferson, NC: McFarland, 2009.

—ML

SPELLBOUND

(1945)
Miklós Rózsa

The Film

Alfred Hitchcock was a top director in Hollywood for almost four decades, with several critically acclaimed films, three of which were produced by David O. Selznick. *Spellbound*, which came five years after the Oscar-winning *Rebecca*, is the second of these films.

Spellbound shares an essential plot point with many other Hitchcock films, namely a leading character who is suspected of having committed a serious crime. Gregory Peck plays a man who arrives at the Green Manors mental clinic claiming to be Dr. Edwardes, its new director. The clinic's staff soon learns that the real Edwardes died at a ski resort and that this impostor is most likely Edwardes's killer, but he remembers nothing except that his initials are J.B. (from a cigarette lighter in his pocket). Ingrid Bergman plays Doctor Constance Petersen, a member of the clinic's psychiatric staff, who becomes convinced of his innocence while trying to cure him of his amnesia. Many plot twists occur in the film, especially when J.B. is convicted of murder and Constance, who loves him, tries to solve the mystery concerning Edwardes's death.

The Music

In creating *Spellbound*'s music, Rózsa employed an electronic instrument called the theremin, named for its Russian inventor, Leon Theremin. The wavy vibrato-like sounds of this instrument, created by hand movements in front of a wooden box to which are attached a pair of electrified metal rods, signify J.B.'s distraught

While Dr. Constance Petersen (Ingrid Bergman) sleeps, the tormented John Ballantyne (Gregory Peck) considers their fate. *United Artists / Photofest © United Artists*

mental condition. Early in the film, J.B. is visibly disturbed by the sight of dark lines against a white background. Whenever he sees such images, the theremin musically projects his feelings of paranoia.

The opening credits begin with ominous chords that lead to the paranoia theme, with the vibrato-like tones of the theremin sounding a melody based on a pattern of four descending tones. This motif, which is accompanied by swirling harp and celesta harmonies, leads directly into the score's main theme, a lyrical idea for strings and harp that connects J.B. and Constance. Note that the first four tones of this love theme are echoed repeatedly by instruments sounding the tones at a lower octave level. This overlapping melodic device is an identifiable aspect of many of Rózsa's film scores.

In addition to these two primary themes, a light-hearted idea for strings is introduced when J.B. arrives at Green Manors and joins his new colleagues in the dining hall. This idea returns when Constance joins him for a walk on the grounds.

The love theme is prominently featured in a nighttime scene where Constance goes to the clinic's library to find a book by Edwardes. When she sees a light on in J.B.'s room, the music swells with strings and harp as she opens the door. Then a solo violin sounds the theme, followed by a soaring emotional statement as he kisses her, with shots of doors opening in the distance. The romantic mood is broken, however, when he detects dark streaks on her white robe. At this point, the theremin idea suggests J.B.'s troubled mental state.

The paranoia motif is also heard in the operating room scene. The sounds of the theremin, celesta, and harp emphatically underscore the moment when J.B. becomes mentally disturbed by the many light-vs.-dark images in the room. This theme returns in many later scenes, as J.B. is forced to confront the traumatic events that have caused his amnesia.

Another theme, based on a rhythmically charged four-note motif for brass, occurs after J.B.'s collapse in the operating room and Constance discovers that J.B. is not Edwardes. Tremolo strings, muted trumpets, and celesta arpeggios add to the dramatic energy of this idea.

A musically memorable scene occurs after Constance and J.B., who is now wanted by the police, arrive at the home of her mentor, Dr. Brulov, who quickly recognizes symptoms of paranoia in the man she introduces as her husband. When J.B. gets up during the night, a sustained theremin vibrato sound begins, accompanied by tremolo strings and repeated pairs of low-pitched tones based on the earlier brass motif. When J.B. stands in front of a bathroom sink and stares into a shaving cup, the music becomes increasingly turbulent as he takes hold of a straight razor. The theremin sounds, abetted by rhythmic strings and accented brass tones, add great tension as J.B. walks toward the sleeping Constance with razor in hand. The wavy theremin sounds continue as he walks down a staircase toward Brulov's office.

Another musical high point comes when Constance and J.B., who has now regained some of his memory, including his name, John Ballantyne, go to a ski resort to solve the mystery of Dr. Edwardes's death. As they ski down a steep slope, he remembers a tragic event from his childhood, with theremin sounds and heavy brass chords in the cue.

Spellbound's music is contemporaneous with Rózsa's scores for such film noir classics as *Double Indemnity*, *The Lost Weekend*, and *The Red House*, the latter two also featuring theremin sounds. Rózsa avoided using the theremin thereafter, but other composers soon began using its otherworldly sounds for sci-fi films.

The combination of the eerie paranoia theme and the emotional love theme helped to make the score of *Spellbound* one of the most significant of Rózsa's career. Additionally, the use of the theremin was an inspired idea that contributed a sound design that was quite unique for its time. For all of these reasons the score of *Spellbound* deserves to be featured in this book.

Recognition

Six Oscar nominations, including Best Picture.
Rózsa won the Oscar for Best Original Score.
Spellbound Concerto is among the most often-recorded works derived from film
music.

Recordings

Miklós Rózsa, *Spellbound*, Intrada, 2009. Recording with Alan Wilson and the Slo-
vak Radio Symphony. Excellent sound and performance. ****
Miklós Rózsa, *Spellbound*, Stanyan, 1988. Ray Heindorf's 1958 studio recording
released on CD, with original thereminist Samuel Hoffmann re-creating the
electronic sounds. Good mono sound. ***½

Bibliography

Alexander, Wade. Liner notes. *Spellbound*. Stanyan STZ116-2, 1988, CD.
Harris, Robert A., and Michael S. Lasky. *The Films of Alfred Hitchcock*. New York:
Citadel Press, 1976.

—LEM

THE SPIRIT OF ST. LOUIS

(1957)
Franz Waxman

The Film

Billy Wilder's *The Spirit of St. Louis* depicts the historic flight by Charles Lindbergh
in May of 1927 that instantly made him the most famous man on the planet.
The film, which is based on Lindbergh's Pulitzer-winning memoir, recreates the
events surrounding his daring attempt to become the first pilot to fly nonstop
from New York to Paris.

Spirit's screenplay uses the final hours of preparation and the actual flight as
a springboard for a series of flashbacks that include Lindbergh's exploits as a
fearless airmail pilot and a barnstorming aerial performer. James Stewart, who
portrays Lindbergh, vocally provides the flyer's thoughts and also the memories
that he recalls before and during the thirty-three-hour flight across the Atlantic
Ocean. The flashbacks illustrate both Lindbergh's courage and his joy of flying at
the dawn of the aviation age.

The Music

Franz Waxman's music is crucial to the viewer's emotional connection with the
film, since much of it involves rather lifeless scenes with Lindbergh sitting alone

James Stewart as aviation hero Charles Lindbergh. *Warner Bros. / Photofest © Warner Bros.*

in the airplane and using his map to calculate his progress while fending off the desire for sleep after being awake for a full day before his takeoff.

The first sounds in the film, which occur as the Warner's logo appears, are those of an airplane. After fifteen seconds, Waxman's music begins boldly with a series of ascending fifths played by brass. This idea can be identified as the *Spirit* motif, since it represents the musical "voice" of Lindbergh's plane. After the *Spirit* motif is heard, a second significant musical idea is introduced. The sounding of this soaring melody, which will be referred to as the flying theme, is based on an ascending series of stepwise tones that signify the heroic nature of Lindbergh's adventure.

The score's two main ideas, the *Spirit* motif and the flying theme, are the most frequently heard melodic elements in Waxman's score. Sometimes they appear separately, and at other times they are combined in the same cue.

The *Spirit* motif arrives in the underscore when one of Lindbergh's financial backers in St. Louis doodles on his notepad the word "SPIRIT" in capital letters. Three times, as "Spirit of St. Louis" is suggested as the proposed plane's name, the *Spirit* motif is sounded softly by woodwinds with a wavy-sounding background played by strings.

This motif returns during a montage sequence as workers at Ryan Aeronautical in San Diego are designing and building the plane. Very energetic and rhythmically driven music for strings accompanies a series of short film clips that illustrate the various stages of the plane's construction. At first the *Spirit* motif is hinted at by French horns. As the nameplate is ready to be bolted onto the plane's fuselage, the horns, trumpets, and timpani along with cymbals heroically sound the *Spirit* motif.

The flying motif is noticeably heard when Lindbergh tests the new plane. With each successive takeoff, swirling strings and fast-repeated piano tones accompany the high tones of a solo trumpet. Then, on a longer flight, the flying theme returns in a soaring string arrangement accompanied by French horns.

Although many of the score's most noteworthy cues occur during the actual flight, there is no music as Lindbergh first attempts to achieve liftoff. When the *Spirit* finally clears telephone wires and trees during its initial climb, the flying theme is sounded gloriously by strings and brass, with a hint of "La Marseillaise" added to suggest Lindbergh's destination. The French national anthem is also heard elsewhere in the film.

One of the score's most heroic cues starts at around 1:58:30 when Lindbergh flies over Dingle Bay on the west coast of Ireland, with an energetic Irish jig melody combined with the *Spirit* and flying motifs in a dynamic orchestral statement. The cue becomes even more dramatic when the jig's first four tones are repeatedly sounded while brass instruments play the *Spirit* motif's rising fifths.

When Lindbergh flies over Paris, both main motifs are merged into a splendidly dramatic cue. Unfortunately, the final moments of this music are almost drowned out by the roar of the crowd as Lindbergh lands at Le Bourget field.

Not all of the score is by Waxman. Roy Webb and Ray Heindorf contributed last-minute short cues that were inserted into flashbacks, including a scene where Lindbergh comically pilots a dilapidated airplane.

Another change in the score involves Waxman's dramatic chordal idea for brass. This music was removed from the opening credits, in place of which Waxman was asked to insert a soaring version of the flying theme. While not heard in the actual film, the discordant brass idea appears in somewhat altered form in the film's theatrical trailer.

Throughout the film, Waxman's music adds a heroic quality to Lindbergh's historic flight. Even with alterations, this score is one of his finest achievements and imminently worthy of inclusion in a list of greatest film scores.

Recognition

Included by the American Film Institute in its 2005 list of best film scores.
Time magazine praised Stewart's ability to convey Lindbergh's flight as "a journey of the spirit."

Recordings

Franz Waxman, *The Film Music of Franz Waxman*, RCA, 1990. Excellent sound. ***½
Franz Waxman, *The Spirit of St. Louis*, Varése Sarabande, 1989. Original soundtrack remastered. Includes original version of the main-title music. Good sound. ***½

Bibliography

Karlin, Fred. *Listening to Movies: The Film Lover's Guide to Film Music.* New York: Schirmer Books, 1994.

Lasher, John Steven. Liner notes. *The Spirit of St. Louis.* Entr'acte LP ERS-6507, 1977.

—LEM

STAR TREK—THE MOTION PICTURE
(1979)
Jerry Goldsmith

The Film

Numerous films have been based on TV series. Noteworthy examples are the *Star Trek* films, the first of which arrived in theaters in 1979. Fans of the original TV series, known as "Trekkies," rejoiced when the show's creator, Gene Roddenberry, succeeded in assembling all of the leading actors from the 1960s series to re-create their original roles in the film.

The plot of the first *Star Trek* film concerns the reuniting of the crew of the USS *Enterprise* for a highly dangerous journey into deep space that occurs several years after the ship's original five-year mission. After an attack by an alien energy force destroys three Klingon warships, the *Enterprise* is commissioned to intercept this mysterious energy cloud before it enters Earth's atmosphere. It is the mission of Captain James Kirk (William Shatner), Chief Science Officer Spock (Leonard Nimoy), Dr. Leonard McCoy (DeForest Kelley), along with Scotty, Uhura, Sulu, Chekov, and the rest of the starship's crew, to save Earth from being destroyed.

The Music

Many composers have scored the various *Star Trek* films. Especially significant is Jerry Goldsmith, who scored five of the ten *Star Trek* films released between 1979 and 2002. The legacy of Goldsmith's exciting score in the first of these films helped to establish the heroic nature of the *Enterprise*'s many voyages into space in the films to come.

The main theme is a rousing march based on a seven-note motif that includes bold jumps in pitch. This motif, which signifies the *Enterprise* itself, is triumphantly sounded by trumpets at the very beginning of the film.

A grandiose version of the *Enterprise* theme begins at 17:20 (in the director's cut edition) when the starship is being refitted for service with Admiral Kirk assuming command. As Kirk and Scotty, the chief engineer, ride in a space shuttle toward the docking station, strings and harp first sound the theme in a slow tempo, with trumpets then repeating the melody. When the *Enterprise*'s silvery surface becomes more fully visible the music shifts into a glorious full-orchestra statement. This cue reaches its majestic concluding point when the melody is played

Resuming their mission: Captain James T. Kirk (William Shatner) and Mr. Spock (Leonard Nimoy).
Paramount Pictures / Photofest © Paramount Pictures

by soaring violins and French horns accompanied by resonant brass chords and pounding timpani.

Another glorious rendition of the *Enterprise* theme, featuring trumpets and pounding timpani, begins around 36:30 to accompany the scene where the refitted starship begins its journey into deep space. The repeated use of an insistently rhythmic accompaniment pattern played by strings and piano helps to increase the music's intensity as the *Enterprise* moves through space.

A second significant theme, which is associated with the Klingons, a warlike race of extraterrestrials, is heard when their spaceships are being attacked in the film's opening scene. The Klingon motif consists of pairs of ascending fifths (as in C to G in the scale), which sound repeatedly in a rhythmically syncopated idea introduced by French horns along with repeated pizzicato string tones and a clacking percussion sound. As the scene continues, the instrumentation includes trumpets along with tuba and flutes, plus rhythmic string tones and pounding drum sounds.

A love theme is introduced around 47:00 into the film, when executive officer Decker, whom Kirk has replaced as the *Enterprise*'s captain, meets his former lover, Ilea, a Deltan who has no hair. This theme, with its stepwise ascending motif of seven tones, is one of Goldsmith's most romantic melodies. It makes several later appearances in the film (and is also prominently featured in the film's overture, which is heard at the start of the director's cut edition).

One additional theme that is woven into the score is Alexander Courage's main theme for the TV series. It is introduced at around 39:20 when Kirk makes an entry in the ship's log. Then at around 52.15 and also at 1:29:30, as Kirk makes further log entries, the TV theme is briefly featured again at a soft dynamic level.

An especially noteworthy scene begins around 1:05:00 when the *Enterprise* enters the mysterious cloud. A fluttery-sounding flute pattern with soft harp tones begins the cue; then a continuing use of piano arpeggios and low brass tones adds a nervous energy to the scene. This eight-minute sequence is perhaps the least-melodic section of the score, but one of its most significant in terms of its dramatic musical impact. The climax of this sequence comes when the ship approaches the center of the cloud, where the mysterious entity called V'Ger resides. Here high-pitched flute sounds and lots of resonant brass tones accompany the arrival of the *Enterprise* at its destination.

In this scene and elsewhere Goldsmith inserted "clangy" sounds produced by an instrument called a Blaster Beam, which consists of a metallic tube that is struck against a strung metal board. The beam's highly resonant and accented sounds punctuate many of the film's most dramatic moments and were ingeniously incorporated into the film's sound design, which also includes a myriad of electronic sound effects.

This score is a superb example of grandly conceived film music, especially in the sci-fi genre. With its rousing melodies and glorious orchestration, Goldsmith's score richly deserves a place in this book.

Recognition

Nominated for three Oscars: Art Direction, Visual Effects, and Original Score.
Score also nominated for Golden Globe and Saturn awards (for science fiction score).
Enterprise theme also heard in *Star Trek V, VIII, IX,* and *X.* Also used as main theme for TV Series *Star Trek: The Next Generation.*

Recordings

Jerry Goldsmith, *Star Trek: The Motion Picture*, Columbia, 1986. Original vinyl soundtrack rereleased on Columbia CD. Good sound. ***½.
Jerry Goldsmith, *Star Trek: The Motion Picture*, Sony Legacy, 1998. Expanded soundtrack released on CD. Excellent sound. ****
Jerry Goldsmith, *Star Trek: The Motion Picture* (Limited edition), La-La Land, 2012. Complete score released on a three-disc set. Excellent sound.****

Bibliography

Bond, Jeff. *The Music of Star Trek: Profiles in Style.* Los Angeles: Lone Eagle Publishing, 1999.
Okuda, Michael, Denise Okuda, and Debbie Mirek. *The Star Wars Encyclopedia: A Reference Guide to the Future.* New York: Pocket Books, 1994.

—LEM

STAR WARS
(1977)
John Williams

The Film

Star Wars almost requires no introduction. Undoubtedly the most renowned science-fiction film of all time, one that has inspired eight sequels (and counting), George Lucas's magnum opus was a revelation in 1977 when it was first unleashed on the world. Little could Lucas, or the actors and actresses involved in the film, have known how colossal the franchise would become on a global scale.

Starring Mark Hamill, Carrie Fisher, and Harrison Ford, *Star Wars* is set "a long time ago in a galaxy far, far away," to quote the now-famous opening captions that precede each film. In the original 1977 film, later titled "Episode IV: A New Hope," the Empire, under the rule of antagonist Darth Vader, holds Princess Leia (Fisher) as prisoner, in an effort to crush the rebellion being fought against it. Luke Skywalker (Hamill) and Han Solo (Ford) work together to rescue the princess, assist the Rebel Alliance, and restore freedom and justice to the galaxy by attempting to defeat the Empire. The film was referred to as Episode IV because it was always Lucas's intention to create a prequel trilogy, which eventually arrived be-

Mark Hamill, Carrie Fisher, and Harrison Ford before they became cinematic icons. *Lucasfilm Ltd. / Twentieth Century Fox Film Corporation*

tween 1999 and 2005. A third trilogy, Episodes VII–IX, scheduled to be completed by 2019, is under the new ownership of Disney. There are also stand-alone films being made, with the first, *Rogue One: A Star Wars Story*, released in 2016 and *Solo: A Star Wars Story* scheduled for release in 2018.

The Music

John Williams, recommended to director George Lucas by his friend and contemporary Steven Spielberg, composed the music for *Star Wars*, and he would eventually compose the music to the seven subsequent films in the series at the time of writing. The score for the original 1977 *Star Wars* was performed by the London Symphony Orchestra with Williams himself conducting. Heavily influenced by late Romantic composers such as Richard Wagner, Gustav Holst, and Richard Strauss, Williams's score, along with Lucas's film, acts as a grandiose space opera. The use of the leitmotif technique, championed by Wagner and adopted by Williams in film scoring, assists the audience in associating and memorizing characters and locations.

The main theme to *Star Wars*, arguably one of the most famous film music themes in the history of the medium, opens every film. The opening brass chord, almost pinning the audience back in their movie theatre seats, is emphasized even more by the silence that precedes it. "A long time ago, in a galaxy far, far away" fades to black, and then we hear it—a fortissimo assault on our auditory nerves as the words STAR WARS appear, along with Williams's triumphant fanfare-esque introduction to the main theme. The scrolling text outlining the context of the plot, a cinematic technique now synonymous with the *Star Wars* series, accompanies the main theme, until it fades out as the camera pans to a behemoth of a spaceship entering the frame. This can be regarded as an overture to the film, if we persist with the comparisons to opera. Aside from the main theme, the *Star Wars* films have a catalog of musical themes (leitmotifs) for characters and locations. Princess Leia, for example, has her own theme, but also one that links her romantically to Han Solo. Every key character is represented musically, and these themes run through all the films where they are present. One exception is Darth Vader, whose infamous Imperial March theme was not composed until 1980 with the release of *The Empire Strikes Back*. In the original *Star Wars* film, Williams composed a much less effective sinister brass theme for Vader and the Empire. The Imperial March became the de facto musical representation of the Empire and Vader from episode five onward, and it has been used in parody and pastiche across a wide range of films and television programs as a representation of evil.

It is clear that the comprehensive score by Williams does more than simply accompany the visual and narrative elements. In *Star Wars*, the music is woven into the film so tightly that it becomes impossible to imagine the film without the score. The music follows the characters' narrative arc throughout and becomes an immovable feature of these science-fiction classics. Williams's scores deserve their place in the very highest echelons of film music. Indeed, the American Film Institute named this first *Star Wars* score number one in its list of 100 Years of Film Scores, and the Library of Congress has included it in the National Recording Registry.

Recognition

1977 Academy Award for Best Original Score.
1977 Golden Globe Award for Best Original Score.
1977 Saturn Award for Best Music.
1978 Grammy for Best Instrumental Pop Recording.
1978 Grammy for Best Original Score.
1978 Grammy for Best Instrumental Composition.
1978 BAFTA Award for Best Film Music.

Recordings

John Williams, *Star Wars: The Ultimate Soundtrack Collection*, Sony Music Classical, 2016. This eleven-disc box set contains music from the first six films (episodes I–VI) and includes a DVD about the music of *Star Wars* as well as a bonus disc containing interviews with Harrison Ford. The definitive recording for fans of the series. ****

John Williams, *Star Wars Episode IV: A New Hope*, Sony, 2004. This remastered, two-disc soundtrack contains over one hundred minutes of music and is almost comprehensive in its coverage. Recommended if only interested in the first film. ***

—ML

A STREETCAR NAMED DESIRE

(1951)
Alex North

The Film

Directed by Eliza Kazan, *A Streetcar Named Desire* stars Marlon Brando and Vivien Leigh as Stanley Kowalski and Blanche DuBois in a film adaptation of the Pulitzer Prize–winning Tennessee Williams play of the same name from 1947.

Stanley (Marlon Brando) works as a traveling salesman when he moves to New Orleans to marry his love, Stella (Kim Hunter). Stanley meets Stella's sister, his sister-in-law, for the first time. Blanche (Vivien Leigh) is perturbed at the cramped apartment, and she and Stanley have an acrimonious relationship from the beginning. Stanley becomes suspicious when it appears Blanche has planned to stay in New Orleans for the rest of her life. He becomes concerned that Blanche is there for unscrupulous reasons and is worried that Stella's claim on the family fortune has gone missing. Stanley investigates Blanche's past and attempts to find out why she was fired from her jobs. The relationship between Stanley and Stella is soured by his treatment of Blanche, and the film concludes with Stanley being blamed for Blanche's downfall from a respected but troubled girl into a destroyed soul.

The film has many memorable scenes, including one set on a staircase where Stella is desperate to hide from Stanley, but she is so dependent on him that she is seductively drawn back down the stairs toward him. The sweaty climate of New Orleans is perfectly represented in this claustrophobic, dramatic film.

The film was overwhelmingly successful and received twelve Academy Award nominations, of which it won four for acting. It was also nominated for three Golden Globes, winning one, and two BAFTAs, winning one. In terms of Academy Award nominations, it is the joint third-most-successful film of all time.

Mentally frail Blanche DuBois (Vivien Leigh) is manhandled by her brother-in-law Stanley Kowalski (Marlon Brando). *Warner Bros. / Photofest © Warner Bros.*

The Music

The music to *A Streetcar Named Desire* was composed by Alex North. The score was not without controversy, as the "lustful and carnal" music found itself a casualty of censorship and was replaced at times with a much less effective, romantic string score. However, North's score was later reinstated, much to the benefit of the film.

A Streetcar Named Desire opens with a sultry, jazzy, passionate exposition of the main musical themes and textures that will follow in the remainder of the film. The opening themes are episodic in nature, something that North favors in his film compositions. These short melodic or harmonic fragments can then be layered or manipulated and are easier to handle than longer, flowing melodies. The score is dense and saturates the film, often appearing below dialogue to give a very complex sound world that combines speech, music, and sound effects. It can almost be suffocating, which is appropriate, considering the cramped living conditions and tense atmosphere shared by the main characters.

The opening music, within seconds, leaves the audience under no doubt that this will be a film of ferocious passion and heated desire. However, North did state that the opening main theme has "nothing to do with the personalities, but the atmosphere of the city."

The score combines jazz and swing, along with song, Romanticism, and modernism, which has been described as containing "harmonic language ranging from simple functional harmony to complex enriched and altered chords." There are also elements of atonality present in the score, which sits well with the time period in which the film was released. The height of tonal and atonal experimentation was in the mid-twentieth century. The rhythms are also complex, in line with the jazz-heavy score. The composer felt very strongly about the use of jazz in the film, claiming: "I thought the play had a very sensuous feeling, and to reflect that best would be by using elements of jazz. . . . The first time that Stanley meets Blanche, there is a club, a little dive, so I tried to combine the fact there was source music, and also this sensuous, sexual undercurrent, and I just felt that jazz could best reflect those particular moments."

The majority of North's material is inspired from the main title theme. The composer called this theme the "germ" or "essence" of the score, and it introduces the diminished fifth (or tritone) interval that is a common occurrence during the score. This interval represents the character of Stanley, but can also be seen as a signifier of Blanche's time at Belle Reve, an idealistic notion she has of a seemingly blissful past.

The music in *A Streetcar Named Desire* has been described as objective or subjective, depending on the scene. On one hand, subjective music conveys the internal struggles of the characters, whereas objective music might be the jazzy signification of the city. There are occasions when subjective music appears an objective scene, and vice versa, which gives the impression of music acting as counterpoint to the overall mood of the narrative or visual scene.

The standout scene in the film, and one that fell afoul of the censors, was the staircase scene where Brando shouts up: "Hey Stella!" In this extremely sensual scene, Stella slowly descends the staircase, accompanied by flute. Brando stands at the bottom waiting for her, accompanied by saxophone. The two instruments' melodic lines writhe around each other in a sexually charged musical moment, until the two finally embrace at the bottom of the staircase. The sultry, sexy sound of the saxophone perfectly represents the raw sexuality of Brando's sweaty, expectant body, while the delicate flute highlights the innocence, perhaps false, of the descending, alluring female on the staircase.

There is little doubt that North's score was risqué, but there is also no doubt that it perfectly represents the very essence of *A Streetcar Named Desire*. It remains one of the classic jazz-inspired scores in film history.

Recognition

Nominated for Academy Award for Best Music.

Recording

Alex North, *A Streetcar Named Desire*, Varese Sarabande, 2014. This is an accomplished performance by the National Philharmonic Orchestra under the direction of Jerry Goldsmith. The forty-six-minute score is spread across fifteen tracks. ****

Bibliography

Davison, Annette. *Alex North's A Streetcar Named Desire: A Film Score Guide*. Lanham, MD: Scarecrow Press, 2009.
Palmer, Christopher. "Film Music Profile: Alex North." *Film Music Notebook* 3, no. 1 (1977): 2–8.

—ML

SUNSET BOULEVARD

(1950)
Franz Waxman

The Film

Directed by Billy Wilder and starring William Holden and Gloria Swanson, *Sunset Boulevard* received critical acclaim on its release.

Joe Gillis (William Holden) is a screenwriter in early post-war Hollywood. He is not able to sell his work and is giving up on the dream of making it in the film industry by considering moving back to his small, sleepy hometown to take up an office job. While escaping from his money woes, his car breaks down on Sunset Boulevard, and he finds himself at the mansion of former silent-movie star Norma Desmond (Gloria Swanson). The actress has delusions of grandeur and invites Joe to live with her so he can write films and she can star in them as a comeback. A romantic relationship develops between them, but Joe falls for another writer, which results in Norma murdering him. Her final delusion is thinking that the police and press are gathered for her big comeback, with her home as a movie set.

The film was nominated for eleven Academy Awards, winning three for Best Story and Screenplay, Best Art Direction, and Best Original Score. It also won four of seven Golden Globe nominations.

The Music

The score to *Sunset Boulevard* was composed by Franz Waxman, one of the great composers of the Golden Age of Hollywood. The score was voted number sixteen on the American Film Institute's 100 years of film scores list of the twenty-five greatest. The composer was suited to the job, according to the director, because

Screenwriter Joe Gillis (William Holden) and faded star Norma Desmond (Gloria Swanson). *Paramount Pictures / Photofest © Paramount Pictures*

of his style. He wrote with a rich German Romanticism, inspired by greats such as Richard Strauss, Richard Wagner, and Erich Wolfgang Korngold. His music was described as "elegant and full," but also "slightly tortured," and he was praised for enhancing the dark psychology and emotional tension in his previous scores. Waxman utilized his belief in orchestral color in this score. He claimed that melody was secondary to him and that he would instead see a scene and "hear" a particular ensemble of instruments, not necessarily a melodic line.

The two main characters in *Sunset Boulevard* have contrasting themes. For Gillis, who is out of hope, Waxman composed an "aimless, nonchalantly syncopated melody—deliberately flat in tone, gray in color." This theme usually features a piano, and it is a wonderful example of how music can express not just exuberance or heroism, but also downright destitution and mediocrity.

For Norma's delusional persona, Waxman created a flute trill. It is jabbed, "pecked out," and at various moments accented or syncopated. This is a musical representation of her madness, and her own musical theme appears underneath this harsh soundscape.

At various points in the film, Waxman brings other musical themes in to underscore the developing narrative. In one witty moment, he takes the old Paramount newsreel theme and slows it down as Gillis and the young writer he falls for walk through the actual Paramount lot. There is an exotic theme for the murder of Gillis, but it is "twisted and tortured." This tango theme may also suggest Norma is something of a femme fatale. In the end, for the final deluded moment of Norma Desmond's narrative, there is a fanfare, muted, as if being played from a great distance. The tango theme reappears, reflecting the murder, but also her apparent ecstasy, as she believes she is starring in a new film.

The two characters' musical themes have been referred to as representing "dead dreams" and "delusions," which summarizes it perfectly. The contrast between the sane character and his mediocrity, underscored by plain, unassuming music, and the madness of the failed actress, whose music is anything but plain, is effective. This contrast extends to scoring man against woman, older against younger, an ideal past against uncertain present and future. The music plays to the narrative, convincing us that Norma Desmond is a glitzy, successful, flamboyant character, when in fact she is no different from the failed screenplay writer Gillis.

Interestingly, the musical themes are switched around at certain points by Waxman. When Gillis first enters Norma's mansion, he says "The name is Gillis," but this is accompanied by Norma's theme. Likewise, when he begins to write her script, seemingly in control and getting his life back on track, Norma's theme dominates the score, showing that she is calling the shots.

The music throughout has an existential strain to it, with gothic and noir undertones, but remains a useful exercise in studying character music in cinema.

Preexisting film music styles were also utilized to complement Waxman's original score. He used distorted arrangements of film music moments from the 1920s and 1930s to underscore Norma's delusional state of mind.

Recognition

Academy Award for Best Original Score.
Golden Globe for Best Original Score.

Recording

Franz Waxman, *Sunset Boulevard: The Classic Film Scores of Franz Waxman*, RCA Red Seal, 2008. This is a compilation album with several of Waxman's most memorable film scores present. A worthwhile purchase for an overview of his musical output. ***

Bibliography

Caps, J. "Soundtracks 101." *Film Comment* 39, no. 6 (2003): 31.
Palmer, C. *The Composer in Hollywood*. London: Marion Boyars Publishers, 1990.
Pelkey, S. C., and A. Bushard, eds. *Anxiety Muted: American Film Music in a Suburban Age*. New York: Oxford University Press, 2015.
Sikov, E. *On Sunset Boulevard: The Life and Times of Billy Wilder*. Jackson: University Press of Mississippi, 2017.

—ML

SUPERMAN
(1978)
John Williams

The Film

Directed by Richard Donner and starring Christopher Reeve, Marlon Brando, and Gene Hackman, *Superman* is a superhero film based on the DC Comics character of the same name. At the time of release, with a budget of $55 million, it was the most expensive film ever made, and was lauded by critics for the use of visual effects.

The movie begins on Krypton, where Superman's father sends him off to Earth as a young child. He grows up to be a newspaper reporter named Clark Kent but has an alter ego, Superman. When the evil Lex Luthor plans to take over the world, Superman is the only one who can stop him. The film was nominated for four Academy Awards, of which it won one, a Special Achievement Award for visual effects. The nominations were for Best Sound, Best Editing, and Best Original Score. It also received nominations for five BAFTAs, winning one for Most Promising Newcomer (Christopher Reeve), and one Golden Globe for Best Original Score.

Superman (Christopher Reeve) saves the day again! *Warner Bros. / Photofest © Warner Bros.*

The Music

The score to *Superman* was composed by John Williams. Originally, Jerry Goldsmith was due to write the music, having collaborated with Richard Donner on *The Omen*. However, scheduling conflicts caused Goldsmith to drop out, and Williams, fresh off the *Star Wars* success of 1977, took over. The score was performed by the London Symphony Orchestra and conducted by Williams. The composer is said to have been attracted to the film because it did not take itself too seriously, and he thought it had a "theatrical camp feel" to it.

There are several words that can summarize the main theme to *Superman*. Bombastic, heroic, noble, or even patriotic. There is no doubting that Williams's fanfare depicting the superhero is timeless. It is a bold claim to make, but there are those who suggest that Superman's musical theme is the most accomplished character music Williams has ever composed, which, given his back catalog, is praise indeed. It is difficult to argue against this opinion, though. With the possible exception of Darth Vader and the Imperial March in the *Star Wars* series, nowhere else does Williams so blatantly apply a musical style to a character that fits so effectively and naturally. Superman is a superhero, so the music is superheroic. Superman is a patriot, so the music is overwhelmingly patriotic. The film is a bombastic romp through a DC Comics adaptation, and so the music follows suit.

The brassy, excessive orchestral might that performs the theme would have completely drawn audiences in at the first showings of the film, and it continues to have a similar appeal today. *Superman* is one of those films where the very mention of it will have a good proportion of people humming or singing the fanfare. The score, like many by Williams, is truly as memorable as the film.

There is, of course, more to the soundtrack than the main theme. The love theme, which appears at various points during the film, is based on a song "Can You Read My Mind," with lyrics by Leslie Bricusse. It was originally intended that the song appear in the film, but the character of Lois Lane speaks the lyrics in the film instead. This love theme appears in the opening main theme, but appears more prominently each time Clark Kent and Lois Lane share screen time. There is also a clever cue entitled "Personal" which links Clark Kent to Superman by musically connecting the heroic main theme and the love theme, highlighting the duality of his personalities. The only minor blip in what can be considered a true Williams classic is the "March of the Villains," which, while playing on Gene Hackman's whimsical, slightly comical portrayal of a villain, borders on slapstick and does not seem to quite fit with the orchestral prowess and power of the rest of the score. It has been referred to as "irritatingly prancing," which perhaps is unjustified, but regardless, film lovers may recall more fondly the main theme and love theme.

Overall, it is yet another Williams score that justifiably makes the final cut for this book, due to one of his most recognizable themes. The main theme to *Superman* remains a staple of orchestral film music concerts around the world. It is eminently hummable, a superhero soundtrack for the ages.

Recognition

Grammy for Best Instrumental Composition.
Grammy for Best Album of Original Score.
Nominated for Academy Award for Best Original Score.
Nominated for Golden Globe for Best Original Score.

Recording

John Williams, *Superman—The Movie* Soundtrack, Rhino/Warner Bros., 2010. This epic soundtrack album covers two and a half hours in thirty-five tracks. It is the original 1978 recording, remastered somewhat, and contains previously unreleased material. The sound quality can be a little dated at times, but this does not detract from an essential album to own. ****

Bibliography

Donner, Richard, and Tom Mankiewicz. *Superman*. DVD audio commentary. Warner Home Video, 2001.

Graydon, D. At Home: Soundtracks: "*Superman the Music: 1978–1988*." *Empire Magazine*, 2008.

London Symphony Orchestra and Film Music. Archived September 30, 2011, at the Wayback Machine. Retrieved November 20, 2017. https://lso.co.uk/orchestra/history/lso-and-film-music.html.

—ML

T

THE THIRD MAN
(1950)
Anton Karas

The Film

Directed by Carol Reed and starring Joseph Cotten, Valli (Alida Valli), Orson Welles, and Trevor Howard, *The Third Man* is a noir film set in post–World War II Vienna.

Holly Martins (Joseph Cotten) arrives in Vienna, Austria, to meet his old school-friend Harry Lime (Orson Welles). Lime has offered the unemployed writer a job in his home city. Unfortunately, as he arrives in Vienna, Martins learns that Lime has died and meets Lime's friend-cum-lover Anna Schmidt (Alida Valli). Seemingly against his character, it is revealed that Lime was the leader of a drug gang that stole penicillin from the military hospital. This had caused many deaths among the child population of Vienna. In a thrilling plot twist, Lime's death is exposed as a fake.

The film was nominated for three Academy Awards, winning one for Best Cinematography. It also won one of two BAFTA nominations.

The Music

The musical score to *The Third Man* was composed by Anton Karas, a Viennese zither player who composed it by pure chance. The director had decided to avoid heavily orchestrated waltzes, despite the film being set in the home of such music, Vienna. While he visited Vienna, he heard a zither player in a wine garden. It was Anton Karas. Reed took Karas to London by invitation, and the two worked together on the score for six weeks, with Karas staying at the director's home.

The resulting score consists of existing songs adapted for zither and new compositions such as "Café Mozart Waltz" and "Harry Lime." When the film was released, Karas's music was the result of as much enthusiastic praise as Reed's directing. William Whitebait in the *New Statesman and Nation* (1949) excitedly stated: "What sort of music it is, whether jaunty or sad, fierce or provoking, it would be hard to reckon; but under its enthrallment, the camera comes into play. . . . The

From left: Holly Martins (Joseph Cotten) and the third man, Harry Lime (Orson Welles). *Selznick Releasing Organization / Photofest © Selznick Releasing Organization*

unseen zither-player . . . is made to employ his instrument much as the Homeric bard did his lyre." Another reviewer claimed that the real hero of the film was the unseen zither player.

James Limbacher, writing in 1974, claims that the music recalled the age of the silent film and its solo accompaniments: "Mr Reed has successfully revived accompaniment by a solo instrument without any of the drawback attaching to its early practice. Many of us can recall the old procedure: 'Hearts and Flowers' for deathbed, 'William Tell' for Fire, Trainwreck, Battle, or Storm." The simplicity of the score, so unusually for solo instrument, is the reason for its success. It does not purport to be anything it is not. It is a simple, atmospheric accompaniment to life in postwar Vienna. Whether it is authentic or not to that time in that city is another question, but the fact that the director heard Karas playing a waltz obviously made an impact, and the background music became a big hit and saw a rise in interest in the zither. *Time* magazine said Karas's playing provided "jangling melancholy," and was "catchy" and "twangy."

Some criticism was aimed at the score for being monotonous after a while, with the sound of the zither alone starting to "oppress the ear long before the tale has been told." But there is enough variation in the different performance techniques and repertoire to make it a classic film score that is as highly regarded today as it was in 1950. Three hundred thousand records were sold in the opening weeks, and street performers could be heard playing Karas's melodies found in the film. According to one report, the Marquess of Blandford at an event in London requested Karas play the Harry Lime theme six times in a row, such was its popularity. This popularity in London overwhelmed the composer with delight, and he reportedly said: "I am so happy; I am so happy. Perhaps the sound of the zither is new. In Vienna, you hear zither music everywhere."

Recognition

The score did not receive any award nominations, but it should be acknowledged that in the early postwar years, there were fewer award ceremonies for films, and as such the chances to be nominated were far lower. Perhaps the enthusiastic critical response through the years is tribute enough. In fact, Roger Ebert once asked, "Has there ever been a film where the music more perfectly suited the action than in Carol Reed's *The Third Man*?"

Recordings

Gertrud Huber, *The Third Man*. Silva Screen Records, 2003. This disc markets itself as the "world premiere digital recording" of *The Third Man* soundtrack. Containing twenty tracks and running to forty-eight minutes in length, the zither is performed with aplomb; however, a digital remastering of Karas's original performances would have been welcomed. ***

Anton Karas, *The First Man of the Zither Plays "The Third Man Theme" and Other Original Recordings*, Jasmine Music, 2002. This recording is the remastered original soundtrack. It is well recommended as the only place to hear the composer himself performing the score. ****

Bibliography

Aspden, Peter. "Sewers, Zithers and Cuckoo Clocks." *Financial Times*, June 13, 2015, Arts 16.
Ebert, Roger. "The Third Man (1949)." *Chicago Sun-Times*, December 8, 1996.
Limbacher, James L. *Film Music: From Violins to Video*. Vol. 1. Metuchen, NJ: Scarecrow Press, 1974.
"Zither Dither." *Time*, November 28, 1949.

—ML

TITANIC
(1997)
James Horner

The Film

James Cameron's epic disaster film, telling the story of the sinking of the RMS *Titanic* in April 1912, surpassed all hopes and expectations at the box office. Indeed, the film held the title of highest-grossing film of all time for over a decade until the release of *Avatar*, also a Cameron film, in 2009. The film focuses on an unlikely romance between third-class passenger and artist Jack Dawson (Leonardo DiCaprio) and sophisticated first-class Rose DeWitt Bukater (Kate Winslet). Rose, being forced into an unhappy marriage for reasons of financial security, attempts suicide when she becomes disillusioned with her lot in life. Jack sees her leaning over the stern of the ship and rescues her. The ensuing narrative juxtaposes the striking of the iceberg and subsequent sinking of the ship with the ongoing battle between Jack and Rose and Rose's fiancé and entourage. The tragedy of the sinking of the ship is heightened by the death of Jack, just as rescue is on its way.

The film was nominated for fourteen Academy Awards and won eleven: Best Picture, Best Director, Best Art Direction, Best Cinematography, Best Visual Ef-

On the top of the world before falling into the icy sea: Jack Dawson (Leonardo DiCaprio) and Rose Dewitt Bukater (Kate Winslet). *Paramount Pictures / Photofest © Paramount Pictures*

fects, Best Film Editing, Best Costume Design, Best Sound, Best Sound Effects Editing, Best Original Dramatic Score, and Best Original Song. This was a joint record for both nominations and wins. The film also won four Golden Globes and was nominated for ten BAFTAs.

The Music

The late James Horner provided the score for *Titanic*, with Celine Dion performing "My Heart Will Go On" for the final credits, a song that arguably became as famous as the film itself by topping charts around the world and winning an Academy Award and Golden Globe for Best Original Song. The success of the song, and the score as a whole, is reflected in thirty million copies of the soundtrack sold, making it the highest-selling primarily orchestral film score of all time. The score is epitomized by its Celtic sound, with the consistent use of Uilleann pipes performing the main theme at various points in the film. The Celtic connection was intentional, with Enya being Cameron's first choice for the score. Her music was used by Cameron as a temp track in the first cuts of the film. James Horner was appointed after Enya refused the commission, and he consciously composed with Enya's musical style in mind.

Music is used effectively for the duration of the film to depict both the grandeur and tragedy of the ship and Jack and Rose's romance. The film opens with sepia footage of the *Titanic* setting sail, with passengers and onlookers waving as the ship departs. The ethereal vocals of Swedish soprano Sissel Kyrkjebø performing the heartbreaking "Never an Absolution" accompany this opening scene, before a transition to the present day takes the viewer to the wreck of the ship. This theme returns at particularly poignant moments in the film and is undoubtedly the predominant musical theme. Another prominent musical theme is titled "Southampton." This is an uplifting, soaring theme that uses synthesized choirs and pulsating percussion to promote a feeling of positivity, progress, and speed. It is the theme played under DiCaprio's famous "I'm the King of the World!" line as he stands at the bow of the ship. However, given the direction of the narrative, it is not heard again after the half-hour mark.

It was not only Horner's original score that made an impact in the film. The historically accurate notion that the "band played on" is represented as the ship goes down, with the ship's string ensemble performing "Nearer My God to Thee." This hymn, written in the nineteenth century by Sarah Flower Adams, is emotively played as a montage of the chaos aboard the sinking ship witnessed by the audience.

The emotional climax of the film brings about the return of Sissel Kyrkjebø's haunting voice. As Rose realizes Jack has died from exposure and lets him sink to the bottom of the Atlantic Ocean, "Never an Absolution" returns to the soundscape. It is a highly moving scene, with a crew member on a nearby lifeboat shouting, "Is anyone alive out there?" as Rose makes the choice between life and death. She lets Jack go and swims toward rescue.

"My Heart Will Go On" only appears in its entirety during the end credits, but there are various moments in the film where the introduction and melody are heard. This wordless rendition of the song is entitled "Rose" on the official soundtrack, as it is used to represent Winslet's character. Noteworthy examples of this music are when Jack is drawing the nude portrait of Rose shortly before the sinking, and when they embrace on the bow of the ship as the *Titanic* sees its last daylight. The piano introduction also makes a brief appearance as Rose looks forlornly at the Statue of Liberty, having finally arrived in New York City, and makes one final appearance as the present-day Rose lies in her bed and, according to which theory you believe, dreams of the *Titanic* or dies and is finally reunited with Jack.

Recognition

1997 Academy Award for Best Original Song ("My Heart Will Go On").
1998 Golden Globe for Best Original Song ("My Heart Will Go On").
Number 1 Chart position in fourteen countries.

Recordings

James Horner, *Back to Titanic*, Sony Music Soundtrax, 1998. Additional music from the film, including a suite, an epilogue, and the inclusion of diegetic music from the film such as "An Irish Party in Third Class" and "Come Josephine, In My Flying Machine." Recorded by the London Symphony Orchestra and Choristers of Kings College Cambridge, it is a worthy addition to the original soundtrack release. ***
James Horner, *Titanic*, Sony Masterworks, 2012. This is a remastered four-CD collector's edition released on the 100th anniversary of the Titanic's sinking. Includes popular music from the era of *Titanic*, as well as all the tracks found on the first two soundtrack releases. ****
James Horner, *Titanic*, Sony Music Soundtrax, 1997. This is the official soundtrack produced by James Horner. ****

—ML

TO KILL A MOCKINGBIRD

(1962)
Elmer Bernstein

The Film

Harper Lee's autobiographical novel *To Kill a Mockingbird* won many literary awards when it was published in 1960, including the Pulitzer Prize. Two years later, Robert Mulligan's film version of the book was released, and it also won acclaim and numerous awards.

The film is faithful to the book, with the adult Scout (voice of Kim Stanley) narrating memories of her childhood in the town of Maycomb, Alabama, where her widowed father, Atticus Finch (Gregory Peck), tries to raise her and her older brother, Jem, during the Great Depression. Scout's narration also includes her father's legal defense of Tom Robinson, a black man, who is accused of raping a white woman. The children, along with Dill, a neighbor's nephew, become witnesses to the story's major events, including Robinson's trial and their father's attempts to see that justice is carried out. During this time, Atticus fears for the safety of his children and ultimately learns that their well-being depends on a most unlikely hero.

Defense lawyer Atticus Finch (Gregory Peck) and his client Tom Robinson (Brock Peters). *Universal Pictures / Photofest © Universal Pictures*

The Music

By the 1960s fewer Hollywood films were being scored in the grand orchestral tradition of Max Steiner and Erich Wolfgang Korngold. Elmer Bernstein's score for *To Kill a Mockingbird* is an example of a film in which the music has a resonance that is intimate rather than symphonic.

Nowhere is this intimacy more noticeable than in the opening credits, at the very start of which there is a lilting melodic line played on a piano; this idea becomes the children's theme, the film's principal musical idea. This short moment is followed by soft vocal sounds made by a child as she begins to take things out of a keepsake box. One minute into the credits the flute, accompanied by piano arpeggios and repeated chords sounded on a small harmonica, plays the children's theme in a lyrical-sounding statement. Strings and French horns soon join in playing a louder version of this theme, and then the piano softly repeats the theme with a background of harmonica chords as the titles come to an end.

This theme is heard throughout the film, but is limited to mostly short cues involving Atticus's children. The most extensive version of this theme occurs at the very end of the film.

Besides the children's theme there are other melodies in Bernstein's score. One of the most noteworthy occurs in an early scene where the children are playing with an old tire. When Scout gets inside the tire and Jem rolls it down the street there is an energetic cue that features multiple layers of motifs. First there is a rhythmic idea for strings and French horns that includes a syncopated effect caused by the use of a sudden silence within the pattern. This rhythmic "hiccup" is heard along with a fast-paced melodic idea for flutes; further layers are sounded by trumpets in a highly accented melody and fast-paced strings that mimic a rapid-sounding dance tune. Altogether this rambunctious cue resembles Bernstein's earlier music for *The Magnificent Seven* and also brings to mind the Western sounds of Aaron Copland's ballet music for *Billy the Kid* and *Rodeo*.

The score's most unusual music is associated with the ominous presence of the Radley house, which is located down the street from the Finch home. According to popular rumor, the Radley's son, whom the children refer to as "Boo," is a frightening and dangerous person, who stays locked up in the family home. Whenever they come near the Radley house, the music reflects the children's anxiety with a four-note fear motif. And yet, when the kids approach the Radley's porch the music reflects a different sound, with the piano playing a minor-key waltz melody that suggests the mystery of the hidden person inside the Radley house. The music suddenly shifts to rhythmically driven low harmonies when the children fear that they have been spotted.

Another memorable cue occurs after the trial, when Atticus's neighbor Maudie sits with the children while Atticus receives word that Tom is dead. The cue begins with the sounds of flute, clarinet, and bassoon, without any accompaniment. Cellos along with other strings soon add a sweet slow-paced melody, followed by the flute and piano, which sound a moment of the children's theme.

In the final sequence of the film, when Jem and Scout are assaulted on the way to a school Halloween party, the music gets extremely dramatic. Following the attack, when Atticus learns that his children were rescued by Boo, the music includes a lyrical version of the children's theme, with a solo cello accompanied by celesta and harp that are heard when Scout takes Boo's hand and brings him toward the bed where Jem is asleep.

Large sections of the film have no music, most especially the trial scenes that dominate a large portion of the film's second hour. But in the scenes with the children, the music adds to the sense of adventure that emanates from their youthful imagination. Ultimately the music serves as a reminder of the endless curiosity of childhood, with its adventures, fears, and sense of discovery. Throughout the film, Bernstein's music enhances the children's playfulness. The various styles of the score effectively enhance Harper Lee's story, which has been transferred to the screen with loving care. This is one of the composer's most subtle scores and also one of his most memorable.

Recognition

Eight Oscar nominations, including citations for Best Picture, Best Actor, and Best Musical Score. It won in three categories, but the film and scoring awards went to *Lawrence of Arabia*.

In 2007 the American Film Institute cited *Mockingbird* as number twenty-five on its list of 100 Years . . . 100 Movies as one of the greatest films of all time.

Recordings

Elmer Bernstein, *To Kill a Mockingbird*, Hallmark, 1996. Studio recording by Bernstein and the Royal Scottish Orchestra. Excellent sound and performance. ****

Elmer Bernstein, *To Kill a Mockingbird*, Mainstream, 1991. Original soundtrack CD. Available on Amazon Prime. Good sound. ***½

Bibliography

Hickman, Roger. *Reel Music: Exploring 100 Years of Film Music*. New York: W. W. Norton, 2006.

Mulhall, Kevin. Liner notes. *To Kill a Mockingbird*. Elmer Bernstein conducting the Royal Scottish Orchestra. Varése Sarabande VSD-5714, 1996, CD.

—LEM

TOM JONES

(1963)
John Addison

The Film

Comedy films have been around since the dawn of filmmaking, but truly inspired comedies such as Tony Richardson's boisterous film version of Henry Fielding's classic novel *Tom Jones* have been a rarity.

The title character (Albert Finney) begins life as an abandoned child who is taken in and raised by Squire Allworthy. Since Tom is illegitimate, he is looked down upon, especially by his neighbor, Squire Western, who objects to the attention Tom pays to Western's daughter, Sophie (Susannah York). When Allworthy orders Tom to leave home and be on his own, many unpredictable adventures occur, including trysts with several women. Throughout the film Tom wants Sophie, but many obstacles are put in his path.

The film is a very compacted version of Fielding's story, with techniques out of the silent era of filmmaking and the cinematic device of having characters wink at or talk to the camera.

Sophie Western (Susannah York) and the hedonist Tom Jones (Albert Finney) *Lopert Pictures Corporation / Photofest © Lopert Pictures Corporation*

The Music

John Addison's music is in many ways a patchwork quilt of musical styles and instrumental (plus some vocal) sounds. In its mixture of styles, the music reflects the film's inclusion of various filmmaking techniques.

The tone of the film is set at the very beginning, with a pre-credit sequence that was shot in the style of a silent movie. In the first scene, when Allworthy retires for the evening, he receives a great shock when he finds a newborn infant in his bed. The music is at first very lighthearted, with a harpsichord sounding a sprightly little tune with numerous fast-repeated pairs of tones, while a piano that sounds like an early eighteenth-century model provides a rhythmically steady background harmony. When baby Tom is discovered, the music shifts to a slow-paced melodic idea for solo piano. The music soon returns to the fast-paced first idea, when the squire demands to know who the baby's mother is. When he decides to raise the child and gives it a name, the film's credits begin.

The credits are accompanied by a rhythmic tune in which the accordion plays a sprightly tune containing sudden rhythmic stops. This start-and-stop sound adds to the lighthearted nature of the music, which also includes a clever background of staccato brass tones and percussion sounds. Toward the end of the credits there is a pompous march-style theme played by French horns with orchestra-bell tones in the accompaniment. This tune is later associated with both Squire Western and his meddling sister, who insistently tries to match Sophie with Allworthy's deceitful nephew, Mr. Blifil.

A sensuously playful tune for alto saxophone accompanies Tom's amorous frolics. It is first heard when Tom has a liaison with a young village lass named Molly, daughter of Allworthy's gamekeeper. This alto sax tune returns during several of Tom's amorous moments.

A lyrically romantic theme is associated with Sophie, who is attracted to Tom despite his apparent lack of social position. This theme features a sweetly flowing idea for piano assisted by the lilting tones of a solo violin. Together the piano and violin state this theme whenever Sophie appears onscreen.

Tom is musically associated with the accordion, which is featured in both full-melodic statements of the main theme as it appears in the opening credits, and in short variants of this idea that are heard as Tom tumbles from one adventure to another. An especially sweet string arrangement of this theme occurs when Tom is banished from Allworthy's estate. The most boisterous version of the idea occurs at a country inn where Tom is accused of making love with Mr. Fitzpatrick's wife and has to escape when Squire Western finds him there. The speeded-up photography is accompanied by a frantically fast-paced version of Tom's theme.

This theme is also heard when Tom and Fitzpatrick meet in London. Here the accordion is joined by trombones and many other instruments as the music keeps pace with the ensuing duel that ends with Tom being arrested.

One of the most amusing cues in the film involves a lively tune based on the hymn "O God Our Help in Ages Past," which follows a scene where the hymn is sung during a church service. This theme is sounded in a truly rowdy style by trombones with a circus-like harmonic background; it is featured when Tom gets into a fight as he wends his way on foot through a local village en route to London.

A second vocal theme occurs late in the film when Tom is wrongly accused of attempting to kill Fitzpatrick and is condemned to be hanged. As he paces about in his jail cell a male voice sings a melancholy ballad that begins, "If he swing by the string he will hear the bell ring, and then there's the end to poor Tommy." The melody of this faux English folk song is shortly thereafter sounded by a solo accordion in unison with a solo woodwind instrument as Tom's execution draws nearer.

One further theme worthy of mention is a jauntily rhythmic tune associated with Mr. Partridge, former barber for Allworthy and once accused of being Tom's father. The plucked tones of a banjo accompany Partridge as he walks about London trying to find someone who can save Tom from the hangman's noose.

There are a few scenes without scoring, especially the hunting scene at the Western estate early in the film. But otherwise the film is filled with an abundance of musical cues that aid immeasurably in keeping Tony Richardson's adaptation of Fielding's novel a memorable romp. John Addison's music is a huge asset to the film and one of the classic comedy scores of all time.

Recognition

Nominated for ten Oscars and winner of four, including Best Picture and Original Score.

In 2009 chosen by the British Film Institute as number fifty-one on their list of the Top 100 British Films of the Twentieth Century.

Recording

John Addison, *Tom Jones*, Kritzenland, 2009. European issue of the original soundtrack on CD. Limited edition. Good mono sound. ***½

Bibliography

Brode, Douglas. *The Films of the Sixties.* Secaucus, NJ: Citadel Press, 1980.

—LEM

U

UNBREAKABLE

(2000)
James Newton Howard

The Film

Hot on the heels of the acclaimed 1999 film *The Sixth Sense* came writer/director M. Night Shyamalan's *Unbreakable*, a film that did not initially impress audiences as much as its predecessor, but in the years since its initial release has become a cult classic.

In *Unbreakable* Bruce Willis plays David Dunn, a security guard in Philadelphia who laments that he has given up a football career to please his wife. His marriage is faltering, as is his relationship with his young son. His life is in a doldrums until he meets Elijah Price (Samuel L. Jackson), a graphic art dealer, who has a theory that in life there are polar opposites. Price suffers from a condition in which his bones break easily, while David seems immune to harm and has never had any ailments, except for a childhood incident in which he nearly drowned. David is eventually persuaded that he may have extraordinary powers. The question is: what will he do with them?

The Music

James Newton Howard's score for *Unbreakable* is unusual in two ways. First, he composed twenty minutes of music after meeting with Shyamalan during the film's initial planning stages. Howard viewed storyboards of the film and went to work even before shooting began. Second, Shyamalan asked that the score have what he called "singularity." Howard resolved this issue by creating a score that would avoid many of the usual orchestral instruments, limiting the instrumental pallet to a string orchestra with no wind instruments except for two trumpets. The only other instruments in the score are a solo piano and timpani, with synthesized percussion sounds. Another unusual scoring ingredient is Howard's use of piano "blings," high-pitched chords used as a form of musical punctuation.

Bruce Willis as the nearly indestructible David Dunn. *Buena Vista Pictures / Photofest © Buena Vista Pictures*

The film's first music occurs in the opening scene, set in 1961, when a black woman gives birth in a Philadelphia department store. As a doctor examines the newborn Elijah and finds the infant's limbs are broken, a soft theme played by piano and strings enters. This idea, primarily based on a descending motif of seven pitches, is soon joined by syncopated drum sounds provided by a synthesizer. This music, the "seeking" motif, leads directly into the film's credits.

This motif is next heard when David, the sole survivor of a train wreck that occurs early in the film, finds a note attached to his windshield after attending a memorial service for the crash victims. This idea carries over into the next scene when David arrives at his workplace. This melodic idea keeps returning as David ponders whether his survival was a fluke or a superhuman occurrence.

Another important thematic idea is introduced when David meets Elijah, who left the windshield note that asks whether David has ever been sick. During this meeting, when Elijah proposes that there are extreme opposites in life between the humanly frail (such as himself) and those who are perhaps like David, a new theme is sounded softly by the upper strings with soft piano tones in the background. This idea, the "hero" motif, which begins with an ascending fifth followed by three more rising pitches, suggests that David may be a hero without realizing it.

The hero idea returns in a bright motif for trumpet and strings when Joseph witnesses his father lifting more and more weight during a barbell workout in the basement of their home.

The closer David comes to realizing his potential powers the more powerful the music becomes. When he breaks into a barricaded facility to examine the damaged train, the seeking theme returns in a dramatic statement. This scene also includes David's memory of a car accident that occurred during his college years. When he tears off a car door to reach the trapped Audrey the hero theme is sounded triumphantly by trumpets and strings along with rumbling drums.

Elijah is musically identified with two ideas; the first is a repeated four-tone motif that is introduced when as a frail teenager he learns about superheroes and villains through comic books his mother has given him.

A lyrical idea for solo cello and strings is heard after Elijah suffers severe injuries from a fall. This idea, based on a smooth-flowing four-note motif, returns when he enters physical therapy and purposely goes to a clinic where Audrey works as a physical therapist.

The most dramatic music in the score comes after David takes Elijah's advice to be among people to test his physical and mental powers. When David enters a train station, synthesized drums provide loudly throbbing accents; the seeking motif then boldly sounds, with high trumpet tones soaring above the strings. When David follows a man in an orange jumpsuit to a private home he has invaded, the seeking motif is sounded repeatedly by strings and choral voices. A new three-note motif for strings is added to the music, with trumpets sounding the hero motif as David approaches the house.

Chilling sound effects are heard when David discovers the body of the homeowner and finds the man's teenage children who are still alive. There is no music when David enters an upstairs bedroom, but the seeking theme dramatically returns when David is pushed off a balcony into a swimming pool. The hero theme loudly returns when the teenagers assist him in climbing out of the pool. The seeking theme, with high trumpets, strings, and timpani, dramatically returns when David begins strangling the villain; the music then subsides as the man stops breathing.

All the music described above greatly enhances *Unbreakable*'s dramatic impact. Of the eight scores that Howard wrote for Shyamalan from 1999 to 2013, this is the most original. It is an audacious work that richly deserves inclusion in this volume.

Recognition

Nominated for Saturn award as Best action/adventure/thriller film.
In 2013 *Time* magazine recognized *Unbreakable* as number four on a list of top ten superhero movies.

Recording

James Newton Howard, *Unbreakable*, Hollywood Records, 2000. Original soundtrack on CD. Excellent sound. ****

Bibliography

MacDonald, Laurence E. *The Invisible Art of Film Music: A Comprehensive History*. Second edition. Lanham, MD: Scarecrow Press, 2013.

—LEM

UP

(2009)
Michael Giacchino

The Film

Up is a 3D computer-animated feature film, directed by Pete Docter. The film received universal acclaim, with critics praising it for including scenes of tragedy, personal discovery, and adventure, while still maintaining its family focus and sense of childlike adventure.

The film opens in 1940, where a young Carl Fredricksen idolizes famous explorer Charles F. Muntz. Carl befriends a girl named Ellie, who also worships Muntz. She tells Carl she wants to move to Paradise Falls in South America, a location that appeared in a travelogue film by Muntz.

In a wonderful, poignant montage scene that spans sixty years, we see Carl and Ellie eventually get married. The tragic element of the film occurs when Ellie suffers a miscarriage, after which the couple decide to visit Paradise Falls to bring some positivity back into their lives. They save for the trip, but the money keeps being spent on more urgent needs, such as repairing the house. Just as Carl saves up enough for the trip, Ellie becomes ill and passes away.

Later, Carl and Ellie's house is surrounded by skyscrapers, and his is the last house obstructing the real estate developers' plans. After pressure to leave, Carl keeps his promise to Ellie by turning his house into an airship using thousands of balloons. Russell, a young boy, becomes an accidental stowaway.

Carl's house lands on a mesa near Paradise Falls. Many adventures follow in the jungle, where Carl and Russell meet Dug the dog and a female bird that they name Kevin. The film finally ends with Carl's house perching on the cliff next to Paradise Falls, finally fulfilling their dream.

The film was nominated for five Academy Awards, of which it won two for Best Original Score and Best Animated Feature. It also won two Golden Globes and two BAFTAs in the same categories.

The Music

The score to *Up* was composed by Michael Giacchino; it was his third Pixar film. The director asked the composer for emotion, resulting in Giacchino composing themes based on the characters of Carl and Ellie but also other minor characters. Because of this style of composition, the composer sees the film as operatic in

Ellie and Carl in their younger years. *Buena Vista Pictures / Photofest © Buena Vista Pictures*

style, as these themes change style and orchestration depending on the situation the character is in.

It is unusual for one scene to summarize what is great about a score, but in *Up*, there is a four-minute montage sequence that indisputably epitomizes why Giacchino's score is so successful.

In this scene, which appears within the first ten minutes of the film, Carl and Ellie are shown to fall in love, get married, decorate a baby nursery, suffer a miscarriage, and grow old, before Ellie passes away. As one reviewer succinctly highlights, "The most noticeable quality of this sequence is its ability to tell a self-contained story that spans nearly 60 years without ever using one line of dialogue. It utilizes music and visuals to tell its narrative, almost feeling like a short film in the silent era of animation." The musical cue Giacchino writes is entitled "Married Life," but in truth, it is much more than the title suggests. While being based around the same melody, the adaptations Giacchino composes for the different stages of their lives create arguably the greatest opening sequence to an animated film in cinema history—and, quite honestly, in cinema history as a whole.

A jazzy, nostalgic take on the Mendelssohn wedding march opens the sequence. This segues immediately into a retro, ragtime variation on the film's main musical theme as they renovate and move into their new home together. The muted trumpet melody is taken over by romantic violin as they lay on the grass together in their twenties and thirties, looking at clouds in the sky. The music continues to evolve through brass and piano versions of the main theme as it shows Carl and Ellie working at the zoo and seeing clouds apparently shaped like babies. As they prepare a nursery for a future new arrival, the music slows almost to a complete stop. The scene transitions to a hospital. Ellie has lost her baby. This then cuts to Ellie sitting in the garden meditating, with Carl comforting her. A solo piano is now performing the main theme in a slow, poignant fashion. An accelerando takes the tempo almost back up to the same speed as the beginning of the clip as they begin saving for their big trip to Paradise Falls. The music continues with a nostalgic feel until Carl finally buys their tickets to Paradise Falls, but Ellie falls as she walks to him. The solo piano, tinged with a sadness of inevitability, shows Ellie in her hospital bed as the now elderly Carl visits her. The piano continues as Carl sits at her funeral, before finally returning to a dark house alone. It is without comparison as an emotionally shattering opening to a film, especially an animated Pixar film, which one would expect to be jovial and child-friendly.

The composer has been vocal about this scene, stating, "In that particular scene, I just remember watching that for the first time . . . and I was feeling very emotional about it because at some point during that scene you realize 'wow, this is not about this movie, this is about us' and everything in this we're all going to go through in one regard on another. We're all going to deal with these things that these characters are doing. You're going to lose someone that you love, that's going to happen. I think a lot of the music in there was a reflection of those feelings."

The remainder of the soundtrack relies on the main theme heavily, but it is the four-minute early scene that propels Giacchino's score into cinema history as one of the most heartbreaking. It is truly memorable and seldom leaves a dry eye in the room where it is being screened. If there is any doubt left as to the power of the score, winning all four major awards for his music settles the argument.

Recognition

Academy Award for Best Original Score.
Golden Globe for Best Original Score.
BAFTA for Best Music.
Grammy for Best Score Soundtrack.

Recording

Michael Giacchino, *Up*, Walt Disney Records, 2009. This twenty-six-track recording is the official soundtrack release of the film. It is wholly recommended for the third track alone, "Married Life." ****

Bibliography

Ciafardini, Marc. Exclusive: Interview . . . Film Composer Michael Giacchino. *Go, See, Talk*, May 14, 2012. http://goseetalk.com/interview-film-composer-michael-giacchino/.

O'Brien, Jon. "Michael Giacchino: *Up* [Original Score]." *Allmusic*. Accessed November 14, 2017. https://www.allmusic.com/album/up-original-score-mw0000819395.

Taylor, B. "How the 'Married Life' Opener Elevates '*Up*' to Great Heights." *Rotoscopers*. Accessed November 25, 2017. http://www.rotoscopers.com/2014/05/06/how-the-married-life-opener-elevates-up-to-animations-greatest-heights/.

—ML

V

The Film

Alfred Hitchcock specialized in making suspense thrillers, but *Vertigo* stands apart from his other films as a unique mixture of mystery and romance. Its plot concerns a man whose love for a supposedly suicidal woman becomes an obsession when after her untimely death he meets someone who bears a striking resemblance to her.

Scottie Ferguson (James Stewart) is a retired detective whose life has been haunted by a tragic accidental death that might have been avoided if he were not afraid of heights. After retiring from the San Francisco police force, he is approached by an old college friend, Gavin Elster, who wants Scottie to secretly follow Elster's wife, Madeleine (Kim Novak). Elster is concerned about his wife's strange behavior and fears she may try to harm herself. In shadowing Madeleine, Scottie saves her from an attempted drowning and then unexpectedly falls in love with her, but his affection leads to unforeseen and ultimately tragic consequences.

The Music

Vertigo, the fourth of Hitchcock's films to be scored by Bernard Herrmann, includes music that alternates between moods that are sinister and those that are romantic. This tonal duality is perceivable in the opening-credits sequence, which begins with art designer Saul Bass's close-ups of a woman's face.

As the Paramount logo appears, strings and flutes introduce a repeated series of tones with skips between the pitches, as in the pattern D-F-A-C#. Both ascending and descending renditions of this skipping motif are heard simultaneously. A moment later, brass instruments loudly sound a descending two-note idea that is superimposed over the skipping motif, which now features the flutes along with two harps. After the lead actors' names and the film's title are shown, further credits appear over a series of abstract figures with rotating circular images accompanied by swirling string tremolos.

Detective John "Scottie" Ferguson (James Stewart) hangs by a thread in the opening moments of *Vertigo. Paramount Pictures / Photofest © Paramount Pictures*

The opening scene includes turbulent music for a nighttime chase that ends with the death of a policeman who falls while trying to rescue Scottie, who is dangling from a roof gutter. The music gets especially dramatic when Scottie looks down. Loud harp arpeggios and muted trumpet tones add to the impact of this brief motif. Both the chase music and the vertigo motif recur later in the film.

The film's first hour includes many scenes with Scottie behind the wheel tailing Madeleine, who drives circuitously around San Francisco in a green car. In these scenes a slow-moving motif that begins with three scale-like tones is sounded alternately by woodwinds and strings.

One of the most significant musical ideas in the score is a Spanish-flavored rhythmic pattern in the style of a habanera, which Herrmann used to connect Madeleine with her supposed ancestor Carlotta Valdes, whose portrait Madeleine spends a lot of time studying in a museum. This rhythmic pattern is introduced when Scottie surreptitiously follows Madeleine to a gallery and finds her looking at Carlotta's portrait. A repeated D is sounded in the habanera rhythm by a harp with a soft minor-key melodic pattern that utilizes close parallel harmonies.

The habanera rhythm is subsequently played by low strings as Scottie follows Madeleine to a hotel where he learns that she often stays in a room rented to a

Carlotta Valdes. A later utterance of the habanera motif is sounded by a solo guitar.

One of the most memorable melodic ideas in the score is a love theme associated with Scottie and Madeleine, which is introduced in the scene where Scottie rescues her from drowning in San Francisco Bay. After some highly dynamic music that accompanies the drowning attempt, strings sound a brief moment of the love theme. After Scottie brings her to his home and relates to her what happened, the strings play a motif based on music from the opening credits, but the mood is entirely different now, as it becomes obvious that Scottie is increasingly infatuated with her.

Also heard in the scene following the rescue are repeated patterns of descending chords played by strings. The mysterious sounds of these chords are a clear foreshadowing of the score of *Psycho*, in which string instruments often play repeated patterns of descending harmonies.

When Scottie joins Madeleine for a drive up the California coast and into a redwood forest, a hint of the love theme returns. Sinister woodwind and brass harmonies, along with the wavy sounds of an electric organ, accompany a moment when Scottie tries to find out what is troubling Madeleine, who seems disturbed about her ancestral connection to Carlotta.

One of the film's most memorable musical moments occurs when the grieving Scottie has a dream about Madeleine's death and his own falling into an open grave. Several of the film's motifs are included in this sequence, including bits of the love theme, the chase music, the habanera rhythmic pattern, and the vertigo motif.

Late in the film, when Scottie obsessively attempts to turn Judy (also Kim Novak) into a facsimile of Madeleine, the love theme returns. When Judy's transformation is complete and Scottie has his lost love back in his arms, an extended cue includes a soaring orchestral rendition of this theme.

Throughout the film Herrmann's music shifts ingeniously between mysterious-sounding cues and romantic-tinged moments. The result is a score that masterfully captures the shifting moods of the film's story. The score for *Vertigo* is one of Herrmann's greatest achievements and richly deserves to be included in this book.

Recognition

AFI ranked *Vertigo* as number twelve on its list of 100 years of film scores.
British magazine *Sight and Sound* in 2012 placed *Vertigo* at the top of its list of greatest films of all time.

Recordings

Bernard Hermann, *Vertigo*, Varése Sarabande, 1996. Restored soundtrack release on CD. Excellent sound. ****
Bernard Hermann, *Vertigo*, Varése Sarabande, 1996. Studio recording by Joel McNeely and the Scottish National Orchestra on CD. Fine performance and sound. ****

Bibliography

Auiler, Dan. *Vertigo: The Making of a Hitchcock Classic.* New York: St. Martin's Press, 1998.

Mulhall, Kevin. Liner notes. *Vertigo* [restored soundtrack]. Varése Sarabande VSD-5759, 1996, CD.

—LEM

Appendix A

100 Additional Film Scores

When we started working on this book, we were confronted with the impossible task of narrowing our selections of films with great music to one hundred. Since there have been so many films with great music, we have prepared a second list of films, many of which were originally considered for this book but had to be set aside because of our selection limit. This list represents our acknowledgment of one hundred other film scores that are worthy of being included in a book such as this one.

The Abyss (1989)—Alan Silvestri
An Affair to Remember (1957)—Hugo Friedhofer
The Age of Innocence (1993)—Elmer Bernstein
The Alamo (1960)—Dimitri Tiomkin
Atonement (2007)—Dario Marianelli
Auntie Mame (1958)—Bronislau Kaper
Avatar (2009)—James Horner
The Bad and the Beautiful (1952)—David Raksin
Birth (2004)—Alexandre Desplat
The Blue Max (1966)—Jerry Goldsmith
A Bridge Too Far (1977)—John Addison
Captain from Castile (1947)—Alfred Newman
Champion (1949)—Dimitri Tiomkin
The Cider House Rules (1999)—Rachel Portman
The Cowboys (1972)—John Williams
Crouching Tiger, Hidden Dragon (2000)—Tan Dun
The Diary of Anne Frank (1959)—Alfred Newman
Double Indemnity (1944)—Miklós Rózsa
Dragonslayer (1981)—Alex North
El Cid (1961)—Miklós Rózsa
Elmer Gantry (1960)—André Previn
The English Patient (1996)—Gabriel Yared
Exodus (1960)—Ernest Gold
Fahrenheit 451 (1966)—Bernard Herrmann
The Fall of the Roman Empire (1964)—Dimitri Tiomkin
Far from the Madding Crowd (1967)—Richard Rodney Bennett
Fateless (2005)—Ennio Morricone
For Whom the Bell Tolls (1943)—Victor Young

Gettysburg (1993)—Randy Edelman
Glory (1989)—James Horner
The Grand Budapest Hotel (2014)—Alexandre Desplat
The Greatest Story Ever Told (1965)—Alfred Newman
Green Dolphin Street (1947)—Bronislau Kaper
The Guns of Navarone (1961)—Dimitri Tiomkin
Halloween (1978)—John Carpenter
Hamlet (1964)—Dmitri Shostakovich
Harry Potter and the Sorcerer's Stone (2001)—John Williams
Hawaii (1966)—Elmer Bernstein
The Heiress (1949)—Aaron Copland
Henry V (1989)—Patrick Doyle
The Hobbit: An Unexpected Journey (2012)—Howard Shore
Hoosiers (1986)—Jerry Goldsmith
How Green Was My Valley (1941)—Alfred Newman
How to Train Your Dragon (2010)—John Powell
The Hunchback of Notre Dame (1939)—Alfred Newman
In Cold Blood (1967)—Quincy Jones
The Incredibles (2004)—Michael Giacchino
The Informer (1935)—Max Steiner
Ivanhoe (1952)—Miklós Rózsa
Jane Eyre (1944)—Bernard Herrmann
Jason and the Argonauts (1963)—Bernard Herrmann
Jezebel (1938)—Max Steiner
The Jungle Book (1942)—Miklós Rózsa
Life Is Beautiful (1998)—Nicola Piovani
Lili (1953)—Bronislau Kaper
The Lost Weekend (1945)—Miklós Rózsa
Madame Bovary (1949)—Miklós Rózsa
Marnie (1964)—Bernard Herrmann
Memoirs of a Geisha (2005)—John Williams
The Miracle Worker (1962)—Laurence Rosenthal
The Molly Maguires (1970)—Henry Mancini
Mr. Holland's Opus (1995)—Michael Kamen
Much Ado about Nothing (1993)—Patrick Doyle
Murder on the Orient Express (1974)—Richard Rodney Bennett
Mutiny on the Bounty (1962)—Bronislau Kaper
The Night of the Hunter (1955)—Walter Schuman
The Nun's Story (1959)—Franz Waxman
Obsession (1976)—Bernard Herrmann
Patton (1970)—Jerry Goldsmith
Peyton Place (1957)—Franz Waxman
Picnic (1955)—George Duning
Poltergeist (1982)—Jerry Goldsmith
The Queen (2006)—Alexandre Desplat
Ragtime (1981)—Randy Newman
Raintree County (1957)—Johnny Green

Rebecca (1940)—Franz Waxman
The Red Shoes (1948)—Brian Easdale
The Reivers (1969)—John Williams
The Return of a Man Called Horse (1976)—Laurence Rosenthal
Richard III (1955)—Sir William Walton
Robin Hood: Prince of Thieves (1991)—Michael Kamen
Romeo and Juliet (1968)—Nino Rota
Sayonara (1957)—Franz Waxman
Sense and Sensibility (1995)—Patrick Doyle
Signs (2002)—James Newton Howard
Silverado (1985)—Bruce Broughton
633 Squadron (1964)—Ron Goodwin
The Snows of Kilimanjaro (1952)—Bernard Herrmann
Sophie's Choice (1982)—Marvin Hamlisch
Taras Bulba (1962)—Franz Waxman
Taxi Driver (1976)—Bernard Herrmann
Time after Time (1979)—Miklós Rózsa
The Treasure of the Sierra Madre (1948)—Max Steiner
The Untouchables (1987)—Ennio Morricone
Wall-E (2009)—Thomas Newman
The Way We Were (1973)—Marvin Hamlisch
The Wind and the Lion (1975)—Jerry Goldsmith
Wuthering Heights (1939)—Alfred Newman
Wyatt Earp (1994)—James Newton Howard
Zulu (1994)—John Barry

Appendix B

Composer Biographies

JOHN ADDISON (1920–1998)

Addison, the son a British military colonel, went to Wellington College, where he studied music. After military service during World War II, he taught composition at the Royal College of Music. He then turned to film composition beginning with *Seven Days to Noon* (1950). His credits include *Look Back in Anger* (1959), *The Entertainer* (1960), *A Taste of Honey* (1962), *Tom Jones* (1963), for which he won an Oscar, and *A Bridge Too Far* (1977).

Entry: *Tom Jones* (1963)

SIR MALCOLM ARNOLD (1921–2006)

Born in Northamptonshire, England, Sir Malcolm Arnold was not known primarily for his film scores, yet he still wrote over a hundred of them. With a back catalog of symphonies, concertos, and chamber music to his name, Arnold was one of the most prolific British composers of the twentieth century. His most famous film score was *The Bridge on the River Kwai* (1957), for which he won his only Academy Award.

Entry: *The Bridge on the River Kwai* (1957)

KLAUS BADELT (1967–)

Born in Frankfurt-am-Main, Germany, Klaus Badelt is best known for his collaborative work with Hans Zimmer. Invited to Zimmer's California studio at the age of thirty-one in 1998, Badelt began a long working relationship with Zimmer, and has since composed over fifty scores for film and television. While not yet enjoying the critical success or achievements of his collaborator, Badelt has an impressive résumé nonetheless.

Entry: *Pirates of the Caribbean: The Curse of the Black Pearl* (2003)

JOHN BARRY (1933–2011)

Born in York, England, Barry's father owned eight movies houses, while his mother was his first piano teacher. He later switched to trumpet and formed a band known as the JB7. He scored his first film, *Beat Girl*, in 1959. In the 1960s, he scored several James Bond films, including *Goldfinger* (1964) and *Thunderball* (1965). He won Oscars for *Born Free* (1966), *The Lion in Winter* (1968), *Out of Africa* (1985), and *Dances with Wolves* (1990).

Entries: *Born Free* (1966), *The Lion in Winter* (1968), *Somewhere in Time* (1980), *Out of Africa* (1985), *Dances with Wolves* (1990)

ELMER BERNSTEIN (1922–2004)

Born in New York City, Elmer Bernstein composed hundreds of scores in a career spanning fifty-three years. A hugely successful and influential composer, he was nominated for fourteen Academy Awards, winning once for *Thoroughly Modern Millie* (1967). To distinguish him from Leonard Bernstein (no relation), he was nicknamed Bernstein West due to his California home. He also pronounced his surname Bern-STEEN, compared to Leonard Bern-STEIN.

Entries: *The Magnificent Seven* (1960), *The Man with the Golden Arm* (1955), *To Kill a Mockingbird* (1962)

LEONARD BERNSTEIN (1918–1990)

Bernstein attended Harvard, and then studied conducting. He wrote scores for Broadway, including *On the Town* (1944), *Candide* (1956), and *West Side Story* (1957). He also wrote three symphonies, the ballet *Fancy Free* (1944), and several other concert works. From 1958 to 1970, he was music director of the New York Philharmonic, and for several years appeared on CBS with a series of *Young People's Concerts*. *On the Waterfront* (1954) is his only film score.

Entry: *On the Waterfront* (1954)

CARTER BURWELL (1954–)

Born in New York City, Carter Burwell is a frequent collaborator with the Coen brothers, having worked with them on fifteen occasions. He has composed the scores for over fifty films, and received his first Academy Award nomination in 2015 for *Carol*. While arguably one of the lesser-known composers in this book, Burwell has composed for successful films such as *The Big Lebowski* (1998), *Being Jon Malkovich* (1999), and *Twilight* (2008).

Entry: *Fargo* (1996)

CHARLIE CHAPLIN (1889–1977)

A stage performer in England from age five, Chaplin came to America in 1910 and soon became a silent film comedian with his tramp character. He directed his first feature film, *The Kid*, in 1921. Without formal training, Chaplin created music for all of his later films, including *City Lights* (1931), *Modern Times* (1936), *The Great Dictator* (1940), and *Limelight* (1952), for which he won a scoring Oscar when it was belatedly released in 1972.

Entry: *City Lights* (1931)

AARON COPLAND (1900–1990)

Copland achieved recognition as America's greatest modern composer for such works as the ballet scores *Billy the Kid* (1938), *Rodeo* (1942), and *Appalachian Spring* (1944). He composed several symphonies, plus concertos for piano and clarinet, and music for solo piano. He also created scores for several films, including *Of Mice and Men* (1939), *The Red Pony* (1949), *Our Town* (1940), and *The Heiress*, for which he won an Oscar in 1949.

Entry: *The Red Pony* (1949)

CARMINE COPPOLA (1910–1991)

Born in New York City, Carmine Coppola composed for just twelve films in his career. However, as the father of famous director Francis Ford Coppola, he wrote the music for the *Godfather* films (1972, 1974, 1990), cementing his place in history as the composer of some of the finest, most atmospheric film scores in cinema history. His other most recognizable work was *Apocalypse Now* (1979), the epic Vietnam War film, also directed by his son.

Entry: *The Godfather* and *The Godfather Part II* (1972, 1974)

JOHN CORIGLIANO (1938–)

Corigliano is the son of musicians. His father was principal violinist of the New York Philharmonic and his mother was a pianist. He studied music at Columbia and the Manhattan School of Music. His works include concertos for piano, oboe, and clarinet, three symphonies, and the opera *The Ghosts of Versailles* (1991). His first film score, *Altered States* (1980) earned him an Oscar nomination. Nine years later, he won the Oscar for *The Red Violin*.

Entry: *The Red Violin* (1999)

RANDY EDELMAN (1947–)

Born in Paterson, New Jersey, Randy Edelman moved to Los Angeles to compose for film and television. Well known for scores to comedy films such as *Twins* (1988) and *Kindergarten Cop* (1990), Edelman also contributed to films such as *The Last of the Mohicans* (1992), *Gettysburg* (1993), *The Mask* (1994), and *Billy Madison* (1995). A popular musician as well as film composer, Edelman has a cult following in Europe and Japan.

Entry: *The Last of the Mohicans* (1992)

DANNY ELFMAN (1953–)

Born in Los Angeles, Danny Elfman is a well-known modern-day film composer, famed for his collaborations with the director Tim Burton. In his career, he has been nominated for four Academy Awards, and has won thirty-five awards from seventy-five nominations. While his film compositions such as *Edward Scissorhands* (1990) are celebrated, perhaps his most famous work is the title theme to the TV show *The Simpsons* (1989–present).

Entries: *Batman* (1989), *Edward Scissorhands* (1990)

HUGO FRIEDHOFER (1902–1981)

Born in San Francisco, Friedhofer followed in his father's footsteps by becoming a cellist and playing in silent-movie orchestras. After studying music composition in Italy, he worked at the Fox studio in the early 1930s and then became an arranger at Warner Bros. After his Oscar for *The Best Years of Our Lives* in 1946, he became a freelance composer. His later nominations include music for *The Bishop's Wife* (1947) and *The Young Lions* (1958).

Entry: *The Best Years of Our Lives* (1946)

MICHAEL GIACCHINO (1967–)

Born in Riverside Township, New Jersey, Michael Giacchino is an American composer with Italian heritage. Starting a career in video game music in 1994, the composer soon expanded his oeuvre to include film and television, culminating in an Academy Award for *Up* in 2009. With an expansive back catalog and full schedule of blockbusters on the horizon, Giacchino looks set to be one of film music's big-name composers for the foreseeable future.

Entry: *Up* (2009)

JERRY GOLDSMITH (1929–2004)

Born in Los Angeles, Jerry Goldsmith has one of the most celebrated résumés of any film composer. His scores include *Planet of the Apes* (1968), *Papillon* (1973),

Chinatown (1974), *The Omen* (1976), *Alien* (1979), *Star Trek: The Motion Picture* (1979), *Poltergeist* (1982), *Gremlins* (1984), *Total Recall* (1990), *Basic Instinct* (1992), *L.A. Confidential* (1997), and *The Mummy* (1999). With eighteen Academy Award nominations, he was one of the most nominated film composers in history.

Entries: *Chinatown* (1974), *The Omen* (1976), *Planet of the Apes* (1968), *Star Trek: The Motion Picture* (1979)

DAVE GRUSIN (1934–)

Born in Littleton, Colorado, Dave Grusin (full name Robert David Grusin) is a composer, arranger, producer, and pianist, who has enjoyed a varied career in the music industry. Grusin won an Academy Award for the relatively unknown *The Milagro Beanfield War* in 1988 and has also received ten Grammy awards. The composer for over fifty films, Grusin's most recent Academy Award nomination came in 1993 for *The Firm*.

Entry: *On Golden Pond* (1981)

BERNARD HERRMANN (1911–1975)

A native New Yorker, Herrmann studied composition at Juilliard. He worked at CBS in the 1930s and became music director for Orson Welles's Mercury Theatre. In 1940, he came to Hollywood to score *Citizen Kane* (1941) and stayed in film composing for the rest of his life. He divided his time between films and such concert-hall works as *Symphony* (1941) and the opera *Wuthering Heights*. He also scored the Hitchcock classics *Vertigo* (1958) and *Psycho* (1960).

Entries: *Citizen Kane* (1941), *The Day the Earth Stood Still* (1951), *The Ghost and Mrs. Muir* (1947), *North by Northwest* (1959), *Psycho* (1960), *The 7th Voyage of Sinbad* (1958), and *Vertigo* (1958).

JAMES HORNER (1953–2015)

Born in Los Angeles, James Horner enjoyed a prolific film-scoring career before dying prematurely. A keen pilot, the light aircraft he was piloting over the California wilderness crashed into a forest. Horner was awarded two Academy Awards, both for *Titanic* (1997), and was nominated eight more times. His final score was the remake of *The Magnificent Seven*, released posthumously in 2016.

Entries: *A Beautiful Mind* (2001), *Braveheart* (1995), *Titanic* (1997)

JAMES NEWTON HOWARD (1951–)

Born in Los Angeles, Howard studied piano as a child and won prizes at the Thatcher School for boys. He majored in piano at USC while also studying composition. He worked with Elton John in the 1970s and began film scoring with *Head*

Office (1986). He won his first Oscar nomination for *Prince of Tides* (1991) and has scored several M. Night Shyamalan films, including *The Sixth Sense* (1999) and *Unbreakable* (2000), plus the *Hunger Games* films.

Entry: *Unbreakable* (2000)

MAURICE JARRE (1924–2009)

Jarre, born in Lyons, France, studied percussion at the Paris Conservatory. His composition career began with works for the theater in the 1950s. He combined classical concert works with film music for director Georges Franju. His first English-language film score was *Crack in the Mirror* (1960). Two years later, he won an Oscar for David Lean's *Lawrence of Arabia* (1962) and won two more Oscars for Lean's films of *Doctor Zhivago* (1965) and *A Passage to India* (1984).

Entries: *Doctor Zhivago* (1965), *Lawrence of Arabia* (1962)

TREVOR JONES (1949–)

Born in Cape Town, South Africa, Trevor Jones is a film composer not known particularly well outside of the film world. Despite this, he has worked on some very successful films such as *Labyrinth* (1986) and *The Last of the Mohicans* (1992). Ironically, perhaps his best chance at winning an Academy Award was with the latter, but as it was co-composed with Randy Edelman, it was ineligible for nomination.

Entry: *The Last of the Mohicans* (1992)

ANTON KARAS (1906–1985)

Born in Vienna, Anton Karas is unique in this book as one of only two composers (the other is Leonard Bernstein) who wrote the music for just one film, in this case *The Third Man* (1950). Karas was happy to write the score after a chance meeting with the director, but disliked the glamour and fame that followed. He toured the world infrequently in later life, but desired nothing more than to live a quiet life back home in Austria.

Entry: *The Third Man* (1950)

ERICH WOLFGANG KORNGOLD (1897–1957)

Korngold, a Viennese pianist and composer, was a child prodigy who composed three sonatas by age eleven and completed two opera scores by sixteen. The Nazi occupation of Austria caused Korngold, of Jewish descent, to relocate to America until the end of World War II. At Warner Bros., he scored his two Oscar winners, *Anthony Adverse* (1936) and *The Adventures of Robin Hood* (1938), plus such other Errol Flynn films as *The Sea Hawk* (1940).

Entries: *The Adventures of Robin Hood* (1938), *Kings Row* (1942), *The Sea Hawk* (1940)

HENRY MANCINI (1924–1994)

Starting at age eight Mancini learned to play both flute and piano and studied composing and arranging at Juilliard. In 1946, he started arranging for the Glenn Miller band and in 1952 joined the music staff at Universal. His music for the Blake Edwards TV series *Peter Gunn* earned him instant fame in 1958. He won Oscars for both "Moon River" and the score of *Breakfast at Tiffany's* and worked on Edwards's films into the 1990s.

Entries: *Breakfast at Tiffany's* (1961), *The Pink Panther* (1963)

JEROME MOROSS (1913–1983)

Born in Brooklyn, Moross was a talented pianist and composer from an early age and attended both New York University and Juilliard. His career parallels that of Aaron Copland in his diverse interests, which included music for the theater, concert hall, and movie screen. Following the success of the stage musical *The Golden Apple* (1954), he scored the films *The Proud Rebel* (1957) and *The Big Country* (1958), for which he received an Oscar nomination.

Entry: *The Big Country* (1958)

ENNIO MORRICONE (1928–)

Born in Rome, Morricone studied trumpet and music composition at the Conservatory of Santa Cecilia, from which he graduated in 1956. His film career began in 1961 with scores for Italian comedies and westerns. His music for the spaghetti westerns starring Clint Eastwood made him famous throughout Europe. He later achieved renown for *The Mission* (1986) and *The Untouchables* (1987), both earning Oscar nominations. He won the award in 2015 for *The Hateful Eight*. He is the only composer (other than Alex North) to ever receive an honorary Oscar for musical achievement in film.

Entries: *Cinema Paradiso* (1989), *The Mission* (1986), *Once Upon a Time in the West* (1968)

ALFRED NEWMAN (1901–1970)

A native of New Haven, Connecticut, Newman studied piano and composition as a youth and started conducting musicals on Broadway at fifteen. He came to Hollywood in 1930 and became music director, first at the Samuel Goldwyn studio and later at Twentieth Century Fox, where he earned many of his forty-five Oscar nominations for musical arrangements. He won the first of two original-score Oscars for *The Song of Bernadette* (1943).

Entries: *How the West Was Won* (1962), *The Prisoner of Zenda* (1937), *The Robe* (1953), *The Song of Bernadette* (1943)

RANDY NEWMAN (1943–)

Born in Los Angeles, this nephew of Alfred Newman began piano lessons at seven and started composing songs at fifteen. By the 1960s his songs were being recorded by Judy Collins and Peggy Lee, among others. In 1969, he recorded his first album and scored his first film, *Cold Turkey* (1971). He won Oscar nominations for the scores of *Ragtime* (1981) and *The Natural* (1984). He has earned Oscars for songs from two Pixar animated films.

Entries: *Avalon* (1990), *The Natural* (1984)

THOMAS NEWMAN (1955–)

Born in Los Angeles, Thomas Newman comes from a musically rich family, and is the youngest son of Alfred Newman. Since the 1980s, following a music education at USC and Yale, Newman has written almost one hundred scores and has been nominated for fourteen Academy Awards. His most prominent compositions include *The Shawshank Redemption* (1994), *Meet Joe Black* (1998), *The Green Mile* (1999), *Finding Nemo* (2003), and *WALL-E* (2008).

Entries: *The Green Mile* (1999), *The Shawshank Redemption* (1994)

ALEX NORTH (1910–1991)

Born in Chester, Pennsylvania, Alex North was a prominent film composer and was nominated for an Academy Award on fifteen occasions across a career that spanned four decades. One of his most famous scores was his earliest, *A Streetcar Named Desire* (1951), but he is also well known for *Spartacus* (1960), *Cleopatra* (1963), and *Who's Afraid of Virginia Woolf?* (1966). It was also North's score that was infamously rejected by Stanley Kubrick in *2001: A Space Odyssey* (1968).

Entries: *Spartacus* (1960), *A Streetcar Named Desire* (1951)

MICHAEL NYMAN (1944–)

Born in London, Michael Nyman is a composer well known for his minimalist style. While not a prolific film composer, Nyman has an extensive back catalog of symphonies, operas, and chamber works. He is also a musicologist, and was the first person to use the term "minimalist" in relation to music. Nyman was appointed Commander of the Most Excellent Order of the Bristish Empire in 2008 for his services to music.

Entry: *The Piano* (1993)

BASIL POLEDOURIS (1945–2006)

Born in Kansas City, Missouri, Basil Poledouris was a Greek-American composer of film and television music. In a career spanning almost four decades, he composed over fifty scores, and won an Emmy Award for the television mini-series *Lonesome Dove* in 1989. His most prominent scores include *Conan the Barbarian* (1982), *RoboCop* (1987), *Spellbinder* (1988), *The Hunt for Red October* (1990), *Free Willy* (1993), and *Starship Troopers* (1997). He died from cancer at age sixty-one in Los Angeles.

Entry: *Conan the Barbarian* (1982)

SERGEI PROKOFIEV (1891–1953)

Prokofiev was a Russian child prodigy who began studying piano at age three. By thirteen he had composed four operas, a symphony, and several piano pieces. Known as an *enfant terrible* for his music from the 1920s, he later modified his style with scores to the films *Lieutenant Kije* (1934) and *Alexander Nevsky* (1938) and the narrated orchestral work *Peter and the Wolf* (1936). He also completed seven symphonies and several scores for operas and ballets.

Entry: *Alexander Nevsky* (1938)

DAVID RAKSIN (1912–2004)

Born in Philadelphia, David Raksin become known as the "grandfather of film music," with over three hundred television and one hundred film scores to his name. He studied composition with Arnold Schoenberg in Los Angeles before launching his prolific film-scoring career. Most of his works can be found in the Golden Age of Hollywood, and in later life he taught in California universities. His most influential scores include *Laura* (1944), *The Bad and the Beautiful* (1952), and *Apache* (1954).

Entry: *Laura* (1944)

LEONARD ROSENMAN (1924–2008)

Born in Brooklyn, Leonard Rosenman was a film composer with well over one hundred works spanning six decades. Rosenman won two Academy Awards, both for adaptations. On receiving the second of these awards, he joked, "I write original music too, you know!" Among his more prominent scores are *Beneath the Planet of the Apes* (1970), the animated version of *The Lord of the Rings* (1978), and *Star Trek IV: The Voyage Home* (1986).

Entry: *East of Eden* (1955)

LAURENCE ROSENTHAL (1926–)

This Detroit native began piano lessons at three, and in his teens performed as piano soloist with the Detroit Symphony. He studied composition at the Eastman School and in Paris under Nadia Boulanger. His incidental music for Broadway plays includes *Becket* (1964), and in 1964 he won an Oscar nomination for the film version of that play. He also scored *A Raisin in the Sun* (1961) and *The Miracle Worker* (1962) and has composed for television.

Entry: *Becket* (1964)

NINO ROTA (1911–1979)

Born in Milan, Italy, Nino Rota was a composer, pianist, and conductor who was most well known for his film scores. With over one hundred fifty scores to his name, he was most prolific in the 1940s and 1950s, where in one year (1954) he wrote an incredible thirteen film scores. Perhaps most well known for the scores to the first two *Godfather* films, Rota also had a significant teaching career, becoming director of the Liceo Musicale in Bari for almost thirty years.

Entry: *The Godfather* and *The Godfather Part II* (1972, 1974)

MIKLÓS RÓZSA (1907–1995)

This Budapest native played violin at five and later studied composition at the Leipzig Conservatory. He composed chamber and orchestral works in the 1920s and 1930s and wrote his first film score in 1937. In 1940, he immigrated to America to complete Alexander Korda's *Thief of Bagdad* (1940). Later 1940s scores include *The Jungle Book* (1942) and several film noir movies. Under contract at MGM he scored the epics *Ivanhoe* (1952) and *Ben-Hur* (1959), his third Oscar winner.

Entries: *Ben-Hur* (1959), *King of Kings* (1961), *Quo Vadis* (1951), *Spellbound* (1945)

HOWARD SHORE (1946–)

Born in Toronto, Canada, Howard Shore is a prolific film composer of over eighty scores. Shore rose most significantly to fame after the scoring of Peter Jackson's *The Lord of the Rings* trilogy in 2001, 2002, and 2003. He also went on to score the three *Hobbit* films in 2012, 2013, and 2014. Shore won three of four Academy Award nominations for his work on *The Lord of the Rings,* and on occasion conducts live performances of the *Ring* music while the film footage is being screened.

Entry: *Lord of the Rings: The Fellowship of the Ring* (2001)

ALAN SILVESTRI (1950–)

Born in New York City, Alan Silvestri is a composer for film and television with well over one hundred films to his name. Known for his collaborative work with director Robert Zemeckis, Silvestri has written the music for all of Zemeckis's films since 1984. These include the *Back to the Future* trilogy (1985–1990), *Who Framed Roger Rabbit* (1988), *Forrest Gump* (1994), and *Cast Away* (2000). Silvestri has received two Academy Award nominations.

Entries: *Back to the Future* (1985), *Forrest Gump* (1994)

MAX STEINER (1888–1971)

This Vienna native began as a pianist but soon turned to composing works for the stage. Conducting musicals became his calling card when he immigrated to New York in 1914. After several years as a stage conductor he came to Hollywood to work on early talkie musicals. He was at RKO until 1935, and then at Warner Bros. By his retirement in 1965 he had written and/or arranged music for three hundred films and won three Oscars.

Entries: *Casablanca* (1943), *Gone with the Wind* (1939), *King Kong* (1933), *Now, Voyager* (1942)

DIMITRI TIOMKIN (1894–1979)

Tiomkin was a gifted piano virtuoso who made spending money by playing in silent-movie houses while attending the St. Petersburg Conservatory. In 1925 Tiomkin came to America as part of a vaudeville piano duo. A hand injury resulted in a shift from playing to composing, and in 1929 he arrived in Hollywood with his wife, who created dance numbers for talkie musicals. He soon began creating dramatic underscores and in the 1950s won four Oscars.

Entries: *Giant* (1956), *High Noon* (1952), *Lost Horizon* (1937)

VANGELIS (1943–)

Born in Agria, in Italian-occupied, wartime Greece, Evángelos Odysséas Papathanassíou (almost always shortened to Vangelis) is a composer of electronic, ambient concert music, but has also contributed to several films. In the film world, he is most well known for his Academy Award–winning electronic score to *Chariots of Fire* (1981), and the eerie, noir sounds of *Blade Runner* (1984). He is considered one of the most important composers of electronic music in history.

Entries: *Blade Runner* (1982), *Chariots of Fire* (1981)

RALPH VAUGHAN WILLIAMS (1872–1958)

One of the most renowned composers of the twentieth century, Vaughan Williams studied English hymns and folk music during his student days, and later incorporated melodies from these sources in his works. In addition to nine symphonies and many other instrumental pieces, he created operas and cantatas. His first film music, *49th Parallel* (1941), composed when he was sixty-eight, led to ten other film scores, of which *Scott of the Antarctic* (1948) is the most noteworthy.

Entry: *Scott of the Antarctic* (1948)

WILLIAM WALTON (1902–1983)

Walton is second only to Vaughan Williams as an important contributor of English symphonic music in the twentieth century. Although Walton composed only two symphonies, they are remarkable works. Walton also wrote several concertos, operas, the *Belshazzar's Feast* cantata, and music for twelve films, including four that are Shakespearean adaptations starring Laurence Olivier. Two of these films, *Henry V* (1944) and *Hamlet* (1948), which Olivier also directed, earned Walton Oscar nominations.

Entry: *Henry V* (1944)

FRANZ WAXMAN (1906–1967)

Born in Upper Silesia (now part of Poland and the Czech Republic), Waxman played piano at an early age. While studying music at the Berlin Conservatory he supported himself by playing in dance bands. In 1930, he started scoring and arranging music for European films. After immigrating to America, he wrote his first Hollywood score for *The Bride of Frankenstein* (1935). After stints at MGM and Warner Bros., he became an independent composer and won back-to-back Oscars in 1950 and 1951.

Entries: *The Bride of Frankenstein* (1935), *Sunset Boulevard* (1950), *The Spirit of St. Louis* (1957).

JOHN WILLIAMS (1932–)

Born in Floral Park, New York, John Williams is arguably the most successful and popular film music composer of all time. With a career spanning six decades, a collaborative relationship with Steven Spielberg, and twenty-three Grammys, seven BAFTAs, five Academy Awards, and four Golden Globe awards, he is undoubtedly one of the most instantly recognizable film composers. Only Walt Disney has been nominated for an Academy Award more times than Williams. To date, the composer has fifty-one nominations to his name.

Entries: *Close Encounters of the Third Kind* (1977), *Empire of the Sun* (1987), *E.T. the Extra-Terrestrial* (1982), *Jaws* (1975), *Jurassic Park* (1993), *Raiders of the Lost Ark* (1981), *Schindler's List* (1993), *Star Wars* (1977), *Superman* (1978)

VICTOR YOUNG (1900–1956)

Born in Chicago, Young studied music in Europe as a teenager and performed as a violin soloist. In the 1920s he was principal violinist of the silent-movie orchestra at Sid Grauman's Million Dollar Theater and also performed on radio. In 1935 he signed contracts with Decca Records and with Paramount. He composed over one hundred fifty film scores and wrote such memorable movie songs as "Stella by Starlight." He was the first musician to win an Oscar posthumously.

Entry: *Around the World in 80 Days* (1956)

HANS ZIMMER (1957–)

Born in Frankfurt-am-Main, Germany, Hans Zimmer has composed over one hundred fifty film scores since the 1980s. He has an Academy Award to his name for *The Lion King* (1994), and his other prominent works include *Gladiator* (2000), the *Pirates of the Caribbean* series (2003–), and *Interstellar* (2014). He is known for pulsating, rhythmic film scores that sometimes make use of timbre and texture rather than recognizable melodies.

Entries: *Gladiator* (2000), *Interstellar* (2014), *Pirates of the Caribbean: The Curse of the Black Pearl* (2003)

Glossary of Film and Music Terms

accelerando—Getting gradually faster.

accent—Emphasis placed on certain tones.

beat—A repeated pulsation that is basic to musical **rhythm**.

cadence—A melodic and/or harmonic progression of music that forms a resting place, which may be a temporary pause or a conclusive ending. It provides punctuation to statements of musical ideas.

canon—Type of contrapuntal music in which melodic lines (or fragments) are repeated in a staggered way, as in a round, with overlapping of the various lines. A canonic moment occurs in the main-title theme in *On the Waterfront* and again at the end of the film.

chaconne—Type of contrapuntal music in which a musical pattern, usually in the bass, is repeated continuously, with ever-changing melodic lines overlaid. Same as passacaglia. It is prominently featured in the score of *The Red Violin*.

chord—Any combination of three or more tones sounded simultaneously as harmony.

chordal style—Music in which the various voices are sounded in a mostly simultaneous rhythm. Can also be referred to as hymn style. A good example is the rhythmic uniformity heard in the main-title theme of *The Red Pony*.

chromatic—Refers to the use of tones not included in the diatonic major and minor scales. The chromatic scale includes all twelve pitches within the octave. A good example is the paranoia theme in *Spellbound*, with the melody sounded by a **theremin.**

consonance—A stable and pleasant-sounding combination of tones (especially triadic tones).

contrary motion—refers to music in which melodic lines move in opposite directions.

counterpoint—Music in which various lines of music overlap; may include the same melody or different melodies sounded simultaneously (also referred to as contrapuntal style).

crescendo—A gradual increase in volume. The opposite of a **descrescendo**.

cue—A single piece of music within a film score; it may last a few seconds or several minutes.

decrescendo (or diminuendo)—A gradual decrease in volume.

diegetic music—see **source music**.

dissonance—An unstable and restless combination of tones. Usually leads to a resolution of musical tones into a more stable **consonance**.

fugue—A type of contrapuntal music in which a basic melodic idea is stated and then two or more additional lines or layers of music repeat the fugue melody in staggered fashion. A good example occurs during the police chase in *A Place in the Sun*. Less strict than a **canon**, a fugue may include other musical ideas besides the basic fugue melody.

harmonic progression—A succession of harmonies that lead toward a musical **cadence**, or resting place in the music. A final progression leading to the conclusion of a musical theme, section, or entire work.

harmony—Music heard as accompaniment or background to a melodic idea.

interval—Difference in pitch between tones. The size of an interval is referred to numerically, such as a second (adjacent pitches), third (a basic building block for triadic harmony), fourth, fifth, and so on. Intervals are both harmonic (simultaneous) and melodic (successive).

key—Refers to the scale the music is based on. The keynote (or tonic), is the first tone of the scale. The composer determines the **key** of a piece by selecting a particular scale pattern for the music.

leitmotif—A basic melodic idea (or **motif**) used in creating a piece of music. Based on Richard Wagner's concept for his operas, the leitmotivic method refers to the use of short melodic ideas to represent characters, places, and things. Used by Korngold and Steiner in films of the 1930s and 1940s. More recently used in the *Lord of the Rings* films.

main title—Refers to music heard during the opening credits of a film. This is often the principal theme of a film score.

major scale—Basic tone pattern used to create a positive mood, with a whole step between steps 1, 2, and 3 (as in "do-re-mi").

meter—The recurring pattern of accented and unaccented beats. The choice of a metric pattern is often related to the use of a specific kind of music, such as a march or a specific type of dance. A metric accent normally occurs on the first beat of the pattern (or measure).

Mickey Mousing—music that mimics action. In Steiner's *King Kong*, the music often reflects physical movement, as when the jungle chief descends steps. Here the music is synchronized with each step he takes and features descending melodic tones. Conversely, a rising action is accompanied by ascending tones.

minor scale—Basic tone pattern used to create a more somber or dramatic mood. Tones 1 and 2 are a whole step apart, while tones 2 and 3, unlike the **major scale**, are a half step apart. Famous minor key theme: "Imperial March" in *The Empire Strikes Back*.

modal scales—Scales based on ancient or medieval patterns that differ from the major and minor scales. One example is the Dorian scale (or mode) which resembles the minor scale, but with a higher sixth step, as in D-E-F-G-A-B-C-D (without a B flat on the sixth step). A good example is the main-title theme in the 1961 film *King of Kings*.

modulation—The changing of key within a piece. Music often has a tonal center from which the music can modulate (or shift); there is often an eventual return to the original key.

motif (motive or motiv)—Short pattern of tones used repeatedly as a basic part of a theme. For example, the opening theme of *The Godfather* features a seven-note idea played by a trumpet. A short three-note motif is heard in the bride theme in *The Bride of Frankenstein.*

non-diegetic music—See **underscore**.

ostinato—A phrase that repeats continuously, usually starting on the same pitch throughout a section of music or an entire piece.

parallel motion—Melodic motion in which tones move in the same direction. Reflects music from ancient or medieval times. For example: the beginning of the Christ theme in Rózsa's *Ben-Hur.*

pitch (also **tone** or **note)**—The relative highness of lowness of a musical sound. Musical sounds have specific pitches, whereas noises lack a specific pitch.

rhythm—The element of time in music, which is basically governed by the choice of rhythmic devices such as **beat, tempo, meter,** and **syncopation**.

Romanticism—A movement in art and music chiefly of the nineteenth century characterized by highly dramatic and emotional themes.

score—The complete musical composition for a film. Individual pieces within a film score are referred to as **cues**. A good example of a score with a large number of cues is *Gone with the Wind,* the score of which includes ninety-nine separate cues.

soundtrack—A film's music as a whole, similar to the **score**. May also refer to a commercial recording of a film's music. Many films release **soundtrack** albums of their music. Other releases are rerecordings of a film's original score.

source music—Music in a film that can be heard by the story's characters. It may emanate from a radio or TV, a band in a nightclub, a church choir, an orchestra in a concert hall, and so on. It can be original music, but often is borrowed from previously existing sources, as in *Casablanca,* which includes several period tunes, most famously "As Time Goes By." Also known as diegetic music.

spotting—The determination of where music should be placed in a film that is in production. Spotting sessions take place, usually with the composer present, to identify the length of cues for specific moments in the film. These timings are crucial to the composer's work.

syncopation—Rhythmic accents that occur in between beats or on usually unaccented ones. It sets up surprising accents and enhances tension and excitement in the music.

temp track—A temporary soundtrack, usually prepared by a film's director, that includes borrowed music from a variety of sources and is used as a temporary score for the rough cut, or early editing stage, of a film. It is usually replaced by an original score. An exception is *2001: A Space Odyssey,* in which the temp track was chosen by Stanley Kubrick as the actual score.

tempo—The rate of speed of the **beat**. Composers designate tempos by metronome markings and also by words, often in Italian, that appear on the printed pages of both solo sheet music and scores for large vocal and/or instrumental ensembles.

theme—A principal melody of a piece of music, or of a section within a larger piece. A thematic idea can be based on short melodic fragments called **motifs**.

theme song—A song written expressly for a film, or borrowed for use in a film.

theremin—An early electronic instrument played by moving the hands near its two sensitive antennas to regulate pitch and volume. It has often been used in science-fiction or mystery films because of the eerie quality of its sound.

triad—A three-note chord, built in thirds. Triads are usually major (as in C-E-G), or minor, as in (C-E flat-G).

underscore—Music that accompanies a film, and cannot be heard by the story's characters, as opposed to **source music**. It provides background, sets the mood, creates pace, and helps to define both characters and situations. Also known as non-diegetic music.

Select Bibliography

Audissino, Emilio. *John Williams's Film Music: Jaws, Star Wars, Raiders of the Lost Ark, and the Return of the Classical Hollywood Music Style*. Madison: University of Wisconsin Press, 2014.

Auiler, Dan. *Vertigo: The Making of a Hitchcock Classic*. New York: St. Martin's Press, 1998.

Bergan, Ronald. *The Coen Brothers*. Second edition. New York: Arcade Publishing, 2016.

Bond, Jeff. *The Music of Star Trek: Profiles in Style*. Los Angeles: Lone Eagle, 1999.

Brode, Douglas. *The Films of the Sixties*. Secaucus, NJ: Citadel Press, 1980.

Brooks, Herb, and Terryl C. Boodman. *Gone with the Wind: The Definitive Illustrated History of the Book, the Movie, and the Legend*. New York: Simon & Schuster, 1989.

Brosnan, John. *Future Tense: The Cinema of Science Fiction*. New York: St. Martin's Press, 1978.

Burlingame, Jon. *Sound and Vision: 60 Years of Motion Picture Soundtracks*. New York: Billboard Books, 2000.

Burt, George. *The Art of Film Music: Special Emphasis on Hugo Friedhofer, Alex North, David Raksin, Leonard Rosenman*. Boston: Northeastern University Press, 1995.

Bushard, Anthony. *Leonard Bernstein's "On the Waterfront": A Film Score Guide*. Lanham, MD: Scarecrow Press, 2013.

Caps, John. *Henry Mancini: Reinventing Film Music*. Urbana: University of Illinois Press, 2012.

Cohn, Art, ed. *Michael Todd's Around the World in 80 Days Almanac*. New York: Random House, 1956.

Cooper, David. *Bernard Herrmann's "The Ghost and Mrs. Muir": A Film Score Guide*. Lanham, MD: Scarecrow Press, 2005.

Costner, Kevin, Michael Black, and Jim Wilson. *Dances with Wolves: The Illustrated Story of the Film*. New York: Newmarket Press, 1990.

Dans, Peter E. *Christians in the Movies: A Century of Saints and Sinners*. Lanham, MD: Rowman & Littlefield, 2009.

Darby, William, and Jack Du Bois. *American Film Music: Major Composers, Techniques, Trends, 1915–1990*. Jefferson, NC: McFarland, 1990.

Davison, Annette. *Alex North's "A Streetcar Named Desire": A Film Score Guide*. Lanham, MD: Scarecrow Press, 2009.

Deutsch, Didier, ed. *VideoHound's Soundtracks: Music from the Movies, Broadway and Television*. Detroit: Visible Ink Press, 1988.

Fhlainn, Sorcha Ni, ed. *The Worlds of Back to the Future: Critical Essays on the Films*. Jefferson, NC: McFarland, 2010.

Flinn, Caryl. *Strains of Utopia: Gender, Nostalgia, and Hollywood Film Music*. Princeton, NJ: Princeton University Press, 1992.

Geist, Kenneth L. *Pictures Will Talk: The Life and Films of Joseph L. Mankiewicz*. New York: Da Capo Press, 1978.

Goldman, William. *Which Lie Did I Tell? More Adventures in the Screen Trade*. New York: Vintage, 2001.

Goldner, Orville, and George E. Turner. *The Making of King Kong*. Cranbury, NJ: A. S. Barnes, 1975.

Hannan, Brian. *The Making of "The Magnificent Seven": Behind the Scenes of the Pivotal Western*. Jefferson, NC: McFarland, 2015.

Harris, Robert A., and Michael S. Lasky. *The Films of Alfred Hitchcock*. New York: Citadel Press, 1976.

Henderson, Sanya Shoilevska. *Alex North, Film Composer*. Jefferson, NC: McFarland, 2003.

Hickman, Roger. *Miklós Rózsa's "Ben-Hur": A Film Score Guide*. Lanham, MD: Scarecrow Press, 2011.

———. *Reel Music: Exploring 100 Years of Film Music*. New York: W. W. Norton, 2006.

Hirsch, Foster. *Otto Preminger: The Man Who Would Be King*. New York: Alfred A. Knopf, 2007.

Hischak, Thomas. *The Encyclopedia of Film Composers*. Lanham, MD: Rowman & Littlefield, 2015.

Jaffé, Daniel. *Sergey Prokofiev*. London: Phaeton Press, 1998.

Kael, Pauline. *The Citizen Kane Book*. New York: Bantam Books, 1974.

Karlin, Fred. *Listening to Movies: The Film Lover's Guide to Film Music*. New York: Schirmer Books, 1994.

Kehr, Dave. *When Movies Mattered: Reviews from a Transformative Decade*. Chicago: University of Chicago Press, 2011.

Korda, Michael. *Making the List: A Cultural History of the American Bestseller 1900–1999*. New York: Barnes & Noble, 2001.

Leonard, Geoff, Pete Walker, and Gareth Bramley. *John Barry: The Man with the Midas Touch*. Bristol, UK: Redcliffe Press, 2008.

Limbacher, James L. *Film Music: From Violins to Video (Essays and Index of Films)*. Metuchen, NJ: Scarecrow Press, 1974.

MacDonald, Laurence E. *The Invisible Art of Film Music: A Comprehensive History*. Second edition. Lanham, MD: Scarecrow Press, 2013.

Mancini, Henry, with Gene Lees. *Did They Mention the Music?* New York: Cooper Square Press, 2001.

Morgan, David. *Knowing the Score: Film Composers Talk about the Art, Craft, Blood, Sweat, and Tears of Writing for Cinema*. New York: Harper Entertainment, 2000.

Okuda, Michael, Denise Okuda, and Debbie Mirek. *The Star Wars Encyclopedia: A Reference Guide to the Future*. New York: Pocket Books, 1994.

O'Steene, Sam. *Cut to the Chase: Forty-Five Years of Editing America's Favorite Movies*. Studio City, CA: Michael Wiese Productions, 2002.

Palmer, Christopher. *The Composer in Hollywood*. London: Marion Boyars Publishers, 1990.

———. *Dimitri Tiomkin: A Portrait*. London: T. E. Books, 1984.

Pelkey, Stanley C., and Anthony Bushard, eds. *Anxiety Muted: American Film Music in a Suburban Age*. New York: Oxford University Press, 2015.

Phillips, Gene. *Beyond the Epic: The Life and Films of David Lean*. Lexington: University Press of Kentucky, 2006.

Polanski, Roman. *Roman by Polanski*. New York: William Morrow, 1984.

Prendergast, Roy. *Film Music: A Neglected Art: A Critical Study of Music in Films*. New York: New York University Press, 1977.

Rothbart, Peter. *The Synergy of Film and Music: Sight and Sound in Five Hollywood Films*. Lanham, MD: Scarecrow Press, 2013.

Rovin, Jeff. *The Fabulous Fantasy Films*. South Brunswick, NJ: A. S. Barnes, 1977.

Rózsa, Miklós. *Double Life*. New York: Wynwood Press, 1989.

Russell, Mark, and James Young. *Film Music*. Waltham, MA: Focal Press, 2000.

Sackett, Susan. *The Hollywood Reporter Book of Box Office Hits*. New York: Billboard Books, 1990.

Santas, Constantine. *The Epic Films of David Lean*. Lanham, MD: Scarecrow Press, 2012.

Sciannameo, Franco. *Nina Rota's "The Godfather" Trilogy: A Film Score Guide*. Lanham, MD: Scarecrow Press, 2011.

Secrest, Meryle. *Leonard Bernstein: A Life*. New York: Alfred A. Knopf, 1994.

Shay, Don, and Jody Duncan. *The Making of "Jurassic Park": An Adventure 65 Million Years in the Making*. New York: Ballantine Books, 1993.

Sherk, Warren. *Film and Television Music: A Guide to Books, Articles, and Composer Interviews*. Lanham, MD: Scarecrow Press, 2011.

Sikov, Ed. *On Sunset Boulevard: The Life and Times of Billy Wilder*. Jackson: University Press of Mississippi, 2017.

Spencer, Kristopher. *Film and Television Scores, 1950–1979: A Critical Survey by Genre*. Jefferson, NC: McFarland, 2008.

Spoto, Donald. *Stanley Kramer: Film Maker*. G. P. Putnam, 1977.

Sullivan, Jack. *Hitchcock's Music*. New Haven, CT: Yale University Press, 2006.

Thomas, Tony. *The Films of the Forties*. New York: Citadel Press, 1975.

———. *The Great Adventure Films*. New York: Citadel Press, 1976.

Tibbetts, John C., and James M. Welsh. *The Encyclopedia of Novels into Film*. New York: Facts on File, 1998.

Vermilye, Jerry. *The Films of the Thirties*. New York: Citadel Press, 1993.

Wegele, Peter. *Max Steiner: Composing, Casablanca, and the Golden Age of Film Music*. Lanham, MD: Rowman & Littlefield, 2014.

Whitmer, Mariana. *Jerome Moross's "The Big Country": A Film Score Guide*. Lanham, MD: Scarecrow Press, 2012.

Index